DISHING UP® MINNESOTA

DISHING UP®
MINNESOTA

150 RECIPES FROM THE LAND OF 10,000 LAKES

TERESA MARRONE

Photography by David Paul Schmit

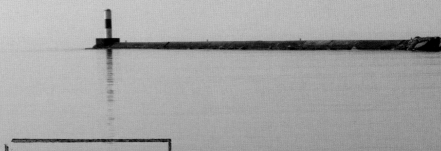

Storey Publishing
Storey Publishing

The mission of Storey Publishing is to serve our customers by publishing practical information that encourages personal independence in harmony with the environment.

Edited by Margaret Sutherland and Sarah Guare
Art direction and book design by Mary Winkelman Velgos,
    based on a design by Tom Morgan of Blue Design
Text production by Jennifer Jepson Smith
Indexed by Christine R. Lindemer, Boston Road Communications

Cover and interior photography by © David Paul Schmit, except © AMB-MD/ iStockphoto.com: 9; © Bill Lindner Photography: 55, 62, 71, 190; © Teresa Marrone: 1 top row center & bottom row right, 57, 73, 79, 90–93, 104, 105, 112, 116, 134, 146, 154, 156, 157, 199, 207, 215, 223, 236, 242, 244 left, 256, 263; back cover (author) by Tracy Walsh (www.tracywalshphoto.com)
Map of Minnesota by © Emma Trithart

Storey Publishing
210 MASS MoCA Way
North Adams, MA 01247
www.storey.com

Printed in the United States by Versa Press
10 9 8 7 6 5 4 3 2 1

LIBRARY OF CONGRESS CATALOGING-IN-PUBLICATION DATA
Names: Marrone, Teresa, author.
Title: Dishing Up Minnesota : 150 Recipes from the Land of 10,000 Lakes / Teresa Marrone.
Description: North Adams, Massachusetts : Storey Publishing, 2016. | Includes index.
Identifiers: LCCN 2016004869 | ISBN 9781612125848 (pbk. : alk. paper)
Subjects: LCSH: Cooking, American. | Cooking—Minnesota. | LCGFT: Cookbooks.
Classification: LCC TX715 .M11587 2016 | DDC 641.59776—dc23 LC record available at https://lccn.loc.gov/2016004869

CONTENTS

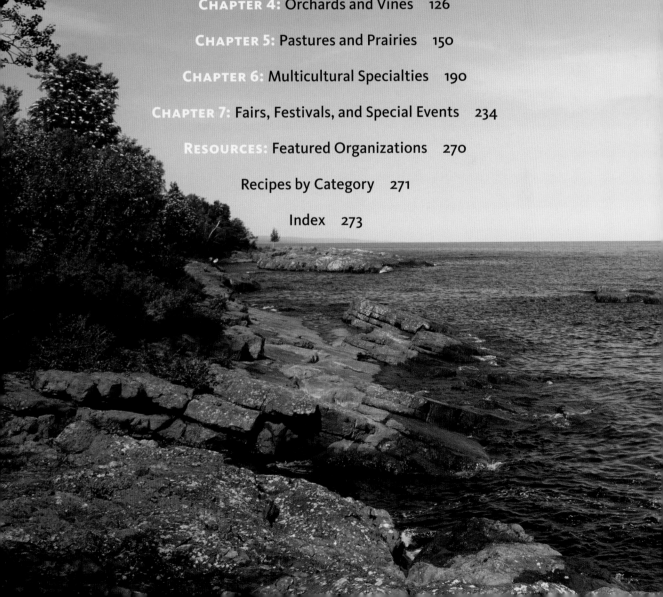

Introduction

Legend has it this walleye was caught by
Paul Bunyan and Babe the Blue Ox
after a three day struggle. Paul finally
wrapped his line around Babe's horns and

THE *NEW YORK TIMES* DEVOTED the majority of its food section on November 18, 2014, to a list of Thanksgiving dishes "that evoke each of the 50 states." Minnesota was saddled with grape salad, a kindergarten-simple dish in which green grapes are mixed with sour cream and brown sugar, broiled, then chilled before serving. Although versions of the recipe did appear in a few old church cookbooks, almost no one had heard of the stuff, much less eaten it.

Reaction was swift and hot. Within hours, social media exploded, and the hashtag #grapegate became a sounding board for outraged Minnesotans.

Across the state, newspaper and magazine columnists joined the fray both in print and online, and the story was covered on news broadcasts, including the *NBC Nightly News*. Grapes?! Where was the wild rice? The pie made with Honeycrisp apples, a Minnesota-born variety? Pheasant in cream? It was the same old story that has quietly annoyed Minnesotans for years: Like Rodney Dangerfield, we can't get any respect.

In reality, Minnesota is a pretty interesting place. It has a rich and vibrant food culture, although it's not always easy to pin down. With divergent influences from native Dakota and Ojibwe peoples, the

Scandinavian and German immigrants of the 1800s, the newest residents hailing from Southeast Asia and Somalia, and current-day chefs, farmers, and artisan producers, Minnesota's food scene is a study in opposites: traditional and contemporary, rustic and elegant, country and city. These threads are woven into whole cloth, however, by the bounty of top-notch local ingredients that appear in the best of each culture's dishes.

Abundant lakes, rivers, and streams give Minnesota its license-plate slogan, Land of 10,000 Lakes — and yes, there really *are* that many. These waterways also provide some of the best regional ingredients. Lake Superior, the largest freshwater lake on Earth, harbors lake herring, trout, whitefish, smelt, and salmon. Inland waters abound with game fish, including walleye, largemouth and smallmouth bass, panfish, and trout. Wild rice is harvested from large, shallow lakes as well as from some rivers and streams. Many lakes boast seasonal populations of waterfowl, which are eagerly hunted — and cooked — by many residents each fall.

Although large expanses of Minnesota are devoted to the production of corn, soybeans, and industrial livestock, the state is home to numerous small farms, many committed to sustainable practices. Minnesota is also the sixth-largest dairy state. Much of the milk is converted into cheese and butter; producers range from huge corporations to small family farms. Minnesota-produced artisan cheese and butter, eggs from free-range hens, grass-fed beef, and top-quality produce are highly prized by discerning chefs and home cooks. Farmers' markets, co-ops, and CSA farms are found throughout the state. Agricultural areas also provide habitat for deer, pheasants, and small game, and the fall hunting season is a major event in the state.

In 2014 (the #grapegate year), over 100 new restaurants were opened in the Twin Cities, the metropolitan area that includes Minneapolis and St. Paul and is home to about 60 percent of the state's population. Craft brewing has also exploded; even Grand Marais, a town of 1,300 on Lake Superior just southwest of the Canadian border, boasts two microbreweries. In restaurants and home kitchens, Minnesota cooks are going back to their roots, crafting bacon, sausage, and other charcuterie, as well as cheese and artisan-style or heritage breads. Foraging, particularly for mushrooms and berries, is a popular pastime for many Minnesotans, who make up a pretty outdoorsy group in general.

We've got a few heavy hitters in the food world, too, both individuals and corporations. Lynne Rossetto Kasper, host of American Public Media's radio broadcast *The Splendid Table*, makes her home in Minnesota. So do television food personalities Amy Thielen (host of *Heartland Table*) and Andrew Zimmern (host of *Bizarre Foods with Andrew Zimmern*). Zoë François, coauthor of *Artisan Bread in Five Minutes a Day* and a string of related titles (many written with fellow Minnesotan Dr. Jeff

Hertzberg), has a long history in the Minneapolis food scene and lives here with her family.

Minnesota megacorporation General Mills is a food manufacturer and marketer whose current brands include Wheaties, Cheerios, Betty Crocker, Häagen-Dazs, Yoplait, Bisquick, and Nature Valley, as well as natural brands Annie's, Cascadian Farm, and Muir Glen. Hormel Foods, based in Austin, Minnesota, is a huge brand name in itself; Hormel also encompasses the Jennie-O Turkey, Spam, Skippy peanut butter, and Di Lusso Deli brands. Other major Minnesota food corporations include International Dairy Queen, Land O'Lakes, Malt-O-Meal, Michael Foods, and Buffalo Wild Wings.

Dishing Up Minnesota celebrates Minnesota's food and heritage, with 150 recipes ranging from traditional to modern. By the way, on November 25, 2014, as a follow-up to its earlier article on Thanksgiving foods, the *New York Times* ran a Web feature on "Thanksgiving Recipes Googled in Every State: Which Foods Are Unusually Popular in Each State on Thanksgiving." Minnesota's was wild rice casserole. You betcha; that sounds about right.

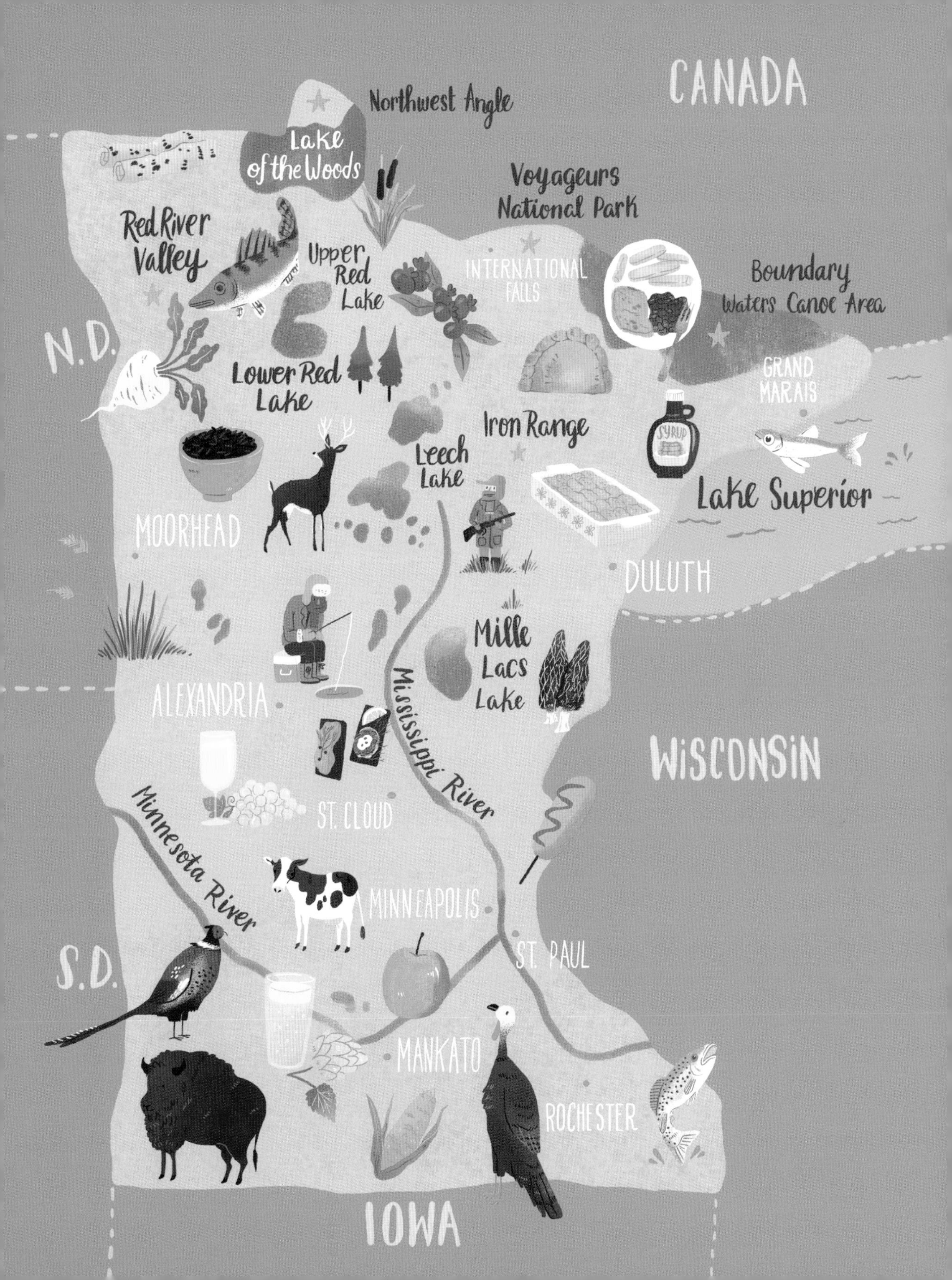

CANADA

Northwest Angle

Lake of the Woods

Voyageurs National Park

Red River Valley

Upper Red Lake

INTERNATIONAL FALLS

Boundary Waters Canoe Area

N.D.

Lower Red Lake

GRAND MARAIS

Iron Range

Leech Lake

SYRUP

Lake Superior

MOORHEAD

DULUTH

Mille Lacs Lake

ALEXANDRIA

Mississippi River

WISCONSIN

ST. CLOUD

Minnesota River

MINNEAPOLIS

ST. PAUL

S.D.

MANKATO

ROCHESTER

IOWA

CHAPTER 1
The Land of 10,000 Lakes

ARE THERE REALLY 10,000 LAKES IN MINNESOTA?

Actually, according to the Minnesota Department of Natural Resources (DNR), our state has 11,842 lakes of at least 10 acres in size (the official dividing point between lake and not-lake) — but "Land of 11,842 Lakes" isn't such a catchy license-plate slogan.

Only 4 of Minnesota's 87 counties have no natural lakes. At 12 acres, Dickey's Lake in Hennepin County is the smallest official lake in the state; according to DNR data, it is populated mostly with bullheads. The largest lake that is wholly inside state borders is Red Lake, a walleye hot spot in Beltrami County; its two basins total almost 289,000 acres.

Minnesota shares majestic Lake Superior with Wisconsin, Michigan's Upper Peninsula, and Ontario; roughly one-quarter of its 20-plus million acres is considered Minnesota water. We also share Lake of the Woods with Ontario and Manitoba; the Minnesota portion of this 950,400-acre lake is in the so-called Northwest Angle, a small rectangular bump in northern Lake of the Woods County that was born from a mapmaker's error.

The Boundary Waters Canoe Area Wilderness, on Minnesota's northeastern border with Ontario, contains more than 1,000 pristine lakes. This roadless, canoe-only area occupies over 1 million acres, and the paddler's paradise continues across the border into Quetico Provincial Park. Lake Vermilion, in St. Louis County, has the state's longest shoreline, listed at 290 miles by the DNR. We also have almost 70,000 miles of rivers and streams, including 589 miles of officially designated Wild and Scenic Rivers and 1,900 miles of trout streams.

Minnesotans love to fish, in open water or through the ice; sales of fishing licenses topped half a million in a recent year. Walleye is the official state fish, but trout, muskie, northern pike, bass, and panfish are eagerly sought by anglers, too. Minnesotans also love to *eat* fish; read on for some tasty ideas for your catch, whether you got it by hook and line or at the fish counter of your local market.

Backyard Fish Fry

A Minnesota lakeside tradition! Deep frying in the backyard means less mess in the kitchen — and no fried-fish odor in the house. Plan on 2 pounds of boneless, skinless fish fillets for every 4 or 5 guests. Crappies and other panfish, such as bluegills, sunnies, and perch, fry up quickly, so the fillets should be cooked whole (that is, 2 fillets per fish). Cut fillets of walleyes, bass, and northern pike into halves or thirds, depending on the size; pieces should be no larger than 3 inches long and no thicker than ½ inch. Rinse the fillets just before cooking, and blot with paper towels; they should be lightly damp when breaded. Coleslaw or other salad, baked beans, potato salad, and fresh fruit and vegetables are traditional accompaniments, along with plenty of cold beer or lemonade; corn on the cob is also welcome. Offer brownies or bars for dessert.

VARIABLE SERVINGS

BREADING (enough for 5 to 6 pounds of fish)

- 1½ cups cornmeal
- 1 cup all-purpose flour
- 2 tablespoons paprika
- 2½ teaspoons salt
- ¾ teaspoon garlic powder
- ¾ teaspoon ground white pepper
- ¼ teaspoon cayenne pepper or other ground hot pepper, optional

  Vegetable oil, for deep frying
  Boneless, skinless crappie fillets or other fish fillets (see headnote)

Variation: Beer-Battered Fish

Mix the breading with beer, using roughly equal amounts of both (1 cup breading to 1 cup beer, for example); the batter should be thinner than pancake batter but not watery. Shake the fillets in a bag of plain all-purpose flour, then add to the bowl of batter. Use tongs to lift out the fish pieces one at a time and allow excess batter to flow back into the bowl before transferring the fish to the fryer.

1. **Make the breading:** Combine the cornmeal, flour, paprika, salt, garlic powder, white pepper, and cayenne, if desired, in a jar or lidded container. Seal tightly and shake to mix. The breading can be stored in a cool cupboard until needed; it will keep for several months.

2. Heat oil in a deep fryer to 350°F and line a dish with paper towels. Pour 1 cup of the breading into a plastic bag. Add as many fish pieces as you plan to cook per batch; a small fryer will hold three or four typical pieces, while a large one may hold up to 10. Shake the bag to coat the fish. Remove one at a time, shaking off excess breading, and carefully slip into the hot oil. Fry until golden brown and cooked through; very thin "potato-chip" sunfish fillets take about 2 minutes, while good-size crappie or perch fillets take 3 to 4 minutes. Thicker fillets from walleye or northern pike may take as long as 6 minutes. (For the first batch, fry just one piece and remove it after a few minutes, then check for doneness; once you've got the timing figured out for the type of fillets you have, you can cook more pieces at once.)

3. Transfer the cooked fish to the dish lined with paper towels, and let guests dig in as soon as you've got enough to get them started; the fish is best eaten right away. Return the oil to 350°F before adding the next batch.

LAKE SUPERIOR AND THE NORTH SHORE

In 1855, Henry Wadsworth Longfellow published his epic poem "The Song of Hiawatha," featuring Gitche Gumee, the "shining big-sea-water." The odd name captivated imaginations again 121 years later in Gordon Lightfoot's haunting song, "The Wreck of the Edmund Fitzgerald." Gitche Gumee stems from *gichigami*, an Ojibwe word meaning "a sea, a large lake"; it is also used to refer specifically to Lake Superior.

LAKE SUPERIOR is the largest and clearest of the Great Lakes. With a surface area of 31,700 square miles, it is also the largest freshwater lake in the world by surface area. Its glacially formed basin contains 3 quadrillion gallons of water — one-tenth of the Earth's fresh surface water. Minnesota's North Shore accounts for half of Superior's northwest shoreline, which continues into Canada. The shipping port of Duluth anchors Superior's southwestern tip; 110 miles northeast, the harbor town of Grand Marais is the other North Shore anchor.

DULUTH is the fourth most populous city in Minnesota. Although visually stunning, with surrounding cliffs, the seemingly endless backdrop of Lake Superior, and the picturesque Lift Bridge in the center of town, it is a working harbor that handles about 38 million tons of water-borne freight annually. Iron ore from Minnesota's Iron Range (page 221) and coal from western states account for about 80 percent of the tonnage. Midwestern grain bound for Europe and Africa, general freight, and bulk commodities fill out the total.

About 3.5 million tourists visit Duluth annually — and like all tourists, they are hungry and thirsty.

The downtown and lakeside areas, including Canal Park and the Lakewalk, feature over 50 restaurants, from casual to cutting edge. Four Duluth brewpubs offer both food and house-made beers; packaged beers from Lake Superior Brewing Co. and Bent Paddle Brewing Co. are available at liquor stores throughout the state. Vikre Distillery, a micro operation housed in an old warehouse next to the Lift Bridge, uses foraged wild botanicals to craft three varieties of gin; it also produces aquavit and specialty whiskeys.

Heading from Duluth toward Grand Marais, opt for the scenic lakeside road rather than the expressway to Two Harbors. The New Scenic Café, about 15 miles from Canal Park, is one of the North Shore's top food destinations. The funky exterior — the building was a 1960s-era drive-in — belies the food excellence within. Chef Scott Graden combines modern-day flair with top-quality seasonal ingredients, locally sourced when possible, to create exceptional, photo-worthy food that delights the senses without feeling pretentious.

GRAND MARAIS — the 2015 winner of America's Coolest Small Town contest — is an artist community, home to several galleries as well as the North House Folk School, a workshop-based school that teaches traditional northern crafts including basketry using indigenous materials, timber framing, and blacksmithing. The town is also the starting point for the Gunflint Trail, a 55-mile corridor that is one of two main gateways to the Boundary Waters Canoe Area Wilderness (page 20). The year-round population of Grand Marais hovers around 1,300, but seasonal residents and tourists swell that number enough to support several excellent dining options including the Angry Trout, a nationally regarded restaurant housed in an old fishing shanty on the harbor. Another lakeside favorite is the Gun Flint Tavern, an eclectic bar and grill that is also a microbrewery with a half-dozen rotating beers including a seasonally available brew crafted with wild rice. A few blocks away, a stunning taproom is home to Voyageur Brewing Company, whose packaged beers are finding their way into bars, restaurants, and liquor stores in other parts of the state. Finally, the Cook County Whole Foods Co-op (no relation to the chain of similar name) offers groceries and excellent ready-to-eat soups, salads, and sandwiches — perfect to tote to the nearby harbor for a picnic.

Plank-Grilled Trout with Cucumber-Dill Sauce

Plank cooking is a technique borrowed from Native tribes in the Pacific Northwest, who cooked fresh fish on a slab of cedar wood. It's perfect for lake trout or a good-size steelhead trout, and also works well with salmon. The warm sauce is a wonderful complement to the grilled fish, which picks up a woodsy taste from the plank. Look for grilling planks at sporting-goods stores, gourmet stores, and large grocery stores; these days, you'll have your choice of not only cedar but also other woods, including maple and alder. **Note:** The grilling plank should be about ½ inch thick and large enough to hold the fillets. It has to soak for at least 4 hours before you can use it for cooking; plan accordingly.

4 SERVINGS

1 quart cold water

¼ cup firmly packed light brown sugar

¼ cup coarse kosher salt

4 (5- to 6-ounce) boneless trout or salmon fillets, skin on or skinless

1 tablespoon vegetable oil

2 tablespoons unsalted butter, melted

1 teaspoon lemon juice

CUCUMBER-DILL SAUCE

½ cup dry white wine

2 tablespoons lemon juice

1 tablespoon heavy cream

1 shallot, minced

1 cup (2 sticks) unsalted butter, each cut into 16 pieces

1 cucumber, peeled, seeded, and diced

1 tablespoon snipped fresh dill fronds

1. **Make the fish:** Soak the plank in clean water for 4 to 8 hours, weighting it to keep it submerged.

2. When you're ready to start preparation, make a brine by combining the cold water with the brown sugar and the salt in a mixing bowl, stirring until the sugar and salt dissolve. Place a 1-gallon plastic food storage bag in a baking dish. Add the fish fillets and the brine. Seal the bag and refrigerate for 25 to 30 minutes. Meanwhile, prepare a grill for direct high heat.

3. When the fish has brined for no more than 30 minutes, remove it from the brine and pat dry; discard the brine. Pat the plank dry and lightly coat the top with the oil. Arrange the fish fillets on the plank in a single layer, skin side down. Stir together the melted butter and lemon juice, then brush it over the fillets.

4. Place the plank on the grill grate directly over the fire. Cover the grill and cook until the fish is just opaque when probed at the thickest part, 15 to 20 minutes. The plank will smolder and may catch fire around the edges; that's okay, but if the fire looks too strong, spray it with water.

5. **Meanwhile, make the sauce:** Stir together the wine, lemon juice, cream, and shallot in a small saucepan. Cook over high heat until the mixture reduces and becomes slightly thick, about 5 minutes. Reduce the heat to low and whisk in the butter, a piece at a time. Remove from the heat and stir in the cucumber and dill. Serve warm with the fish.

Freshwater Fish Chowder

This chowder doesn't use any cream or other dairy, which makes it taste lighter and fresher than other chowders and really allows the flavor of the fish to shine. The Yukon Gold potatoes remain firmer after cooking, while the russets tend to crumble into the broth. Choose whichever you like.

4 thick-cut bacon strips, chopped

1 yellow or white onion, diced

1 large or 2 medium carrots, peeled and diced

1 celery stalk, diced

1 small shallot, minced

½ cup dry white wine

¾ pound russet or Yukon Gold potatoes, peeled and cut into ½-inch cubes

1 quart reduced-sodium chicken broth

½ teaspoon dried thyme

½ teaspoon salt

¼ teaspoon paprika (smoked paprika is very good here)

¼ teaspoon ground white pepper

1 bay leaf

¾–1 pound boneless, skinless walleye, trout, eelpout, or other freshwater fish, cut into ¾-inch chunks

Snipped fresh chives, for garnish

Oyster crackers, for serving

Hot pepper sauce, for serving

1. Cook the bacon in a 1-gallon soup pot over medium heat, stirring frequently, until crisp. Remove half of the bacon with a slotted spoon and set on a paper towel–lined plate; leave the remaining bacon in the pot. Spoon off all but about 1 tablespoon of the bacon drippings.

2. Add the onion, carrots, celery, and shallot. Cook over medium heat, stirring frequently, for about 5 minutes. Stir in the wine. Continue cooking until the wine has reduced by half, 4 to 5 minutes. Add the potatoes. Cook, stirring several times, until the pot is mostly dry, 3 to 4 minutes. Add the broth, thyme, salt, paprika, pepper, and bay leaf. Increase the heat to high and bring to a boil, then adjust the heat so the mixture bubbles gently. Cook until the potatoes are tender, about 15 minutes. Remove and discard the bay leaf. Use a potato masher to partially mash about one-half of the vegetables.

3. Add the fish chunks. Cook, stirring several times, until the fish just begins to flake, about 5 minutes. Ladle into heated soup bowls or wide, shallow soup plates. Garnish with the reserved bacon and the chives. Serve with oyster crackers and hot sauce.

Variations

- To make a semivegetarian version for people who eat fish but no red meat or poultry, omit the bacon and substitute vegetable broth for the chicken broth. Use 1 tablespoon vegetable oil to cook the vegetables in step 2.

- Substitute snipped fresh dill fronds for the chive garnish.

Fish Fillets on Garlic Toast with Vegetables and Saffron Broth

Attractive, tasty, and simple, this dish is perfect for an intimate supper for two as well as a casual weekday meal. The perfect fish for this is a walleye fillet that weighs 8 to 10 ounces; simply cut it in half for two portions. If you are using smaller fillets, such as those from perch or crappie, make a single serving by arranging two fillets so the rib portions overlap.

2 SERVINGS

2 teaspoons extra-virgin olive oil

⅔ cup diced onion

½ cup diced carrot

½ cup diced fennel bulb

1¼ cups diced fresh tomatoes (peeled and seeded before dicing), or 1 cup drained canned diced tomatoes

1 cup Chardonnay or other dry white wine

¼ teaspoon dried thyme

¼ teaspoon crumbled dried oregano

2 garlic cloves

1¾ cups chicken broth

6–8 saffron threads

2 slices firm Italian bread, about 3 by 4 inches and ¾ inch thick

8–10 ounces boneless, skinless walleye or other fish fillets (see headnote)

Salt and freshly ground black pepper

⅓ cup shredded mozzarella cheese

1. Preheat the oven to 400°F. Heat the oil in a large skillet over medium heat. Add the onion, carrot, and fennel. Reduce the heat to medium-low and sauté the vegetables for about 5 minutes. Add the tomatoes, wine, thyme, and oregano. Bring the mixture to a gentle boil. Cook, stirring occasionally, until the liquid is saucy but not soupy, about 15 minutes. Cover the skillet and reduce the heat; simmer until the vegetables are tender, about 10 minutes.

2. Meanwhile, mince one garlic clove. Combine the minced garlic and broth in a small saucepan; crumble the saffron threads into the broth. Bring the broth to a boil, and boil until reduced by half, 7 to 10 minutes. Set aside and keep warm. While the broth is cooking, place the bread slices on a baking sheet. Bake until crispy and lightly brown, about 10 minutes total, turning once midway through. Halve the remaining garlic clove and rub the bread on both sides with the garlic halves, then place each piece of bread in a wide, shallow, oven-safe soup plate.

3. When the vegetables are tender, sprinkle the fish generously with salt and pepper. Place the fish in the skillet with the vegetables, and spoon some of the vegetables over the fish. Cover the skillet and simmer until the fish is just opaque, 5 to 10 minutes.

4. When the fish is just opaque, spoon some of the vegetables evenly over the bread. Use a spatula to place individual portions of fish carefully on top of the vegetable-topped bread. Divide the remaining vegetables evenly over the fish. Sprinkle with the cheese. Place the soup plates on a baking sheet. Bake until the cheese is melted and beginning to bubble, 4 to 6 minutes.

5. As soon as the cheese has melted, place the soup plates on heatproof mats on the table. Ladle the hot broth evenly around the sides of the bread. Be aware that the bowls are very hot.

Wood-Grilled Stream Trout

Using actual wood in your charcoal grill (rather than charcoal briquettes) allows you to bring the taste of the campfire home. You will need about 2 quarts of smoking-wood chunks (or dry hardwood or fruitwood chunks) ranging from golf ball size to baseball size, some newspaper to start the fire, two inexpensive 10- by 14-inch metal cake-cooling racks (buy cheap ones made of thinner bars, which allow the racks to flex enough to be wired together on the edges without crushing the fish), and a handful of twist ties from a box of plastic sandwich bags.

2 SERVINGS

2 (½- to ¾-pound) whole dressed rainbow or other stream trout, rinsed and patted dry

1 tablespoon extra-virgin olive oil

Salt and freshly ground black pepper

4 sprigs parsley

2 multibranched sprigs thyme

2 sprigs dill (fronds, not seed heads)

Note: To serve four, use another rack setup and rotate the two racks over the hot part of the fire, increasing the cooking time slightly to compensate. If you want to try this with a larger fish or with fillets, plan on about 10 minutes cooking time per inch of thickness.

1. Cut three slashes in the thicker meat on both sides of each fish, perpendicular to the spine, cutting down just until you encounter the spine. Rub the fish inside and out with the oil. Sprinkle inside and out with salt and pepper, also sprinkling some into the slashes. Stuff two sprigs parsley and one sprig each thyme and dill into the body cavity of each fish. Place the fish in a dish; cover and refrigerate for 1 to 2 hours.

2. When you're ready to start cooking, crumple some sheets of newspaper and place them on the coal grate of a charcoal grill. Pile the wood chunks on top in a pyramid. Light the newspaper and let the pile burn until the wood pieces are flaming and beginning to burn down. Spread the wood out slightly and add the cooking grate. Cover the grill, keeping the vents in the lid about halfway open, and let burn until the wood is lightly ashed and no longer flaming, 5 to 10 minutes longer.

3. Meanwhile, place the fish back to back on a metal cake-cooling rack, about 1 inch apart. Place a second rack over the fish. Wire the edges together tightly along the sides and ends with wire twist ties, twisting the ties tightly enough to pull the racks together and secure the fish.

4. Place the rack assembly with the fish on the cooking grate, directly over the coals. Cover the grill and cook for 5 minutes. Carefully flip the rack assembly and re-cover the grill. Cook until the fish is flaky at the thickest part, 4 to 6 minutes longer. Transfer the rack assembly to a baking sheet and cover loosely with foil. Let stand for about 5 minutes. Cut the twist ties and open up the racks. Transfer the fish to individual plates. Serve at once, warning diners to be aware of the bones in the whole fish.

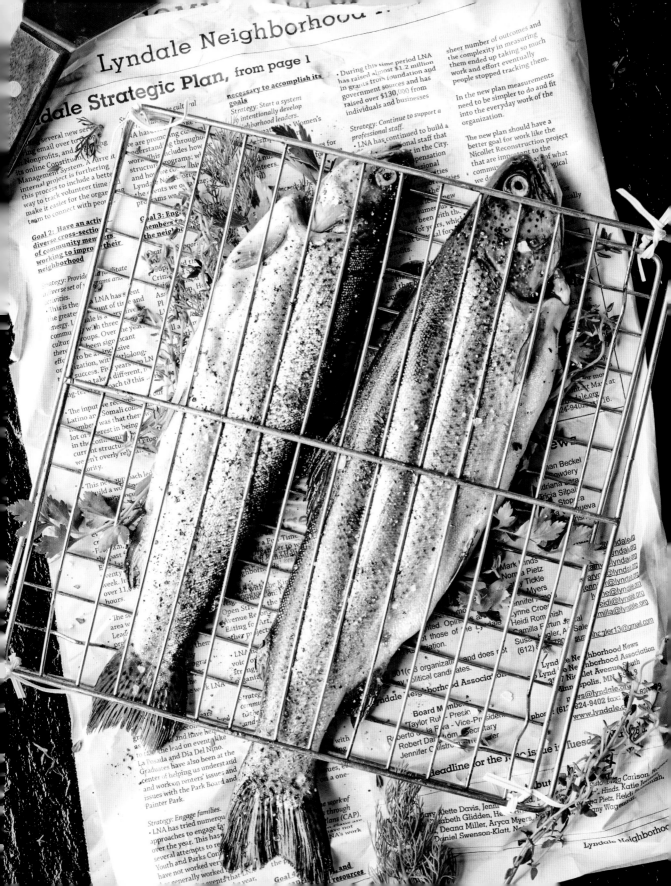

Crab-Style Fish Cakes

Fresh fish is chopped by hand to yield fish cakes with an appealing, somewhat flaky texture similar to crab cakes (in contrast to the smooth, fluffy Traditional North Shore Fish Cakes on page 25). Walleye is probably the most common choice, but this dish works just as well with panfish, smallmouth bass, trout, or completely boned northern pike.

3 eggs

¼ cup plus 2 tablespoons heavy cream

1 cup cubed French bread or firm white sandwich bread (½-inch cubes; remove crusts before cubing and measuring)

1½ pounds boneless, skinless walleye or other firm freshwater fish (see headnote)

¾ teaspoon salt

⅛ teaspoon ground white pepper

¼ cup finely minced onion

¼ cup finely minced roasted red bell pepper, jarred or homemade

2 tablespoons minced fresh parsley

½ teaspoon finely grated fresh gingerroot

½ cup all-purpose flour

1 teaspoon paprika

1 cup panko (Japanese-style breadcrumbs) or finely crushed crackers

Vegetable oil, for frying

1. Beat together one of the eggs and ¼ cup of the cream in a mixing bowl. Stir in the bread cubes. Set aside at room temperature for about 15 minutes, stirring occasionally with a fork to break up the bread.

2. Meanwhile, cut the walleye into 1-inch chunks. Sprinkle with the salt and pepper. Use a *very sharp* heavy knife to chop the mixture until the largest pieces are about ¼ inch in size; about half of the mixture should be finer, similar to very coarsely ground beef in texture. Transfer to a large mixing bowl.

3. Line a baking sheet with parchment paper. Mash the softened bread into a smooth paste with the fork, then scrape it into the bowl with the chopped fish. Add the onion, bell pepper, parsley, and gingerroot; mix very well with a wooden spoon. Scoop out ⅓ cup (packed) of the fish mixture, then pat between your hands into a cake about 3 inches across. Place on the prepared baking sheet. Repeat with the remaining fish mixture to make 10 cakes. Cover with plastic wrap and refrigerate for 1 to 2 hours; this helps firm up the fish cakes.

4. When you're ready to cook, preheat the oven to 300°F. Stir together the flour and paprika in a wide, shallow bowl. Beat the remaining two eggs with the remaining 2 tablespoons cream in another bowl. Place the panko into a third bowl. Dredge both sides of a fish cake first in the flour, gently

shaking off excess. Dip into the egg mixture, allowing excess to drip back into the bowl. If the fish cake starts to break apart while working with the egg mixture, use a slotted spatula to lift it out of the egg mixture, then flip it gently into your hand and place it back into the egg mixture to coat the second side; use the spatula to lift it out of the egg mixture again. Gently dip the egg-coated fish cake into the panko, turning to coat both sides. Set the panko-coated fish cake on a clean plate. Coat four more fish cakes in the same way.

5. Warm ¼ inch of oil in a large skillet over medium heat until shimmering. Carefully add the panko-coated fish cakes. Fry the patties until golden brown on both sides and firm to the touch, 8 to 10 minutes total. Transfer to a clean plate and keep warm in the oven while you coat and fry the remaining fish cakes. Serve immediately.

RED LAKE NATION FISHERY, REDBY

Walleye is Minnesota's official state fish, and justifiably popular on the dinner table due to its firm, flaky white meat. What few people know is that when they order fresh walleye at a restaurant — even one that's perched on one of Minnesota's many walleye lakes — they're probably feasting on Canadian walleye, because it's illegal to sell this protected game fish if it was taken in Minnesota waters.

An exception to this is the wild-caught walleye from Red Lake Nation Fishery, a Native-run business on the Red Lake Indian Reservation, which is exempt from the rule due to its tribal status.

Fish are caught and hand-filleted by band members, then shipped daily to restaurants and individual customers in Minnesota and many other states. The tribally owned company also provides jobs and much-needed income on the reservation. In addition to the famous Red Lake Nation walleye, the fishery supplies perch, northern pike, whitefish, and crappie, as well as smoked whitefish.

Recipe from KATE MARRONE

Salmon or Trout Mousse with *Sauce Verte*

Use Lake Superior salmon or any native trout, such as brook trout, steelhead, lake trout, or rainbow trout, to prepare this elegant appetizer. The mousse is a lovely pink color when prepared with salmon or pink-fleshed trout. This dish was one of the most-requested hors d'oeuvres that my sister, Kate Marrone, prepared when she ran a catering service in Minneapolis a number of years ago. **Note:** A food processor is required to prepare this dish.

8–12 APPETIZER SERVINGS

2 tablespoons unsalted butter, softened

2 pounds boneless, skinless salmon or trout, cut into 1-inch cubes

¼ teaspoon cayenne pepper

⅛ teaspoon nutmeg, preferably freshly grated

Salt and ground white pepper

3 cups heavy cream

2 eggs

1 recipe *Sauce Verte* (page 96)

1. Preheat the oven to 400°F. Begin heating a saucepan of water to boiling. Butter a 2-quart ring mold, or two smaller fish molds, very generously. Cut parchment paper to fit inside the top of the mold. Butter the parchment on the side that will be directly on top of the mousse mixture when it is poured into the mold.

2. Combine the salmon, cayenne, nutmeg, and salt and pepper to taste in a food processor. With the machine running, slowly pour the cream through the feed tube. Add the eggs, one at a time. Process until the mixture is smooth and fluffy.

3. Spoon the fish mixture into the prepared mold(s), ensuring that the mixture is pressed into all crevices of the mold. Smooth the top with a spatula. Place the buttered parchment directly on top of the fish mixture.

4. Place the mold(s) into a baking dish that fits them comfortably. Pull out the oven rack slightly and place the baking dish on the rack. Add boiling water to come halfway up the sides of the mold(s). Carefully slide the rack back in. Reduce the oven temperature to 350°F. Bake for 1 hour for the 2-quart mold, or 45 minutes for smaller molds, then test for doneness by lifting the paper up and inserting a skewer or cake tester into the center of the mousse. The mousse is done when the tester comes out clean. Do not overcook, or the mousse will become dry. Let the mousse cool on a wire rack for 15 minutes before unmolding. Cool completely, then refrigerate until well chilled. Slice and serve with the *Sauce Verte*.

Smoked Trout or Salmon Cakes

Shele Toftey owns and operates Dockside Fish Market in Grand Marais with her husband, Harley. Shele has fished commercially in both Alaska and in Minnesota's Lake Superior, and now runs Dockside's retail and food operations. She certainly knows how to handle fish, whether in a boat or in the kitchen. (See page 26 for more information about Dockside Fish Market.)

4 OR 5 SERVINGS

¼ cup finely chopped green bell pepper

¼ cup finely chopped red bell pepper

¼ cup mayonnaise

¼ cup Dijon mustard

4 scallions, thinly sliced

1 garlic clove, minced

2 tablespoons lemon juice

1 teaspoon Old Bay seasoning

Pinch of cayenne pepper

1 pound smoked trout or smoked salmon

1 cup panko (Japanese-style breadcrumbs)

2 tablespoons olive oil, or as needed

1. Stir together the green and red bell peppers, mayonnaise, mustard, scallions, garlic, lemon juice, Old Bay seasoning, and cayenne in a mixing bowl.

2. Remove the skin and bones from the fish, and flake the meat into small pieces; you should have about 2 cups. Add the flaked fish and panko to the bowl with the bell pepper mixture, and mix thoroughly. Shape the mixture into 2-inch patties, packing firmly; you should have about 16 patties.

3. Warm the oil in a large skillet over medium heat. Fry the patties until golden brown on both sides and firm to the touch, 9 to 12 minutes total; you may need a little more oil, especially if you have to cook the fish cakes in two batches. Serve immediately.

THE BOUNDARY WATERS CANOE AREA WILDERNESS

Stretched like a tiara across Minnesota's border with Ontario, the Boundary Waters Canoe Area (BWCA) is Minnesota's premier destination, annually attracting over 250,000 visitors who come to canoe, fish, and observe nature. A 1.1-million-acre roadless area, the BWCA is dotted with more than 1,000 lakes and streams that are connected by 1,500 miles of canoe routes. No motors are allowed. Visitors portage between lakes, carrying their canoes and gear over rocky paths to reach the next lake, heading ever farther into the wilderness.

The BWCA was formed by glaciers that scoured the region 2 million years ago, leaving depressions in the bedrock that became lakes. Scour marks from glacial till are still visible on exposed granite, testifying to the immense power of ice and rock. Along the rocky shores, white and red pine, balsam fir, and white cedar tease their roots down between cracks in bare granite to gain purchase. A short walk inland, thin soil supports more conifers, as well as birch, aspen — locally called popple, or poplar — and plants such as blueberries, sarsaparilla, Labrador tea, and wildflowers. From a canoe, the BWCA is a three-color canvas: sky blue water, gray rock, and green trees, with scudding white clouds as an accent.

Most canoeists spend a week or so in the wilderness, carrying enough food to last the whole time. Many hope to supplement their packed, non-refrigerated foods with freshly caught walleye, trout, or smallmouth bass, all of which are abundant in the clear, cold lakes. A shore lunch of fresh fish, seasoned by the scenery, is a meal worthy of a five-star restaurant.

Herbed Fish and Carrots in Foil

This is similar to cooking fish *en papillote,* but instead of a parchment envelope, the fish is cooked in foil, on a bed of carrots. Foil cookery is a classic campfire technique. It's particularly appropriate for a trip to the BWCA (opposite page), because the seasoning is folded into the foil, so it's easy to put together when you've got fresh fish. At home, you can use the same technique on a charcoal or gas grill. This recipe is adapted from my book *The Back-Country Kitchen: Camp Cooking for Canoeists, Hikers, and Anglers.*

2 SERVINGS (1 PACKET)

½ teaspoon mixed dried herb blend, such as *fines herbes*

¼ teaspoon lemon pepper or garlic pepper

A good pinch of kosher salt

2 small whole carrots

Small chunk of onion

1 garlic clove, optional

1½ tablespoons butter

8–10 ounces smallmouth bass, walleye, northern pike, or other fish fillets, skin and rib bones removed (a single fillet from a moderately sized walleye or pike, or several fillets from smaller fish)

1. Tear off an 18-inch square of heavy-duty foil. Place the herbs, pepper, and salt in the center of the shiny side. Fold the foil to enclose the herb mixture completely, or, if you're cooking at home, proceed as directed in step 3.

2. When you're packing the food pack, place the foil packet where it won't be punctured. Tuck the carrots into the center of the pack; they will keep for several days. Whole onions and garlic also travel well; once the onion is cut, store it in a plastic bag and use within 2 days. Place the butter in a small plastic container with a tight lid, and place that in a plastic bag; push the container into the center of the food pack (or keep it in a cooler, if you're using one).

3. Prepare a campfire or grill for direct high heat. Open the foil and push the herb mixture off to one side. Peel the carrots and cut into ¼-inch slices. Arrange them down the center of the foil. Cut the butter into chunks and scatter half over the carrots. Scatter a few slices of onion over the carrots; slice the garlic thinly, if using, and add to the onion slices. Place the fish on the carrots, arranging smaller fillets so the thinner portions overlap. Sprinkle the herbs and remaining butter over the fish.

4. Fold the long edges of the foil together, then roll-fold toward the fish, making three or more roll-folds. Roll-fold each end toward the center.

5. Place the packet, seam side up, on a grate over the coals. Cook for 15 minutes, moving the packet around occasionally. Flip the packet and cook for 8 to 10 minutes longer. Open the packet and distribute the fish, vegetables, and juices between serving plates.

Classic BWCA Walleye Shore Lunch

This is prepared on an open fire built underneath a Forest Service iron grate, found at most official Boundary Waters Canoe Area (BWCA) campsites. The first key to preparing this meal in the rough outdoor setting is a little advance preparation, which means bringing along the right ingredients. The second key, of course, is catching walleye to cook; I leave that up to your skills with a rod. You will also need a cast-iron skillet, a small plastic bottle of liquid dish soap, utensils for cooking and serving, a sharp fillet knife, paper towels, and a plastic bag for garbage.

4 SERVINGS

FISH BREADING

1 cup all-purpose flour

¼ cup cornmeal

2 teaspoons onion powder

2 teaspoons salt

1 teaspoon garlic powder

1 teaspoon paprika

POTATO PACKETS

4 tablespoons butter, cut into 8 pats

2 large russet potatoes, peeled, boiled, cooled, and sliced ½ inch thick

3 bacon strips, cooked until crisp, then crumbled

½ cup sliced onion, cut crosswise from a wedge

Salt and freshly ground black pepper

½ cup (1 stick) butter, cut up and packed in a tightly sealing plastic container

4 small to medium walleye fillets (or 2 larger fillets, cut in half crosswise), skin and rib bones removed

Apples and cookies for dessert, optional

1. **Prepare the fish breading:** Combine the flour, cornmeal, onion powder, salt, garlic powder, and paprika in a 1-gallon ziplock bag. Hold the top of the bag together and shake to mix. Roll up and seal the bag.

2. **Prepare the potato packets:** Tear off two 24-inch lengths of heavy-duty foil. For each packet, fold one piece of foil in half crosswise with the shiny side in. Place two pats butter on the foil. Top with one-quarter of the potatoes. Scatter half of the bacon and half of the onion over the potatoes. Sprinkle with salt and pepper to taste. Top with another one-quarter of the potatoes and two more pats of butter. Fold the long edges of the foil together, then roll-fold toward the potatoes, making three or more roll-folds. Roll-fold each end toward the center.

3. When you head out to fish, wrap the potato packets and the butter container in a towel with a small frozen ice pack. Tuck the rolled-up bag of breading into the skillet, and wrap with a towel.

4. To prepare lunch, build a good-size fire under a fire grate. Let it burn until you have a lively bed of coals with a few flames licking out; feed the fire as needed during cooking to maintain a hot, but not roaring, fire. Put the packets on the grate and cook until you hear sizzling, then turn and cook until the second side sizzles. Cook for about 10 minutes longer, turning frequently. Move them to the edge of the grate to keep warm.

Recipe continues on page 24

5. Rub the outside of the skillet with dish soap; this makes it easy to clean off the soot that will accumulate on the skillet. Place the skillet on the grate. Add about 2 tablespoons of butter. Shake two fish fillets in the bag of breading. Add to the skillet. Cook until golden brown and crisp on both sides, adding a bit more butter if needed. Poke the fish at the thickest part; if the flesh is opaque, the fish is done.

6. Serve the fish and one of the potato packets to the first two lucky diners while you cook the second batch of fish. Remove the skillet from the heat and set it on a rock to cool while you enjoy your lunch. Give everyone an apple and a cookie for dessert, if desired.

7. Wipe the skillet inside and out with paper towels. Burn the paper towels, or put them in the garbage bag. Crush the foil and place in the garbage bag. Pour water on the fire and stir with a stick until it is *completely cold*. This is very important; fires can smolder for hours and reignite forest duff. The 2007 Ham Lake Fire, which was started by a campfire, burned for weeks in the BWCA, adjoining Quetico Provincial Park, and inhabited parts of the Gunflint Trail area, consuming over 75,000 acres of forest and about 130 structures.

Traditional North Shore Fish Cakes

These Scandinavian-inspired fish cakes are made with fresh lake herring or whitefish, typically from Lake Superior but also found in some of the larger "inland" lakes along the North Shore. Be sure to remove all the bones from the fish, paying particular attention if using whitefish (which have pinbones along the center of each fillet; remove these with tweezers). These fish cakes have a smooth, fluffy consistency that is typical of many fish cakes prepared on the North Shore (for a version with more texture, see Crab-Style Fish Cakes on page 16). You could also prepare these with any freshwater fish.

4 OR 5 SERVINGS

1 (½-pound) russet potato, peeled and cut into thirds

1¼ pounds boneless, skinless lake herring or whitefish, cut into 1½-inch chunks

2 tablespoons finely minced onion

2 tablespoons finely minced celery

½ cup heavy cream

2 eggs

1½ teaspoons salt

¼ teaspoon ground white pepper

⅛ teaspoon ground nutmeg, or a bit more

½ cup all-purpose flour

Vegetable oil, for frying

1. Preheat the oven to 300°F. Bring a pot of lightly salted water to a boil, and boil the potato until tender, then drain and mash until smooth. Transfer ¾ cup to a mixing bowl and set aside to cool. Refrigerate any remaining mashed potato for another use.

2. Combine the fish chunks, onion, and celery in a food processor. Pulse a few times, then add half the cream. Pulse a few more times, until the fish is coarsely chopped. Add the eggs, salt, pepper, and nutmeg. With the motor running, add the remaining cream through the feed tube, and process until smooth. Add the fish mixture to the mashed potato and stir until well mixed. Place the flour in a wide, shallow dish.

3. Scoop out ⅓ cup of the fish mixture, then pat between your hands into a cake about 3 inches across. Dredge both sides in the flour, gently shaking off excess. Transfer to a plate. Repeat until all the fish mixture has been used.

4. Warm ¼ inch of oil in a large skillet over medium heat until shimmering. Carefully add as many cakes as will fit comfortably. Fry the patties until golden brown on both sides and firm to the touch, 8 to 10 minutes total. Transfer to a clean plate and keep warm in the oven while you fry the remaining fish cakes.

HERRING OR CISCO?

The lake herring (*Coregonus artedi*) is a freshwater species native to Lake Superior and some of Minnesota's larger inland lakes; it is from the Salmonidae family, which also includes salmon and trout. It is not the same as ocean herring, part of the Clupeidea family, which also includes sardines and shad. Ocean herring is more common; pickled herring from the grocery store is made with ocean herring. To prevent confusion between ocean herring and lake herring, the scientific community changed the official common name of *C. artedi* to cisco in 2004. It hasn't quite stuck yet, though; along the North Shore, most people still refer to the tasty Lake Superior fish as lake herring, bluefin herring, or, simply, herring.

DOCKSIDE FISH MARKET, GRAND MARAIS

In 1982, Oregon native Shele Clapp was a rarity: a woman — and a petite one, at that — who worked as a crewmember on commercial fishing boats in Alaska, doing the heavy work of hauling lines and nets full of fish alongside what was typically an all-male crew. She picked up the skill as a teenager, fishing with her then boyfriend's family in the Pacific and on Oregon's Columbia River.

In 1990, while fishing in Alaska, she met Harley Toftey, the captain of another boat that was fishing in the same area. A lifelong fisherman from Grand Marais, Harley is a descendant of Norwegians who arrived on Minnesota's North Shore in the late 1800s and who were the namesake of the charming lakeside village of Tofte, 25 miles southwest of Grand Marais. Each year, Harley traveled to Alaska to spend 2 months fishing, and in 1990 he caught more than fish; he caught the eye of the petite fisherwoman on the other boat.

Harley and Shele Toftey now own and operate Dockside Fish Market, on the harbor in Grand Marais. Until she gave birth to twin girls in 1998, Shele joined Harley on their boat every morning at 5:00 during fishing season to fish Lake Superior for lake herring (also called cisco; see page 25).

HARLEY AND HIS CREW still head out every morning during the season. In spring, the herring — his main target, although he also catches some lake trout and whitefish — are suspended over deep water, and the crew sets 250-foot-long nets perhaps 200 feet down, anchoring them in up to 600 feet of water. Nets are brought up daily, and the fish are hand-filleted back on shore.

As the season progresses, the herring move from the depths, coming into relatively shallow water to spawn in late fall. That's the busiest time for Lake Superior fishing, because herring roe fetches a high price from Sweden. Each fall, Dockside's

Harley and Shele Toftey

fish-processing plant swings into gear to process the catch from Harley's boat as well as that from other commercial fisherman along the North Shore.

Inside the plant, workers line up along a conveyor-belt system, each with a specific task. The silvery, foot-long fish are carried individually down the belt. The egg sacs are pulled out to be cleaned and sent to Sweden; the meat is destined for the Manischewitz Company, where it will be turned into gefilte fish. Heads and scrap are sold to a fertilizer factory. "It's a no-waste fishery," Shele notes with pride.

SHELE NOW RUNS THE MARKET END of the business, selling fresh fish to many North Shore restaurants as well as to individuals who choose their catch from the market's refrigerated case. The market's café serves some of the best — and freshest — fried fish on the North Shore, as well

as soups, salads, sandwiches, smoked fish spread, and other treats. Their cozy deck overlooks the harbor and is a pleasant place to enjoy lunch while watching the boats lazing by. Dockside also sells gourmet goods, including bottled sauces, jams, and mustards, and cheese from several top-notch Wisconsin creameries. Their freezer case is stocked with local and not-so-local delicacies, including scallops, shrimp, squid, and crab.

They also smoke brown sugar–brined fish at their smokehouse next to the market, using maple wood from the hillsides above Lake Superior; on smoking days, the woodsy aroma perfumes the nearby Lake Walk. Dockside ships fresh and smoked fish to Coastal Seafoods in Minneapolis, who sells it to restaurants, co-ops, and grocery stores as well as directly to consumers at their storefronts in South Minneapolis and West St. Paul.

Butter-Fried Herring

This method is a particularly good choice for lake herring, although it works with nearly any fresh-water fish fillets that are not too thick. Use only scrupulously fresh fillets; there is nothing here to disguise off flavors. Serve with homemade tartar sauce; if you like, also put a bottle of Frank's RedHot sauce on the table for diners to add as they wish. On the side, try potato pancakes and a fresh green vegetable.

6 boneless, skinless lake herring fillets (about 1 pound total)

4 ounces saltine crackers (1 sleeve) or oyster crackers (have more on hand in case you run short)

2 eggs

⅓ cup all-purpose flour

½ cup (1 stick) unsalted butter, or as needed

Tartar sauce, for serving

Hot pepper sauce, for serving

1. Preheat the oven to 250°F. Rinse the herring fillets and pat dry. Cut into halves crosswise; this makes it easier to turn the fillets without breaking them apart.

2. Place the crackers in a plastic bag. Crush with a rolling pin until they are a medium uneven texture; there should be some fine crumbs, and some as large as ¼ inch across. Transfer to a deep plate. Beat the eggs in a shallow bowl with a fork. Place the flour in the plastic bag used to crush the crackers. Add half of the herring fillets to the bag. Shake gently to coat the herring with flour. Remove three pieces of herring at a time and dip into the beaten egg, coating both sides; let excess egg drip back into the bowl. Dredge both sides of the herring in the cracker crumbs. Place the coated fish on a plate. Repeat with the remaining three pieces of floured herring.

3. Melt 3 tablespoons of the butter in a large skillet over medium heat (a nonstick skillet works best but is not essential). Arrange a single layer of herring in the skillet. Cook until nicely golden on the first side, about 3 minutes, adding more butter around the edges of the skillet if it seems to need it. Carefully turn each piece and add a little more butter around the sides. Cook until golden brown on the second side and cooked through; the fish should just flake when probed in the thickest part with a fork. Transfer to a serving plate and keep warm in the oven.

4. Wipe the skillet quickly with paper towels to remove any burned butter. Melt 3 tablespoons butter in the skillet as before. Fry the remaining herring as you did the first batch. Serve without delay, with tartar sauce and hot pepper sauce.

Whitefish *Sous Vide* with Basil-Saffron Sauce

Sous vide is a method of cooking that involves immersing vacuum-packed food in hot water (see page 162 for more information). Fish cooked with this method is deliciously moist and silky. Serve with a simple mix of hot cooked white and wild rice.

4 SERVINGS

5 tablespoons unsalted butter

2 (¾-pound) boneless, skinless whitefish fillets

Salt and ground white pepper

1 tablespoon minced shallots

1½ tablespoons all-purpose flour

⅓ cup reduced-sodium chicken broth

⅓ cup dry white wine or Champagne

⅓ cup heavy cream

A good pinch of saffron threads

10–12 fresh basil leaves, coarsely chopped

1. Prepare a cooler for *sous vide* cooking as described on page 162, using a target temperature of 143°F. Melt the butter in a heavy-bottomed medium saucepan over medium-low heat. Cook, swirling the pan occasionally, until the butter begins to show brown flecks, 5 to 8 minutes; don't let the butter burn. Remove from the heat and let cool for a few minutes.

2. Cut each fillet crosswise to make two portions. Sprinkle both sides with salt and pepper to taste. Arrange the fish in two 1-gallon ziplock bags (page 162), placing two portions in each bag side by side without overlapping. Add 1 tablespoon of the browned butter to each bag, gently massaging so the butter coats both sides of the fish. Set the bags aside.

3. Add the shallots to the saucepan with the remaining browned butter and cook over medium-low heat, stirring constantly, for about 30 seconds. Whisk in the flour and cook, whisking constantly, for 2 minutes. Whisk in the broth, wine, and cream. Finely crumble the saffron threads into the broth mixture. Cook, whisking constantly, until the sauce thickens and bubbles, 3 to 5 minutes. Cover and remove from the heat.

4. Partially seal the bags and lower them into the hot water, then seal tightly as described on page 162. Close the lid and let cook for 10 minutes. Check the temperature of the fish at the thickest area. It should read 135 to 140°F; if it is not quite done, reseal the bag and return to the cooler, checking again after 5 minutes. Stir the basil into the sauce, then rewarm the sauce over medium heat. Use a spatula to transfer the fish to warmed serving plates. Pour the juices from each bag into the sauce, then stir to blend. Taste and add salt if needed. Spoon the sauce over the fish. Serve immediately.

Walleye with Pea Mash and Crispy Prosciutto

This is a melding of several recipes I've prepared over the years. The primary concept comes from a cod recipe in *Kitchen of Light: The New Scandinavian Cooking* by Andreas Viestad. Many other cooks, including Martha Stewart and Jamie Oliver, have published versions that are very similar to Viestad's recipe, with variations. Among other changes, my own version substitutes walleye for the cod — a delicious pairing with the prosciutto and bright green peas. This recipe is easy to double, and it makes a lovely dish to serve for a dinner party; dish up individual plates and present them to your guests rather than serve it family-style.

2 SERVINGS

- 2 tablespoons plus 2 teaspoons unsalted butter, or as needed
- 2 ounces thinly sliced prosciutto, cut crosswise into ½-inch strips and separated
- ¼ cup all-purpose flour
- A few pinches of paprika
- Salt and freshly ground black pepper
- 1 (10- to 12-ounce) boneless, skinless walleye fillet, cut in half crosswise
- 1¾ cups frozen green peas, thawed
- 3 tablespoons snipped fresh chives
- 1½ tablespoons heavy cream
- 2 teaspoons minced garlic
- ⅛ teaspoon nutmeg, preferably freshly grated
- 1½ tablespoons chopped fresh mint

1. Melt 1 tablespoon of the butter in a medium skillet (preferably nonstick) over medium heat. Add the prosciutto and cook, moving it around and breaking it apart with tongs, until the prosciutto is beginning to crisp up nicely, 3 to 5 minutes. Use the tongs to transfer it to a plate.

2. Combine the flour, paprika, and salt and pepper to taste in a large plastic bag. Close the bag and shake to blend. Melt 1 tablespoon of the butter over medium heat in the same skillet used to cook the prosciutto. Add the walleye pieces to the bag with the flour and shake to coat. Add the floured walleye to the skillet and cook until lightly golden on both sides and cooked through, 8 to 10 minutes, adding a little more butter if needed; when the fish is done it will look just opaque when probed with a fork at the thickest point.

3. While the walleye is cooking, combine the peas, chives, cream, garlic, nutmeg, and 2 teaspoons butter in a medium saucepan. Cook, stirring frequently, until the peas are just tender but still bright green, about 4 minutes. Remove from the heat and mash to a coarse consistency with a potato masher. Stir in the mint. Taste, and add salt and pepper if needed.

4. To serve, divide the mashed peas between serving plates, mounding them slightly. Top each with a walleye fillet. Drizzle any juices from the skillet over the walleye. Scatter the prosciutto over the walleye. Serve immediately.

ICE FISHING

It's one of the small joys of living in Minnesota in the wintertime: taking friends from, say, Georgia out onto a frozen lake in the dead of winter. Trepidation turns to amazement when they realize they are *not* going to fall through the ice to a cold, watery death. And if we're going ice fishing, it's even more fun to watch their eyes as they gauge the progress of the ice auger as it drills through the frozen surface. "Why, there's nearly a foot of ice here!" they exclaim, clearly impressed. We chuckle silently, recalling times when we needed an extension on the auger to drill through ice that was twice as thick — or more.

Ice fishing can be a solitary pursuit, especially when extreme cold keeps all but the most fervent diehards indoors. It can also be a party sport, with friends gathering in clusters of heated fish houses — some replete with bunk beds, satellite TV, and cookstoves — and enjoying pickup ice-hockey games, cookouts on the ice, impromptu snowman construction, and general carousing. Lake Mille Lacs (Minnesota's second-largest inland lake, with an area of over 132,000 acres) is like a village in winter, complete with plowed roads that lead to fish houses set up on reefs far from shore; in recent years, there were as many as 5,500 fish houses on the lake.

Quarry for the ice angler ranges from 4-ounce bluegills to monstrous, toothy northern pike that may be 20 pounds or more. Walleye and trout fall in the middle of the size range and are probably the most popular targets, both for the excitement of landing these nice-size fish through a small hole and for the top-quality meal they promise.

For the smaller species, simple "jiggle sticks" and a handful of tiny lures can be picked up inexpensively, making this type of fishing a family pursuit enjoyed by young and old alike. On the other end of the spectrum, serious pike anglers use chainsaws to cut large openings in the ice, then sit in a "dark house" placed over the opening and hold a multi-pronged spear at the ready, watching for fish that come to inspect a lure dangling in the opening.

The reward for all of this is some of the best eating of the year. Fish caught through the ice have firm, clean, sweet flesh, with no hint of the muddiness or softness that can taint some species caught in the heat of summer.

Smoked Fish Spread

Use any smoked fish you like for this delicious spread. I like it best with whitefish; a whole, smoked 1½-pound whitefish will provide about the right amount of boneless fish. This spread is fabulous served with crackers, toasted baguette slices, or small squares of dense pumpernickel bread. Or you could place a scoop on a bed of lettuce leaves and serve it as a first course, accompanied by a basket of warm rustic bread and a glass of chilled crisp white wine.

¾ pound boneless, skinless smoked fish chunks

4 ounces chive and onion cream cheese spread (about ⅓ cup)

1–2 tablespoons mayonnaise or sour cream

1 tablespoon snipped fresh dill fronds, optional

2 teaspoons lemon juice

½ teaspoon prepared horseradish

¼ teaspoon hot pepper sauce

1. Place the fish in a medium mixing bowl. Mash with a fork until evenly flaked; the texture should be somewhat like tuna salad.

2. Add the cream cheese spread, 1 tablespoon mayonnaise, the dill (if desired), lemon juice, horseradish, and hot pepper sauce. Stir with a large spoon until well mixed. Add a little more mayonnaise if you want a looser texture. Chill for at least 1 hour before serving. This will keep, refrigerated, for up to 1 week.

Open-Faced Smoked Fish Melt Sandwiches

PER SANDWICH

⅓ cup Smoked Fish Spread (above)

1 sandwich-size slice of bread, lightly toasted

1–2 very thin slices of tomato, depending on size

Thinly sliced Muenster or Swiss cheese to cover the bread

Position an oven rack about 6 inches from the broiler, and pre-heat the broiler. For each sandwich, spread the Smoked Fish Spread on the bread, spreading all the way to the edges to prevent burning. Top with a slice of tomato (or two, depending on the size of the tomato). Place a layer of the cheese on top, using enough to cover the fish spread. Place the sandwich(es) on a baking sheet. Broil until the filling is hot and the cheese is bubbly, 3 to 4 minutes. Serve immediately.

Recipe from BRIAN MURPHY

Pickled Northern Pike

Northern pike have delicious, firm white meat, but the finely textured flesh is held together with a network of very fine Y-bones that are difficult to remove during filleting — and easy to accidentally swallow at the dinner table. That probably explains why so many anglers in Minnesota make pickled northern from their catch: The pickling process softens the bones completely, making a tasty snack that goes great with crackers and beer. This recipe is based on notes from Brian Murphy, who spends a lot of his free time fishing the lakes around his home near Glenwood. Brian mentioned that walleye also works well in this recipe. You will need two clean pint jars and one half-pint jar, with lids. **Note:** The Extension Service at the University of Minnesota recommends freezing all fish that will be pickled for 48 hours prior to pickling, to kill parasites that may be found in pike and other freshwater fish.

ABOUT 2½ PINTS

2 cups spring water or distilled water

¼ cup plus 1 tablespoon canning/pickling salt

1 pound skinless northern pike fillets, cut into 1-inch chunks

2 cups distilled white vinegar

2 cups white wine vinegar

1¼ cups sugar

½ cup white wine (a sweet wine is traditional, but Brian notes that "any drinkable white wine would be okay")

1 small white onion (you can try a red onion instead, but the pickled fish may turn pink if you use too much)

5 teaspoons pickling spice

1. Stir together the spring water and salt in a plastic food-storage container or glass bowl. Add the pike and stir gently. Cover and refrigerate for 48 hours, stirring once or twice each day.

2. Drain and rinse the fish, discarding the salt solution. Return the fish to the container. Add enough distilled white vinegar to cover the fish completely. Cover and refrigerate for 24 hours, stirring once or twice.

3. Make the marinade by combining the white wine vinegar and sugar in a nonreactive saucepan. Bring to a boil, stirring until the sugar dissolves. Remove from the heat and let cool completely. Stir in the wine.

4. Drain the fish, discarding the plain white vinegar in which it was steeping. Cut the onion in half horizontally (through the equator); refrigerate one half for another use. Cut the remaining half vertically into ¼-inch-thick wedges, removing the tough root end.

5. Pack the fish and onion wedges into the jars, alternating layers and sprinkling some pickling spice between the layers; use 2 teaspoons for each pint jar and 1 teaspoon for the half-pint jar. Pour in enough cooled marinade to cover the fish completely. Seal the jars with their lids. Refrigerate for at least 3 days to allow the flavors to develop, shaking occasionally. The pickled pike will keep in the refrigerator for up to 6 weeks.

CHAPTER 2

On the Wild Side

ABOUT 25 PERCENT OF THE LAND IN MINNESOTA is public, made up of mostly forested areas, along with some prairie lands. Whether they're hiking, gathering wild edibles, or hunting, Minnesotans love getting out to enjoy the state's abundant natural resources. Along with freshwater fish, wild foods including wild rice, game, maple syrup, wild berries, and wild mushrooms remain central to the state's identity.

Wild rice is very closely associated with Minnesota; the most productive wild rice beds in America are found on White Earth Nation land in northwestern Minnesota. Ojibwe Indians migrated from the East Coast to the Upper Midwest, stopping when they found "the food that grows on water," which they called *manoomin*. Legend says that the Ojibwe learned of its value when a duck dropped some grains into a pot of boiling water, to show the people that it was a good food.

Minnesota is one of the top states in numbers of hunters per capita. About half a million Minnesotans hunt deer annually. Ruffed grouse (also known as partridge) and pheasant are the main upland species hunted in the state, with wild turkeys a distant third. In fall, about 80,000 hunters hit the marshes, fields, and lakes in search of ducks and geese.

Although Minnesota is barely within the maple syrup range (it is the most westerly state where maple syrup can be produced), maple sugaring is a popular hobby. In early spring, people across the state head out to woodlots and urban yards to tap trees. Minnesota has a handful of boutique commercial syrup producers, some of whom have won awards at the national maple syrup competition held annually in Vermont.

Wild berries and mushrooms give Minnesotans a chance to collect the makings of some very tasty meals while enjoying the great outdoors. This chapter contains more than 30 recipes, including favorites such as Minnesota Wild Rice Soup and updated dishes including Duck Carnitas Tacos.

Maple-Cinnamon Apples

A little maple syrup goes a long way in this easy skillet dish. It makes a wonderful breakfast, served alongside some bacon or pork sausage. For dessert, top it with a scoop of vanilla or butter pecan ice cream.

2 SERVINGS

1 large apple
1 tablespoon butter
2 tablespoons pure maple syrup
⅛ teaspoon ground cinnamon
½–¾ cup granola

1. Cut the apple into quarters, then cut away the core. Slice each quarter into four wedges.

2. Melt the butter over medium heat in a medium or large skillet; a nonstick skillet works best. Add the apple slices in a single layer and cook until golden brown on one side, about 4 minutes. Turn and cook until the second side is beginning to brown, about 3 minutes longer.

3. Add the maple syrup and cinnamon, stirring gently to mix and to coat the apples. Cook until the syrup is bubbly and somewhat reduced, 3 to 5 minutes, stirring occasionally.

4. Divide between serving plates. Sprinkle the granola over each. Serve immediately.

MINNESOTA MAPLE SYRUP

Most people are surprised to learn that the only place in the world where maple syrup is commercially produced is a narrow band straddling the U.S.-Canada border, from the Atlantic to Minnesota. Although maples grow elsewhere, the climate isn't right for syrup production; for good sap flow, days must be above freezing and nights well below freezing, and once the trees start to bud, the sap becomes bitter and unsuitable for syrup.

Maple sap straight from the tree is colorless and watery, with a slightly sweet taste. Syrup is made by boiling off (or otherwise removing) most of the water, leaving behind the sugar and minerals that the groundwater picked up from the tree's wood as it traveled from roots to branch tips. It typically takes 40 gallons of sap to make 1 gallon of syrup.

Minnesota is at the western edge of maple syrup production; the maple species that are tapped commercially don't grow any farther west. Hundreds of Minnesota hobbyists tap trees, many within urban areas. Small-scale sugaring operations sell their products at local markets, but only a few producers make enough syrup to distribute beyond their immediate area. Wild Country Maple Syrup in Lutsen is the state's largest; it has also taken first place at the North American Maple Syrup Council's annual competition, held in Vermont. That's pretty impressive, coming from a state that accounts for about 1 percent of the nation's total syrup production.

Like wine, maple syrup has *terroir*, a term used to describe the effects of soil, climate, and groundwater on the flavor of foods produced in specific locales. Syrup made in Lutsen tastes different from syrup made in Minneapolis, or in Vermont; even syrup from Caribou Cream, another Lutsen syrup company, tastes different from Wild Country's. Many North Shore locals have strongly held preferences for one or the other.

If you see locally produced maple syrup at a farmers' market or other venue, take a chance and buy a bottle. Who knows; you may discover the next blue-ribbon syrup from the North Star State.

Pasta with Fiddleheads and Shiitake Mushrooms

Fiddleheads are the curled top portion of certain emerging ferns, particularly the ostrich fern (*Matteuccia struthiopteris*); when cooked, they have a taste reminiscent of asparagus (which works as a substitute in this recipe). When you're looking for ostrich-fern fiddleheads — whether in the wild or at a farmers' market — be certain that the straight part of the stem is deeply grooved on the inside, as the inedible interrupted fern (*Osmunda claytoniana*), which resembles the ostrich fern in many other ways, lacks the deep groove. Choose fiddleheads with a tightly coiled head; once they open up, they are no longer good to eat. I like to serve this with cup-shaped or curly pasta, to play off the shape of the fiddleheads, but you can use fettuccine or linguine if you like.

4 SERVINGS

1–1¼ cups fiddlehead fern coils, brown scales rubbed or rinsed off

2 tablespoons unsalted butter

1 tablespoon sunflower oil or olive oil

5 ounces shiitake mushroom caps, sliced into strips (about 2¼ cups sliced)

Coarse kosher salt

2 tablespoons minced shallots

1 teaspoon minced garlic

1 teaspoon lemon juice

1 quart reduced-sodium chicken broth (the lower in sodium, the better)

8 ounces orecchiette, cavatappi, or other pasta, cooked according to package directions

Freshly ground black pepper

2–3 tablespoons snipped fresh chives, plus a few chive blossoms if available

Freshly grated Parmesan cheese, for serving

1. Bring a pot of salted water to a boil. Prepare an ice-water bath. Cook the fiddleheads in the boiling water for 8 minutes. Drain and rinse under cold water, then add to the ice-water bath.

2. Heat 1 tablespoon of the butter and the oil in a large skillet over medium heat until the butter melts. Add the mushrooms and sprinkle with a little salt. Stir to coat the mushrooms, then spread out in an even layer and cook without stirring until any liquid released by the mushrooms has cooked away and the mushrooms are richly browned, 3 to 8 minutes. Stir the mushrooms and cook, stirring several times, until browned overall, about 3 minutes longer. Remove from the heat and set aside.

3. Melt the remaining 1 tablespoon butter in the same skillet over medium heat. Add the shallots and garlic. Cook, stirring frequently, until fragrant and golden, 3 to 4 minutes. Add the lemon juice and stir until the juice has mostly cooked away, about 30 seconds. Add the broth. Increase the heat to high and bring to a boil. Cook until the broth has reduced to just under 1 cup, 20 to 25 minutes.

4. Meanwhile, drain the fiddleheads. When the broth has reduced, add the drained fiddleheads, browned shiitakes, and cooked pasta to the skillet. Cook for about 2 minutes, stirring once or twice. Sprinkle with salt and pepper to taste, if needed. Transfer to a serving dish. Sprinkle with the chives, and tuck the chive blossoms around the dish. Serve immediately, passing grated Parmesan separately.

Pickled Ramps

Ramps (*Allium tricoccum*) grow throughout much of Minnesota, although they are absent in the far north and the southwest. Often called wild leeks, they have a distinct onion-garlic-chive aroma and taste. Both the leaves and the bulbs are edible and delicious. Ramps are gathered from the wild in spring, at about the same time as morels and often in the same general locations. You can also find them at many farmers' markets and co-ops. For this dish, cut the bulbs off at the midpoint of the stemlike maroon neck, and trim off the roots. Use the leaves for another dish; they can be sliced thinly and added to salads, or chopped and sautéed for sauces, soups, or other cooked dishes. Pickled ramps are lovely on a charcuterie platter or cheese tray, and they make a wonderful lunch served with a chunk of country bread, a wedge of good cheese, and a dab of coarse mustard. For this recipe, you will need two clean half-pint canning jars, with lids.

2 HALF-PINTS

1 quart plus ¾ cup spring water or distilled water

1 cup canning/pickling salt or kosher salt

2 cups ramp bulbs with part of the maroon neck (see headnote)

6 (⅛-inch-thick) slices peeled fresh gingerroot

2 small dried red chile peppers

1 teaspoon mustard seeds

¼ teaspoon whole black peppercorns

1 cup unseasoned rice vinegar

¾ cup sugar

1. Stir together 1 quart of the water and the salt in a nonreactive saucepan. Bring to a boil, stirring until the salt dissolves. Add the ramps and gingerroot. Adjust the heat so the liquid boils gently and cook for 2 minutes. Remove from the heat and set aside until cool. Transfer the ramps, gingerroot, and liquid to a glass, ceramic, or plastic bowl. Cover and refrigerate for 48 hours, stirring several times each day. Don't be alarmed if the ramps turn blue during this period; the blue is a reaction to copper compounds in the water and salt and will disappear after the final step.

2. After 48 hours, drain the ramps, discarding the brine. Pack the drained ramps and gingerroot into two half-pint canning jars, slipping one chile pepper into each jar vertically, pressed against the outside so it is visible. As you pack the jars, distribute ½ teaspoon mustard seeds and a few black peppercorns evenly among the ramps in each jar.

3. Combine the rice vinegar, sugar, and remaining ¾ cup water in a small nonreactive saucepan. Bring to a boil, stirring until the sugar dissolves. Remove from the heat and let cool slightly, then pour the hot liquid into the jars, covering the ramps. Seal with the lids. Let mellow in the refrigerator for 1 week, shaking occasionally, before serving. The pickled ramps will keep in the refrigerator for about 1 month.

Morel Cream Sauce with Roasted Shallots and Garlic

Other than a simple dish of morels sautéed in butter, morel cream sauce is probably the most common way of preparing morels. This sauce is very versatile and can be used to accompany roast chicken or pan-fried fish. It's one of the best gravies there is for mashed potatoes, and it also dresses up plain rice or pasta. I love it over a split flaky biscuit or hot buttered toast for a fabulous breakfast or brunch.

4 SERVINGS

6 medium shallots, peeled

4 garlic cloves, peeled

2 tablespoons sunflower oil or olive oil

½–¾ pound fresh morel mushrooms, halved or cut up

1 teaspoon minced fresh rosemary or ½ teaspoon crumbled dried

1 teaspoon rubbed dried sage

½ cup dry Marsala

½ cup dry sherry

1 cup chicken broth

½ cup heavy cream or half-and-half

Salt and ground white pepper

1. Preheat the oven to 300°F. Combine the shallots and garlic in a small baking dish. Add the oil, stirring to coat. Cover the dish with foil. Bake for 1 hour, or until the shallots and garlic are very soft. Remove from the oven, uncover, and set aside until cool enough to handle. Slice the shallots and garlic, and reserve the oil. **Note:** This may be prepared up to 2 days in advance; refrigerate the garlic and shallots separately from the oil.

2. Warm 1 tablespoon of the reserved oil in a large skillet over medium heat; refrigerate any remaining oil for other uses. Add the morels, rosemary, sage, and sliced shallots and garlic. Cook, stirring frequently, until the liquid released by the mushrooms has cooked away, about 5 minutes. Add the Marsala and sherry. Increase the heat to medium-high and cook until the liquid reduces to about 1 tablespoon, 5 to 10 minutes. Stir in the broth and cream. Cook until the liquid reduces by about half, 10 to 15 minutes. Season to taste with salt and pepper.

CLEANING MOREL MUSHROOMS

Morels have a tendency to trap dirt or sand in the honeycombed pits on the cap. The interior may also be gritty or may harbor insects. Morels (and all other wild mushrooms) should be gently washed before cooking; in most cases, it's best to split morels vertically before washing.

Submerge them in cold water, swooshing them to dislodge any grit or debris; take care not to break the caps. Remove from the water and check the insides, dislodging any stubborn grit with the tip of a paring knife and rinsing again if necessary. Place the morels, cut side up, on a paper towel–lined baking sheet and set aside to dry.

Morel Rings in Clarified Broth

This is an elegant first course, and it also pairs well with homemade biscuits for a nice luncheon. If you have rich homemade chicken broth, use about 4½ cups of that instead of the enriched broth. For more flavor when making the enriched broth, roast the chicken, carrots, and onion in a hot oven until browned before simmering in the broth. **Note:** If you have the time, prepare the enriched broth a day in advance, then refrigerate overnight. The next day, skim off the hardened fat from the surface.

ENRICHED BROTH

- 1 pound chicken wings, cut apart at the joints
- 2 carrots, cut into 2-inch lengths
- 1 small white onion, quartered
- 1 quart reduced-sodium chicken broth
- 1 cup water
- ¼ cup white wine
- 1 bay leaf

- ¾ pound fresh whole morel mushrooms
- 2 scallions
- 2 egg whites
- ¼ cup cold water
- 1 teaspoon white wine vinegar

1. **Make the enriched broth:** Combine the chicken wings, carrots, onion, broth, water, wine, and bay leaf in a 1-gallon soup pot. Heat over medium heat until the liquid is just simmering, then reduce the heat and cook at a near simmer for 1 hour (do not boil at any time). Strain the broth through a fine-mesh strainer into a 2-quart saucepan. Pick the meat off the chicken wings and refrigerate for another use. Discard the bones and vegetables. Rinse the soup pot and the strainer.

2. Slice the morel caps into rings and set aside. Coarsely chop the morel stems. Skim any fat from the surface of the broth. Add the morel stem pieces and any broken cap pieces to the broth. Cut the greens off the scallions and set aside. Add the scallion bulbs to the broth. Simmer over medium-low heat for about 20 minutes. Strain through the cleaned strainer into the cleaned soup pot. Refrigerate the cooked morel mixture for another use. Thoroughly clean the saucepan and the strainer.

3. Beat the egg whites with the cold water and the vinegar in a small bowl until frothy, about 30 seconds. Stir the egg mixture into the hot broth in the soup pot. Bring to a boil, then remove from the heat and set aside for 5 minutes. Meanwhile, line the cleaned strainer with a triple layer of cheesecloth, and place over the cleaned saucepan. Slice the scallion greens very thinly.

4. Strain the broth mixture through the cheesecloth-lined strainer into the saucepan. Add the morel rings to the broth. Cook over medium heat for 5 minutes. Ladle the mixture into soup plates. Sprinkle the scallion rings over the soup. Serve immediately.

WILD MUSHROOMS

In late spring, Minnesotans take to the woods in large numbers to search for the elusive morel mushroom (*Morchella* spp.). Not only is the morel the official Minnesota state mushroom, but it's also one of the very best on the table, commanding high prices when it is available at farmers' markets and co-ops. It grows for just a few weeks, and in dry years, it won't appear at all. With its honeycombed cap and completely hollow interior, it is easy to identify, making it one of the safest mushrooms to forage.

Happily, there is also a good handful of other wild mushrooms that are easy to identify and make good table fare. Brightly colored chicken of the woods (*Laetiporus* spp.) is found growing on trees from late spring through fall. Pale oyster mushrooms (*Pleurotus* spp.) have a similar growing season; they are one of the few wild mushrooms that can be cultivated, and are often sold in grocery stores. Apricot-scented chanterelles (*Cantharellus* spp.) appear scattered on the forest floor, their bright yellows and oranges peeking out from leafy duff from summer through fall. Sharp-eyed fungi fanatics who scour the woods at that same time may also find black trumpets (*Craterellus fallax*), fragrant, trumpet-shaped mushrooms whose dark

colors make them very difficult to spot on the forest floor. Hen of the woods (*Grifola frondosa*) grows at the base of oak trees (primarily) as large clusters of fan-shaped tan or gray caps; they begin appearing in late summer and continue until the first frosts.

Gathering wild mushrooms is not an amateur sport, as many mushrooms are inedible or mildly toxic, and some are lethal, even in small quantities. Common names may also be confusing, because the same name may be used to refer to different species; the scientific (Latin) names listed above are used by serious foragers.

It's best to learn about mushrooms from an experienced forager. The Minnesota Mycological Society (see Resources on page 270) is an excellent resource. Year-round meetings teach about mushrooms, and members can go on forays (field trips) where experts help identify mushrooms of all kinds — some edible, others appreciated solely for their beauty. Another good resource is the book *Mushrooms of the Upper Midwest,* a pocket-size photographic field guide I coauthored with fellow mushroom enthusiast Kathy Yerich.

Golden Toasts with Crispy Morels, Green Pea Spread, and Ham

I bet most Minnesotans remember a dish I used to call chipped beef on toast: a stovetop concoction of Carl Buddig shaved beef and green peas, bound together with cream of mushroom soup and served over toast. Here is a much-improved version with those same basic flavors, featuring fresh morel mushrooms. It's an elegant appetizer or first course.

GREEN PEA SPREAD

- 2 teaspoons unsalted butter
- 1 teaspoon minced shallots
- ⅔ cup frozen green peas, thawed
- ½ teaspoon fresh thyme or a scant ½ teaspoon dried
- Pinch of nutmeg, preferably freshly grated
- Salt and freshly ground black pepper

- 2 tablespoons unsalted butter, or as needed
- 8 (¼-inch-thick) slices French or Italian bread (3 to 3½ inches across)
- 3 tablespoons cream cheese, or as needed, softened
- 1–2 slices medium-thick deli ham
- 1 tablespoon extra-virgin olive oil
- 8 small to medium fresh morel mushrooms, halved vertically
- Sea salt or coarse kosher salt, for garnish

1. **Make the green pea spread:** Melt the butter in a small skillet over medium-low to medium heat. Add the shallots and cook, stirring frequently, for about 1 minute. Stir in the peas and continue cooking until the peas are just tender, 3 to 4 minutes longer. Remove from the heat and stir in the thyme, nutmeg, and salt and pepper to taste. Mash to a medium-coarse texture with a potato masher. Set aside until cooled to room temperature.

2. Melt 1 tablespoon of the butter in a medium skillet over medium heat. Add the bread slices, turning to coat. Cook until nicely golden on both sides, 4 to 5 minutes. Arrange in a single layer on a serving plate. Spread each with 1½ to 2 teaspoons cream cheese. Slice the ham into strips that are as long as each bread slice and a bit narrower. Place one slice on top of the cream cheese on each toast.

3. Combine the remaining 1 tablespoon butter and the oil in the same medium skillet. Heat over medium heat until the butter melts. Add the morels and cook, turning once, until they are golden brown and crisp around the edges, about 5 minutes. Meanwhile, place about 2 teaspoons of the green pea spread on top of each ham-topped toast. Arrange two crispy morel halves on each toast, putting them slightly to one side of the pea spread. Sprinkle lightly with sea salt. Serve immediately.

Crab-Stuffed Morel Mushrooms

Over the years, Bret Bannon has distinguished himself as a serious cook, learning from many notable chefs and authors along the way and sharing his passion for cooking with others. He currently teaches private cooking classes in the Twin Cities and leads culinary tours to France. Bret is also an accomplished food stylist who worked on many of the photos in this book.

6–8 APPETIZER SERVINGS

1 teaspoon unsalted butter

1 teaspoon olive oil, plus more for drizzling

12 fresh morel mushrooms, halved vertically

1 small celery stalk, finely diced

1 shallot, finely diced

¾ cup fresh breadcrumbs (see note on page 95 for instructions on how to make fresh breadcrumbs)

⅓ cup lump crabmeat, picked over to remove any cartilage

1 teaspoon Dijon mustard, optional

2 tablespoons finely grated Parmigiano-Reggiano cheese

1 teaspoon minced fresh thyme

Zest of 1 lemon

¼ cup mayonnaise, or as needed

Salt and freshly ground black pepper

Dill sprigs, for garnish (fronds, not seed heads)

Drawn butter, for serving, optional

1. Position an oven rack at the top of the oven and preheat the broiler. Warm the butter and oil in a skillet over medium heat. When the butter melts, add the morel halves, cut side down. Cover and cook until the mushrooms are just tender, 2 to 3 minutes. Use a slotted spoon to carefully transfer the morels to a plate.

2. Add the celery and shallot to the skillet. Cook, stirring frequently, until just beginning to turn translucent, about 2 minutes. Transfer the celery mixture to a bowl and set aside until just cool. Set aside 1 tablespoon of the breadcrumbs.

3. Add the crabmeat, mustard (if desired), remaining bread-crumbs, Parmigiano-Reggiano, thyme, and lemon zest to the celery mixture, stirring to combine. Add the mayonnaise, 1 tablespoon at a time, gently mixing after each addition, until the mixture is just moist enough to cling together when gently pressed into a spoon. Season with salt and pepper to taste.

4. Scoop up a spoonful of the crabmeat mixture and press firmly into the cavity of a morel half, mounding it up above the mushroom. Repeat with remaining ingredients, arranging the mushrooms on a baking sheet, stuffed side up and slightly separated. Sprinkle with the remaining breadcrumbs and drizzle with a little oil.

5. Broil just until the tops are golden brown. Garnish with dill sprigs. Serve with drawn butter, if you like.

Warm Mushroom Salad with Toasts

This recipe features a trifecta of late-summer mushrooms: chanterelles, oyster mushrooms, and hen of the woods. If you don't have these specific varieties, feel free to substitute something else; you can even use domestic cremini, shiitake, or portabellas for one of the species. Note that chanterelles take a little longer to sauté than the oyster mushrooms or hen of the woods, so adjust timing for any substitutions according to their texture.

4 SERVINGS

1 loaf coarse-crumbed Italian or French bread, sliced ¼ inch thick

4 tablespoons butter, or as needed, melted

¼ cup finely grated Parmesan or Romano cheese

3 tablespoons extra-virgin olive oil, or as needed

3 large shallots, thinly sliced

½ pound fresh chanterelle mushrooms, cut into into large bite-size pieces

½ pound fresh oyster mushrooms, cut into ¼-inch strips

½ pound fresh hen of the woods, torn into bite-size pieces

1 tablespoon lemon juice

2 teaspoons red wine vinegar

½ teaspoon salt

Freshly ground black pepper

6 cups tender mixed salad greens

1. Preheat the oven to 375°F. Arrange the bread in a single layer on a baking sheet. Brush both sides lightly with the melted butter. Sprinkle the tops with the Parmesan. Bake until golden brown, about 10 minutes; remember to keep an eye on it while you cook the mushrooms.

2. While the bread is toasting, heat the oil over medium heat in a large skillet. Sauté the shallots for about 2 minutes. Add the chanterelles and increase the heat to medium-high. Cook for about 4 minutes, stirring once or twice. Add the oyster mushrooms and hen of the woods. Cook, stirring occasionally, for about 5 minutes longer; add a little more oil if needed. Remove from the heat. Stir in the lemon juice, vinegar, and salt, and season with pepper to taste. Adjust the seasoning as necessary.

3. Arrange the salad greens down the center of the serving plates. Tuck the toasted bread alongside the greens. Divide the mushroom mixture evenly among the plates. Serve immediately.

Chanterelles with Parmesan Grits

You can substitute other wild mushrooms such as morels, oyster mushrooms, black trumpets, or hen of the woods for the chanterelles; cremini mushrooms from the grocery store also work well if you're not a forager. The instructions are written for stone-ground grits or coarse cornmeal, both of which require slow, lengthy cooking. You may substitute any coarse grits, but some cook more quickly, so you'll have to adjust the cooking time according to the package instructions (also use a bit less chicken broth than the water called for on the package; the milk added at the end makes up the difference). Don't use instant grits; both texture and taste are inferior.

4 SERVINGS

2 cups chicken broth

1 tablespoon olive oil

¾ cup white or yellow stone-ground grits or coarse cornmeal (see headnote)

1½ tablespoons unsalted butter, or as needed

1 pound fresh chanterelle mushrooms, cut into large bite-size pieces

1 tablespoon minced shallots

½ teaspoon sea salt

½ cup whole milk

¼ cup freshly grated Parmesan cheese

Freshly ground black pepper

1. Combine the broth and oil in a heavy-bottomed saucepan. Bring to a boil over medium-high heat. Add the grits in a slow, steady stream, stirring constantly. Return to a boil, then cover, reduce the heat to very low, and cook for 30 minutes, stirring frequently.

2. Near the end of the cooking time for the grits, heat a large skillet over medium-high heat. Add the butter and swirl the skillet until the butter melts. Add the chanterelles, stirring to coat evenly. Cook, stirring occasionally, until most of the liquid produced by the mushrooms has evaporated, 5 to 8 minutes. Stir in the shallots and salt, and continue cooking until the mushrooms are beginning to turn golden brown in spots, about 5 minutes longer. (If the mushrooms are done before the grits, cover and keep warm.)

3. When the grits have cooked for 30 minutes, stir in the milk and cook over medium heat, uncovered, for a few minutes, stirring frequently. Add the Parmesan and cook, stirring constantly until the cheese melts, about 1 minute. Season with pepper to taste and stir well. Serve the mushrooms over the grits.

Free-Form Chicken Pie with Chanterelles and Wild Rice

This is a wonderful dish for a dinner party: impressive to look at and very tasty. If you like, you can amp up the wild quotient by substituting pheasant or grouse for the chicken.

1 (13-ounce) sheet frozen puff pastry, thawed according to package directions

3 tablespoons all-purpose flour, plus more for handling pastry

3 cups chicken broth

¾ pound boneless, skinless chicken breast

½ cup diced onion

½ cup diced carrot

¼ cup diced celery

5 tablespoons unsalted butter

2 tablespoons minced shallots

½ pound fresh chanterelle mushrooms, quartered or halved if large

Salt and freshly ground black pepper

⅓ cup frozen peas, rinsed briefly in warm water

¾ cup cooked wild rice

1. Preheat the oven to 400°F. Line a baking sheet with parchment paper. Unfold the puff pastry onto a lightly floured work surface. Cut on the fold lines into three strips, then cut each strip in half crosswise for a total of six rectangles. Place the rectangles on the baking sheet, ½ inch apart. Prick each several times with a fork. Bake for about 15 minutes, or until the pastry is golden brown. Remove from the oven and set aside.

2. Combine the broth and chicken breasts in a 1-gallon soup pot. Bring to a simmer over medium heat. Adjust the heat as needed and simmer until the chicken is cooked through, 10 to 15 minutes. Transfer the chicken to a plate.

3. Measure the broth, and return 2½ cups to the soup pot (add water if needed to equal 2½ cups). Add the onion, carrot, and celery to the broth. Cook over medium heat until the vegetables are tender-crisp, about 10 minutes. Reduce the heat to very low.

4. While the vegetables are cooking, melt 2 tablespoons of the butter in a large skillet over medium heat. Add the shallots and cook, stirring a few times, for about 30 seconds. Add the chanterelles, stirring to coat. Sprinkle with salt and pepper to taste. Cook, stirring occasionally, until any liquid released by the mushrooms cooks away. Continue to cook, stirring occasionally, until the chanterelles begin to brown in spots, about 5 minutes longer. Use a slotted spoon to transfer the chanterelles to a bowl.

5. Add the remaining 3 tablespoons butter to the skillet, and melt over medium heat. Whisk in the 3 tablespoons flour. Cook, whisking constantly, until the mixture is golden brown and smells nutty, 5 to 8 minutes.

6. Increase the heat under the soup pot so the broth is boiling gently. Add the flour mixture to the broth, stirring constantly. Adjust the heat as needed so the mixture bubbles gently and cook, stirring frequently, until the mixture thickens to a gravylike consistency, 7 to 10 minutes. Meanwhile, pull the chicken apart with your fingers into bite-size chunks.

7. Add the peas, wild rice, chanterelles and any juices, and chicken chunks to the gravy. Cook over medium-low heat, stirring several times, until everything is hot, about 5 minutes. Taste the gravy and add salt and pepper if needed.

8. To assemble the dish, split the puff-pastry rectangles with a fork so the top can be separated from the bottom. Place the bottoms on serving plates. Divide the chicken mixture among the plates, spooning it over the pastry. Place a puff-pastry top on each portion, offsetting it slightly. Serve immediately.

Cream of Chanterelle Soup

I picked up the concept of slowly infusing stock and cream with mushrooms from Chef Tyler Shipton, who helped found the highly lauded Minneapolis restaurants Borough and Coup d'Etat and has also been a chef at several other acclaimed restaurants. This recipe is my home-style adaptation of a dish he prepared at a mushroom-cooking demonstration for an enthusiastic crowd at a 2014 meeting of the Minnesota Mycological Society. Tyler steeped the soup on a warm cooktop, not in the oven as I do (and you can do it on a very low burner, if you prefer). He strained the soup after puréeing and topped servings with popped sorghum kernels. My version isn't strained, and it includes the addition of sautéed mushroom pieces for additional texture. **Note:** This recipe would also work well with morels.

4–6 SERVINGS

1–1¼ pounds fresh chanterelle mushrooms

2 tablespoons extra-virgin olive oil

1 celery stalk, coarsely chopped

1 carrot, coarsely chopped

1 small onion, coarsely chopped

1 garlic clove, chopped

1 tablespoon chopped shallots

½ cup dry sherry

3 cups chicken broth

1 bay leaf

2 sprigs parsley, coarsely chopped

½ teaspoon fresh thyme

1½ cups heavy cream

2 tablespoons unsalted butter

2 teaspoons white balsamic vinegar or sherry vinegar

Sea salt or coarse kosher salt and freshly ground black pepper

1. Preheat the oven to 175°F. Chop about three-quarters of the chanterelles coarsely, refrigerating the remaining one-quarter. Warm 1 tablespoon of the oil in a 1-gallon soup pot over medium-high heat. Add the chopped chanterelles and cook, stirring occasionally, until any liquid released by the mushrooms cooks away.

2. Add the remaining 1 tablespoon oil. Stir in the celery, carrot, and onion. Reduce the heat to medium and cook, stirring frequently, until the vegetables have begun to brown in spots, about 10 minutes. Stir in the garlic and shallots and cook for about 1 minute longer. Add the sherry and scrape to loosen anything stuck to the bottom of the pot. Cook until the wine evaporates, about 1 minute. Stir in the broth, bay leaf, parsley, and thyme. Increase the heat to medium-high and bring to a simmer. Place the uncovered pot in the oven to steep for 1 hour.

3. Stir the cream into the pot. Heat on the stovetop over medium heat until steaming but not boiling. Return to the oven and steep for 30 minutes. Near the end of the 30 minutes, cut the reserved whole chanterelles in half, or quarters if large. Melt the butter in a medium skillet over medium-high heat. Add the chanterelles. Cook until nicely browned, stirring several times. Remove from the heat.

4. When the cream mixture has steeped for 30 minutes, fish out and discard the bay leaf. Purée the mixture in a blender in small batches until smooth, covering the lid of the blender with a towel and taking care to avoid being burned by the hot liquid. As each batch is processed, pour it into a saucepan. When all of the purée has been added to the saucepan, stir in the vinegar, and season with salt and pepper to taste. Divide the soup among wide, shallow soup plates or soup bowls. Place a small pile of the sautéed mushrooms over the center of each serving. Serve immediately.

Perfect Blueberry Pie

Precooking half of the berries gives this pie a particularly intense, jammy flavor. It's best when made with fresh wild blueberries, but purchased berries will also work. The pie is delicious warm, but the filling will be somewhat runny; for perfect slices, let it cool completely before cutting.

1 (9-INCH) PIE

5 cups fresh blueberries

¾ cup sugar, plus more for sprinkling crust

1 tablespoon lemon juice

½ teaspoon ground cinnamon

½ teaspoon ground nutmeg

Generous pinch of salt

¼ cup quick-cooking tapioca

Pastry for two 9-inch piecrusts

2 tablespoons unsalted butter, cut into small pieces

1 egg, lightly beaten

1. Position an oven rack in the lowest position and preheat the oven to 400°F. Combine 2½ cups of the blueberries, the sugar, lemon juice, cinnamon, nutmeg, and salt in a medium saucepan. Crush about half of the berries with a potato masher. Cook over medium heat, stirring occasionally, for 5 minutes. Stir in the tapioca. Reduce the heat and simmer for 5 minutes. Remove from the heat and let cool for about 10 minutes.

2. Fit one pastry portion into a 9-inch pie plate. Stir the remaining 2½ cups blueberries into the cooked mixture. Scrape into the crust. Dot with the butter. Moisten the pastry edges and cover with the remaining pastry portion, crimping to seal and fluting the edges decoratively. Brush the top and edges with the beaten egg, then sprinkle lightly with sugar. Cut a few slits in the top.

3. Place the pie on a rimmed baking sheet. Bake on the lowest oven rack for 25 to 30 minutes, until the filling bubbles through the slits. Transfer to a wire rack to let cool for at least 1 hour. Serve warm or at room temperature.

PICKING WILD BLUEBERRIES IN THE NORTH

Starting in mid- to late July, wild blueberries ripen on small shrubs throughout northern Minnesota. The best areas are east of an arc from Pine City to Roseau. Families often plan their vacation around this event, traveling to Ely, Grand Marais, or Duluth to pick berries on public lands in the surrounding areas.

Aficionados believe that wild blueberries are tastier than their domesticated cousins. Plus, there's something thrilling about heading out into the wild and returning with a bucket full of blue goodness, free for the taking. All that's needed is a bucket, plenty of bug repellent, a water bottle, and a trail into appropriate state or federal land.

Blueberries thrive in sunny, open spots and are abundant in areas that have been swept by forest fire the previous year. Pick only deep blue berries; if a berry won't release easily from the shrub, it's not ripe enough. Pluck the berries gently, taking care not to damage the branches. For positive identification, check the bottom of the berry; all blueberries have a star-shaped crown at the base. Wild blueberries can be devoured raw or used in any blueberry recipe you like.

Small-Batch Wild Cherry Jelly

This recipe works with any of the wild cherries that are native to Minnesota: chokecherries, pin cherries, and black cherries. It's scaled down from traditional jelly recipes so that you don't need to gather gallons of wild fruit. Homemade chokecherry jelly is a common entry at county fairs across Minnesota, and it also shows up at the Minnesota State Fair homemade jelly competition in the Creative Activities building. Pin cherry jelly and black cherry jelly are less common, but some think they are even better than chokecherry jelly.

You will need four clean half-pint canning jars with bands and lids for this recipe; if you want to can the jelly, you'll need to sterilize the jars and lids and have a water-bath canner.

4 HALF-PINTS

2 quarts fresh chokecherries, pin cherries, or black cherries (stems removed before measuring)

1 quart water

3 cups sugar

1 (1.75-ounce) box powdered pectin

2 tablespoons lemon juice

1. Place the cherries and water in a nonreactive 1-gallon soup pot. Bring to a boil over high heat. Reduce the heat to medium-low, cover the pot, and simmer for 30 minutes. Near the end of cooking, gently crush the fruit with a potato masher. Line a fine-mesh strainer with a double layer of dampened cheesecloth and place it over a clean, nonreactive saucepan. Transfer the fruit mixture to the strainer and let it drip for 30 minutes; don't squeeze the fruit or the jelly will be cloudy. Meanwhile, clean the soup pot.

2. Measure the sugar and set it aside so it is ready when you need it. Measure the pectin by weight in grams (preferred) or in tablespoons, then measure out two-thirds of the total; discard the remaining one-third. Measure 2½ cups of the cherry juice; refrigerate any remaining juice to sweeten and serve as a beverage. Add the 2½ cups cherry juice and the lemon juice to the cleaned soup pot, then whisk in the measured pectin until it dissolves. Bring to a boil over high heat, stirring frequently. When the juice comes to a full, rolling boil that can't be stirred down, add the sugar and cook, stirring constantly, until the mixture comes to a full, foaming boil. Boil for 1 minute, stirring constantly. Remove from the heat and stir for about 1 minute to settle any foam.

3. Pour the hot juice into the prepared jars, leaving at least ¼ inch of space at the top. Seal with a lid and a clean band, sealing finger-tight (don't crank down on it too hard). Let cool, and refrigerate until ready to use; it keeps for a month or longer. To can the jelly, process in a boiling-water bath for 10 minutes.

Blue Ox Pancakes

Babe the Blue Ox was the mythical companion to the mythical Paul Bunyan, a giant lumberjack whose feats were the subject of many stories told round the campfire by Minnesota lumberjacks in the late 1800s. Giant statues of Babe can be found in Bemidji, where the ox appears alongside an equally gigantic Paul Bunyan figure, and Brainerd, where the great beast stands alone in the parking lot of Paul Bunyan Land, a tourist attraction. No doubt Babe had a huge appetite for the wild blueberries that still grow in abundance in the northern Minnesota forests, and which provide color to these pancakes made with blue cornmeal. If you use purchased blueberries, buy the smallest ones you can find. For the full lumberjack-style breakfast, accompany the pancakes — known by lumberjacks as monkey blankets — with steaming coffee, eggs cooked to order, and fried steak, sausages, or bacon.

ABOUT 14 PANCAKES

1 cup all-purpose flour

¾ cup finely ground blue cornmeal, such as Whole Grain Milling blue cornmeal

1 teaspoon baking powder

½ teaspoon baking soda

½ teaspoon salt

¾ cup buttermilk

2 eggs

3 tablespoons sunflower oil or vegetable oil, plus more for frying

½ cup room-temperature Coca-Cola (regular, not diet), or as needed

1½ cups fresh or frozen wild blueberries (do not thaw if frozen)

Unsalted butter, for serving

Pure maple syrup, for serving

1. Preheat the oven to 300°F. Whisk together the flour, cornmeal, baking powder, baking soda, and salt in a large mixing bowl. In a small bowl, whisk together the buttermilk, eggs, and oil.

2. Heat a griddle or large skillet over medium heat until a drop of water dances on the surface; if you have a temperature-controlled griddle, set it for 375°F.

3. When the griddle is hot, pour the buttermilk mixture and the Coca-Cola into the flour mixture, stirring with a wooden spoon until the flour is combined. Add the blueberries and stir gently until just combined; if the batter seems too thick, add a little more Coca-Cola, but don't make it too thin or the berries will stick out of the pancakes too much. Lightly oil the griddle. Pour ¼-cup batches on the griddle, allowing room for spreading. Cook until the bottoms are golden brown and the edges are crisp, 1½ to 2 minutes; there will be a few bubbles on the surface but not as many as you'd expect with a traditional pancake batter. Gently flip the pancakes and cook the second side until the pancakes are cooked through, about 1½ minutes longer. Transfer to a baking sheet and keep warm in the oven while you prepare the remaining pancakes. Serve with butter and maple syrup.

MANOOMIN: WILD RICE

The official Minnesota state grain, wild rice is the seed of certain aquatic grasses native to North America — primarily, the northern states from Minnesota eastward and adjacent Canadian provinces. This border-straddling band is similar to the zone where maple syrup is produced. It's no coincidence that both wild rice and maple syrup were used extensively by the Woodland Indian tribes, particularly the Ojibwe, who call wild rice *manoomin* (also spelled *mahnomin*) and consider it a sacred gift from the Creator.

America's largest concentration of native wild-rice beds is in northern Minnesota, where the plants grow in shallow, calm areas of lakes and slow-moving streams. Genuine wild rice is rich, nutty, roasty, and earthy, with a heady fragrance. In her important and unique cookbook, *Original Local*, Ojibwe poet Heid Erdrich describes the "wonderful aroma of toasted nut and lake and smoke" given off by cooked *manoomin*.

The appearance and flavor of wild rice vary, depending on where and when it was harvested and how it was processed. One thing that does not vary in Minnesota is the method used to harvest genuine wild rice, which is regulated by state law. Except in very rare, specific cases, no mechanical devices such as motorboats may be used. Maximum size of watercraft and other equipment is specified, and regulations help maintain the health of the resource.

In a method that has been used for centuries, wild rice is harvested in late summer from canoes (or small flat-bottomed skiffs), usually in two-person teams. The person in the rear uses a long pole to slowly move the canoe through a stand of wild-rice plants, which typically grow 3 to 8 feet above the water's surface. The person in front uses long, thin sticks to bend the supple stems over the canoe and to brush ripe kernels off the plants and into the bottom of the canoe (see photo on page 190).

Traditionally, fresh rice is sun-dried for a few days, then parched in open kettles over a wood fire to harden the inedible hull. Parched rice is transferred to an area where a "jigger" wearing soft moccasins treads on it. The rice is then transferred to a birch-bark basket or other container and tossed into the air so breezes can blow away the lightweight hulls while the heavier kernels fall back into the basket. The resulting rice may be light brown, dark brown, or greenish tan, and often appears mottled. Wild rice processed in this way is identified as hand-finished or hand-parched, to separate it from rice that was harvested traditionally but finished with mechanical methods. While still genuinely wild, that rice lacks the woodsy flavor imparted by traditional parching.

In contrast, "cultivated wild rice" is not wild at all. It has been selectively bred to produce a high-yielding crop that is typically grown in large, artificially made paddies designed for mechanical harvesting. All the grains are a uniform size and color, generally black. It is tougher and takes longer to cook (an hour or more, compared to 15 to 20 minutes for most *manoomin*), and it lacks the distinctive taste and aroma of natural wild rice. Most cultivated wild rice is grown in California, but some is grown in Minnesota, so you can't always rely on a "made in Minnesota" tag when you're looking for the genuine article; instead, look for words like *naturally wild* or *genuine* on the label. Most co-ops carry genuine wild rice; you may also buy it online from Ojibwe Indian bands including White Earth and Bois Forte (see Resources, page 270, for website addresses).

Breakfast Skillet with Wild Rice, Hazelnuts, and Wild Berries

When you're roaming the Minnesota woods in summer, you can often gather a mixed bag of wild berries. You might not get enough (particularly of any one kind) to make a pie with, but a mixture works really well in this easy breakfast dish. If you are substituting purchased blueberries, buy the smallest ones you can find. When buying strawberries, choose only small, locally grown berries; cut store-bought raspberries or blackberries in half before using. Hazelnuts also grow in the wild throughout most of Minnesota and can be harvested in late summer to early fall — if you can beat the deer and squirrels to them! Otherwise, you'll find whole, skin-on, unsalted hazelnuts (also called filberts) in the grocery store with the nuts sold for baking. **Note:** Be sure to use genuine wild rice for this dish; paddy-grown rice takes a lot longer to cook (and isn't nearly as good as the real stuff).

4¾ cups water

2½ tablespoons baking soda

2 ounces whole, skin-on, unsalted hazelnuts (not quite ½ cup)

1 tablespoon sunflower oil or vegetable oil

1 tablespoon unsalted butter

1 cup genuine wild rice, rinsed (see headnote)

¼ cup diced dried apples

3 tablespoons pure maple syrup, plus more for serving

¼ teaspoon salt

1½ cups mixed fresh wild berries, such as blueberries, blackberries, raspberries, serviceberries, and strawberries (see headnote for substitution of domestic berries)

Heavy cream or half-and-half, for serving, optional

1. Bring 2 cups of the water to a boil in a nonreactive medium saucepan. Add the baking soda; the water will foam up. Add the hazelnuts. Cook for 3 minutes. Drain in a strainer and rinse with cold water. Rub the skins off with your fingers, holding each nut under a thin stream of running water. Squeeze each nut firmly as you're skinning, to split it into halves. Place on a paper towel–lined plate, then blot the nuts dry.

2. Warm the oil in a large skillet over medium-low heat. Add the split hazelnuts. Cook, stirring frequently until the nuts are turning golden brown, about 5 minutes. Transfer the nuts to a bowl.

3. Add the butter to the same skillet and heat until melted. Stir in the wild rice and the remaining 2¾ cups water. Adjust the heat so the water boils very gently and cook, stirring occasionally, for 15 minutes. Stir in the dried apples, maple syrup, and salt. Reduce the heat slightly and continue cooking, stirring occasionally, until the rice is tender and the liquid has cooked away, 10 to 15 minutes longer. Stir in the hazelnuts. Remove from the heat and let cool slightly, for about 5 minutes.

4. Scatter the berries over the top. Serve with cream, if desired, and more maple syrup, so each person can add some to taste.

Wild Rice Spaetzle

Chef Ron Berg notes that this spaetzle is the perfect accompaniment to his Ultimate Roast Breast of Grouse with Sherry-Mushroom Cream Sauce (see page 72 for the grouse recipe, as well as more information about Chef Ron). It also works well as an accompaniment to a stew or any saucy meat dish. **Note:** You will need a tool to form the spaetzle as they drop into the boiling water. Special spaetzle makers work well, but you can improvise. A colander with ¼-inch holes works well. Otherwise, use a flat or box-style cheese grater with ¼-inch holes.

4–6 SERVINGS

- ½ cup finely chopped cooked wild rice (from about ⅔ cup before chopping)
- 2 eggs
- ⅓ cup whole milk
- 1 teaspoon salt
- ¼ teaspoon baking powder
- ⅛ teaspoon ground nutmeg
- Ground white pepper
- 1 cup plus 1–2 tablespoons all-purpose flour, sifted
- 2 tablespoons unsalted butter, or as needed

1. Whisk together the chopped wild rice, eggs, milk, salt, baking powder, nutmeg, and white pepper to taste in a mixing bowl. Gradually stir in enough of the flour to make a loose but fairly elastic dough; it should be thicker than cake batter but more fluid than cookie dough. Set the dough aside to rest while you bring a large pot of salted water to a boil. Have a large bowl of ice water handy.

2. Coat the tool you'll be using to form the spaetzle with cooking spray. **If using a colander,** spoon about one-quarter of the dough into the colander and place it over the boiling water; scrape a rubber spatula through the dough, pressing it through the holes. **If using a cheese grater,** scoop up about one-quarter of the dough with a rubber spatula, transferring it to the *non-sharp* side of the grater. Hold the grater over the boiling water and scrape the spatula across the large holes, forcing the dough through.

3. The spaetzle will float to the top. Cook for about 2 minutes, then use a slotted spoon to transfer it to the ice water. Repeat with another portion of dough; while one batch is boiling, transfer the cooled spaetzle from the ice water to a strainer set over a bowl. When all the spaetzle has been cooked and drained, spread it on a baking sheet lined with several cloth towels. Let stand for a few minutes, then transfer the spaetzle to a dish. Cover and refrigerate if not serving right away.

4. To serve, melt the butter in a large skillet over high heat, then add the spaetzle and sauté until the edges are lightly browned and crisp, 5 to 10 minutes. Serve hot.

Minnesota Wild Rice Soup

A cookbook about Minnesota foods would be sadly incomplete without a recipe for wild rice soup. Many say that it was first popularized in the 1960s at the Oak Grille, the restaurant in Dayton's downtown Minneapolis department store, but I think the recipe is a lot older than that. The version here features turkey, a major product of Minnesota, but you can substitute chicken, pheasant, or whatever you like. It's all good. This is a thinner wild rice soup than some other versions, which are downright gloppy in my opinion. It's still plenty rich!

6 tablespoons unsalted butter

¾ cup thinly sliced celery

¾ cup finely diced carrot

¾ cup chopped onion

6 cups turkey broth or chicken broth, homemade or purchased

½ teaspoon dried thyme

¼ cup all-purpose flour

3 cups cooked wild rice

1½ cups heavy cream

1½ cups diced cooked turkey

2 tablespoons minced fresh parsley

Pinch of ground nutmeg

Salt and ground white pepper

1. Melt 2 tablespoons of the butter in a 1-gallon soup pot over medium heat. Add the celery, carrot, and onion. Cook, stirring occasionally, for 5 minutes.

2. Add the broth and thyme to the pot. Increase the heat to high, and bring to a boil. Adjust the heat so the broth bubbles gently but not furiously and cook for 15 minutes.

3. Meanwhile, melt the remaining 4 tablespoons butter in a small heavy-bottomed saucepan over medium-low to medium heat. Whisk in the flour. Cook, whisking constantly, until the mixture is golden brown and smells nutty, about 8 minutes. Set aside until needed.

4. When the broth has cooked for 15 minutes, add the flour mixture in a thin stream, stirring constantly. Cook for 15 minutes longer, stirring occasionally.

5. Stir in the wild rice and cream. Heat until simmering, then adjust the heat and simmer for about 10 minutes. Add the turkey and cook for about 5 minutes longer. Stir in the parsley, nutmeg, and salt and pepper to taste. Serve immediately.

Variations

• The cream is certainly traditional and expected with this soup, but it's also quite good without any cream at all. Simply omit the cream, adding a little more broth if needed for the number of people you're serving.

• For a mushroom option, sauté ¼ pound thinly sliced mushrooms in 1 tablespoon butter until golden. Stir into the soup along with the turkey.

Wild Rice Casserole

This is a wonderful accompaniment to roast chicken or turkey; it's somewhat like bread stuffing but lots better. You may prepare the sausage, onion, and celery mixture in advance and refrigerate it for a day or two. The bread cubes can be toasted several hours in advance; transfer them to the large bowl as directed, and cover it with foil or plastic wrap until you're ready to mix everything together. Hazelnuts grow wild in many parts of Minnesota and are wonderful in this dish; you can also buy them in the baking aisle, where they are often called filberts. Pecans or walnuts also work well.

6 SERVINGS

4 cups cubed day-old French bread (½-inch cubes)

2½ tablespoons unsalted butter, melted

½ pound Lamb and Pork Breakfast Sausage (page 159) or other uncased breakfast-style sausage

1 cup chopped onion

¾ cup diced celery

¾ teaspoon crumbled dried thyme

¼ teaspoon rubbed dried sage

¼ teaspoon salt

2 cups cooked wild rice

1 small apple, peeled, cored, and diced

½ cup chopped hazelnuts, pecans, or walnuts

1½–2 cups chicken broth

1. Preheat the oven to 400°F. Coat a 2½- to 3-quart casserole dish with cooking spray.

2. Spread the bread cubes on a rimmed baking sheet. Drizzle with the melted butter, stirring to coat evenly. Bake, stirring every 5 minutes, until golden brown and toasted, about 15 minutes. Transfer the toasted bread cubes to a large mixing bowl.

3. Fry the sausage in a medium skillet over medium heat, breaking up the meat with a spatula until it loses its raw color, 4 to 5 minutes. Stir in the onion and celery and continue cooking, stirring frequently, until the vegetables are tender-crisp, 3 to 4 minutes longer. Drain excess grease if necessary, then stir in the thyme, sage, and salt. Transfer the sausage mixture to the bowl with the bread cubes.

4. Add the wild rice, apple, and nuts to the bowl with the bread cubes. Stir until well mixed. Add 1½ cups of the broth and stir well. The bread should be well moistened but not wet; stir in some of the remaining broth if needed. Transfer the bread mixture to the casserole dish. Cover and bake for 45 minutes, then remove the cover and bake for 15 minutes longer, or until the top is lightly crisped.

Northland Venison Burger with Wild Rice

The inspiration for this comes from the delicious Pete's Cabin Burger, served at Town Hall Tap in South Minneapolis. That burger, which is made with Angus beef, is also topped with sautéed mushrooms under the blanket of melted cheese, which is a particularly excellent option if you enjoy mushrooms.

1 pound ground venison

1 cup cooked wild rice, cooled

½ cup finely crumbled blue cheese (about 2 ounces), such as Shepherd's Way Big Woods Blue or Caves of Faribault St. Pete's Select

1 garlic clove, pressed or very finely minced

¼ teaspoon salt

¼ teaspoon freshly ground black pepper

¼ teaspoon paprika, preferably smoked Spanish paprika

4 thin sandwich-style slices Muenster, provolone, or Swiss cheese

4 split hamburger rolls

Condiments as desired, such as ketchup, sliced pickles, mustard

1. Prepare a grill for direct medium-high heat (for broiling, position an oven rack near the top of the oven and preheat the broiler). Combine the venison, wild rice, blue cheese, garlic, salt, pepper, and paprika in a mixing bowl. Mix thoroughly with your hands. Divide into four equal portions. Form each into a patty about 4 inches across and ¾ inch thick. Press the center in to flatten it somewhat, so it is a bit thinner than the edges.

2. Grill the burgers (or broil them), turning once, until they are the desired doneness, 6 to 8 minutes per side; note that food safety experts say that ground meat products should be cooked to an internal temperature of 160°F. When the burgers are cooked as you prefer, place a piece of cheese on each burger and let cook just until the cheese melts.

3. Serve the burgers in the split hamburger rolls, with condiments as desired.

Recipe from BERNITA BOHNENSTINGLE

Pheasant Baked in Cream

Pheasant in cream gravy is much loved throughout Minnesota. In modern times, the birds are often baked in a covering of canned cream soup, but in earlier days, Minnesota farm families prepared pheasant with heavy cream, which was plentiful on farms that kept a few cows. This version comes from my mother-in-law, Bernita Bohnenstingle, a first-generation German (with a dash of Danish) who was raised on a farm in Monson Township in western Minnesota. Sophie Petersen, Bernita's mother, used lard for frying pheasant. These days, Bernita uses bacon drippings.

3 OR 4 SERVINGS

½ cup all-purpose flour

½ teaspoon salt

¼ teaspoon freshly ground black pepper

¼ cup bacon drippings, lard, or vegetable oil, or as needed

1 dressed skinless pheasant, cut up (for better distribution of the highly prized white meat, bone the breast and cut it into quarters)

1½ cups water

2 cups heavy cream

Seasoned salt, optional

1 teaspoon cornstarch mixed with 2 teaspoons water

Mashed potatoes, for serving

1. Preheat the oven to 325°F. Whisk the flour, salt, and pepper together in a wide, shallow bowl. Heat 2 tablespoons of the fat in a large skillet over medium heat. Dredge half of the pheasant pieces in the flour, shaking off excess, and add them to the skillet. Cook until golden brown on both sides, 5 to 8 minutes. Transfer the browned pheasant to a Dutch oven. Repeat with the remaining pheasant, using additional fat as needed; lower the heat slightly if the drippings threaten to burn.

2. When all of the pheasant has been browned and transferred to the Dutch oven, add ¾ cup of the water to the skillet, stirring to mix with the browned bits. Stir in 1¼ cups of the cream and cook until the cream is hot but not boiling. Pour the cream mixture evenly over the pheasant. Sprinkle generously with seasoned salt, if desired. Bake for 1½ hours, turning the pheasant pieces halfway through. Poke several pieces with a fork; the pheasant should be very tender. Older birds may require additional cooking. If the meat is not yet tender, return it to the oven and check every 15 minutes until it is fork-tender; add a little water if it seems dry.

3. Use tongs to transfer the pheasant to a serving platter. Tent loosely with foil. Stir the cream mixture remaining in the Dutch oven. If you want more to serve with the pheasant and potatoes — which you probably will — add some of the remaining ¾ cup cream and ¾ cup water to the Dutch oven, using equal parts cream and water. Stir in a little of the cornstarch-water mixture. Cook on the stovetop over medium heat for a few minutes, until thickened, stirring frequently. Check for seasoning and add additional salt if needed. Serve the cream gravy with the pheasant and mashed potatoes.

COMMUNITY PHEASANT BANQUET

Ring-necked pheasants, an Asian species introduced as a game bird to the United States in 1881 and successfully established in Minnesota in 1916, are beloved by hunters and cooks alike. These gaudy birds are found near agricultural areas, inhabiting brushlands, wetland edges, and woody shelterbelts; in Minnesota they are most prevalent in western and southern farmlands.

In the days before large-scale, monoculture farming, pheasants thrived in areas surrounding small farms. Minnesota hunters bagged over 1.5 million wild pheasants in 1958, and the pheasant population remained strong even under that level of hunting pressure. Community pheasant dinners were often held in rural areas, sponsored by sportsmen's clubs, fire stations, and civic organizations.

Modern agricultural practices have decimated pheasant habitat and, consequently, pheasant numbers. Discontinuation of government programs that paid farmers to set aside land for wildlife habitat has also negatively affected numbers of pheasants and other game.

Despite the decline of pheasant numbers, an annual pheasant banquet is still held in December by the Traverse County Sportsman's Club, a group of over 100 members based in Wheaton, a small western Minnesota farming community. In years past, club members were able to provide enough wild-harvested pheasants for the banquet, but these days the club relies on purchased game-farm birds. A dozen or so club members gather at the American Legion kitchen to prepare a feast of pheasant with cream gravy, homemade mashed potatoes, corn, coleslaw, rolls, cranberry sauce, and homemade desserts.

Guests come from Wheaton as well as from the surrounding communities. "It used to be a fundraiser for the club, but these days it's more about bringing the community together," said DeWayne Groneberg, a member of the Sportsman's Club and an officer with the local Pheasants Forever chapter. (Pheasants Forever, Inc., a nonprofit, grassroots wildlife conservation organization, was founded in St. Paul in 1982 with the mission to help restore and improve habitat for pheasants and other upland birds. More than 700 Pheasants Forever chapters now exist across the country.)

Recipe from CHEF RON BERG

Ultimate Roast Breast of Grouse
with Sherry-Mushroom Cream Sauce

Over the past two decades, Chef Ron Berg has delighted diners at several noted restaurants in the Grand Marais area, including the Gunflint Lodge, Old Northwoods Lodge, and Chez Jude. Ron notes that brining produces a juicier bird, a bonus when preparing wild grouse (which is very lean and can be dry when cooked). This dish is excellent when served with Ron's Wild Rice Spaetzle (page 66) or a wild rice pilaf; it also goes well with baked squash or sweet potatoes roasted with maple syrup and butter.

4 SERVINGS

BRINE

- 2 cups cold water
- 3 tablespoons sugar
- 2 tablespoons coarse kosher salt
- 1 tablespoon finely chopped fresh rosemary, optional
- 1 garlic clove, pressed or very finely minced

- 2 bone-in whole grouse breasts, skin on or skinless
- 1 tablespoon unsalted butter, very soft
- 1 teaspoon finely chopped fresh rosemary, optional
- Freshly ground black pepper
- Sherry-Mushroom Cream Sauce (opposite)

1. **Make the brine:** Combine the water, sugar, salt, rosemary (if desired), and garlic in a medium mixing bowl. Stir until the sugar and salt dissolve.

2. Place the grouse breasts in a ziplock bag, then place the bag in a bowl that holds it comfortably. Add the brine and seal the bag, pressing out the air. Refrigerate for 3 to 4 hours (but no longer than 4 hours). Rinse the breasts in cold water, then pat dry with paper towels. Discard the brine. Refrigerate the rinsed, dried breasts until you're ready to cook.

3. Preheat the oven to 400°F. Place the breasts, bone side down, in a small baking dish. Smear the butter over the breasts. Sprinkle with the rosemary, if desired, then season with pepper to taste. Roast, uncovered, for 15 to 20 minutes, until the internal temperature of the meat is 145°F. (The temperature will rise while it is resting, and the meat will also be cooked further in the final step.) Remove from the oven. Tent loosely with foil and set aside to rest while you prepare the sauce. Reduce the oven temperature to 350°F.

4. While the grouse is resting, prepare the cream sauce; if you like, add the juices from the baking dish to the sauce along with the chicken broth.

5. Use a boning knife to slice the breast meat away from the bones so you have two halves per breast; discard the bones. Place the boneless breast halves in a single layer in a small casserole and pour the sauce over them. Bake, uncovered, for 15 to 20 minutes, until the sauce is bubbling around the edges and the breasts are hot and cooked through. Serve immediately.

Recipe from CHEF RON BERG

Sherry-Mushroom Cream Sauce

This sauce is an integral part of the Ultimate Roast Breast of Grouse on the facing page. It's also great with roast chicken and will elevate mashed potatoes or wild rice to new heights. Chanterelles, morels, oyster mushrooms, hedgehog mushrooms, and hen of the woods are all excellent choices. Shiitakes and cremini mushrooms, while not wild, also work well.

4 SERVINGS

3½ tablespoons unsalted butter

4–5 ounces sliced chanterelles or other wild mushrooms (3–5 cups, depending on variety)

2 tablespoons all-purpose flour

1½ cups reduced-sodium chicken broth

2 tablespoons heavy cream or sour cream

1½ tablespoons dry sherry

Salt

1. Warm 1½ tablespoons of the butter in a large skillet over medium heat until the butter melts and becomes foamy. Add the mushrooms and stir to coat them with butter. Cook, stirring occasionally, until the liquid released by the mushrooms has cooked away. Spread the mushrooms out evenly and cook without stirring until the mushrooms are nicely bronzed underneath, 3 to 5 minutes. Stir well, and cook for 3 to 5 minutes longer, stirring once or twice. Remove from the heat.

2. Melt the remaining 2 tablespoons butter over medium-low heat in a heavy-bottomed medium saucepan. Whisk in the flour and cook, whisking constantly, for 2 minutes. Whisk in the broth. Increase the heat to medium-high and bring to a boil, whisking occasionally. Cook, whisking occasionally, until the mixture thickens, about 3 minutes. Stir in the sautéed mushrooms. Reduce the heat and simmer for 5 minutes. Stir in the cream and sherry, and cook for about 2 minutes longer. Taste, and add salt if necessary. Keep warm until needed.

WILD ACRES, PEQUOT LAKES

Tuck into a meal of duck or pheasant at a Twin Cities restaurant, and it's likely that you're enjoying a bird from Wild Acres, a game farm in Pequot Lakes, a central Minnesota town of about 2,000.

Pat Ebnet and his wife, Kelli, own and operate Wild Acres Processing, part of the Wild Acres brand that also includes a shooting preserve. They breed and raise all their own pheasants, ducks, geese, chickens, and turkeys, hatching nearly 100,000 birds annually. According to Pat, Wild Acres was the first to introduce free-range chickens to area restaurants in the 1980s, and they have built their reputation for top-quality poultry since then. Pat harvests birds three times each week, delivering them farm to restaurant twice weekly.

Noted area chef J.P. Samuelson once quipped, "I think Pat's duck ranks up there with any food product in the United States." One factor is that the birds are fresh, making them juicier and more flavorful than birds that have been frozen. Another key is that many of the birds spend much of their time outdoors. Pheasants live in a natural outdoor habitat, protected from predators by tentlike canopy nets. Geese roam the farm freely until they are harvested. Ducks spend spring through fall in roomy outdoor pens; they're brought inside during winter.

Although they are geared to providing poultry to restaurants, Wild Acres Processing distributes poultry through Clancey's Meats and Fish in South Minneapolis; Seward Community Co-op in Minneapolis (page 124) also carries Wild Acres duck products.

Wild Acres began in 1978 as a shooting preserve, catering to hunters who were looking for a good place to hunt without fighting congestion on public lands. As founder Mary Ebnet (Pat's mom) says, "At Wild Acres you know the birds are here, but it still requires a great deal of skill to flush and bag them." Mary and her crew still provide hunting opportunities for upland game from August through March, as well as trap shooting and sporting clays from spring through fall.

Pat Ebnet

Slow-Roasted Duck

Duck — particularly wild duck — can be tough and gamy if overcooked, and is generally best served rare; unfortunately, the legs and thighs are pretty awful at that stage of doneness, so many cooks set them aside for cooking with another method (and shamefully, some hunters discard them, retaining only the breast). This recipe takes it to the other extreme, using low-and-slow oven roasting to produce a roasted whole bird that's unbelievably succulent, with crisp skin and buttery meat. Even the thighs and legs are delicious, worthy of serious bone chewing. This recipe is best with ducks that have a moderate layer of fat; early-season wild mallards, canvasbacks, or pintails just coming off their feeding grounds in Canada are perfect, as are game-farm mallards. Barnyard breeds such as Pekin have very thick layers of fat and are much larger, so they aren't the best choice for this recipe.

1 DUCK YIELDS 2 SERVINGS

1 skin-on whole mallard or other appropriate duck (see headnote)

¼ teaspoon dry mustard

¼ teaspoon garlic powder

Salt and freshly ground black pepper

Half of an apple

¼ cup apple juice or orange juice

½ teaspoon dried thyme

1. Preheat the oven to 275°F. Use the tip of a sharp paring knife to poke the duck skin all over, about ½ inch apart or closer, taking care not to poke into the meat. Sprinkle the dry mustard and garlic powder over the outside, then rub in with your fingertips. Sprinkle the outside and inside generously with salt and pepper. Cut the apple half into several wedges and stuff inside the cavity. Place the duck, breast side down, on a rack in a shallow roasting pan.

2. Roast for 4 hours, turning over each hour and pricking the skin again each time you turn the duck. After 4 hours, brush the breast side, which should be facing up, with the apple juice. Sprinkle the duck with the thyme, crumbling it between your fingertips as you sprinkle; also add a light dusting of salt and pepper. Continue roasting, breast side up, for 45 minutes longer. Remove from the oven and tent loosely with foil. Let stand for 15 minutes.

3. Cut in half with kitchen shears, cutting through the center of the breastbone and the backbone. Discard the apple. Serve immediately.

Duck Carnitas Tacos

This is written for game-farm Pekin duck breasts, which have a nice layer of fat under the skin. Game-farm Muscovy and mallards, or wild ducks with a fair amount of fat under the skin, also work well, but you'll probably have to add lard for the frying phase, and you may not have to pull off the skin to crisp it separately. Lean wild ducks, or skinned duck breasts, can also be used; add lard as needed for frying. **Note:** Strain and save the duck fat at the end of step 4. Refrigerate it for frying potatoes; it's wonderful stuff.

3–6 SERVINGS

2 boneless, skin-on Pekin duck breast halves (1¼–1½ pounds total)

¾ teaspoon salt

2 cups chicken broth, or as needed

1 cup cold water

2 tablespoons distilled white vinegar

1 tablespoon sugar

¼ red onion, cut vertically into ¼-inch-thick wedges

1–2 teaspoons vegetable oil

6 corn tortillas

½ cup fresh cilantro

½ cup crumbled Cotija cheese

Roasted Ranchero Sauce (page 228) or other salsa, for serving

1. Cut the duck breast halves in half lengthwise, then cut crosswise into ¾-inch pieces. Place the duck pieces in a Dutch oven and sprinkle with the salt. Add enough of the broth to barely cover the meat. Bring to a boil, then adjust the heat so the liquid bubbles gently and cook, stirring frequently, until the broth has cooked away, about 1 hour. The meat should be tender enough to break a chunk in half with a wooden spoon; if it isn't, add a bit more broth and continue cooking until the meat is tender and the broth has cooked away.

2. Reduce the heat to low and fry, turning frequently; as the pieces begin to brown, use two forks to pull the skin away from the meat. Transfer individual pieces of meat to a dish as they become nicely browned on all sides, about 1 hour, leaving the skin pieces in the pot.

3. While the meat is browning, stir together the water, vinegar, and sugar in a mixing bowl. Add the onion slices. Let stand for about 30 minutes, then drain, rinse, and pat dry. Transfer to a small serving dish.

4. When all the meat has been removed, continue frying the skin pieces until they are shrunken, browned, and firm, 10 to 15 minutes longer. Transfer to the dish with the meat. Pour off all but 2 teaspoons of the fat. Return the meat and skin pieces to the pot and keep warm over low heat.

5. Heat a medium skillet over medium heat. Add the oil to film the skillet. Add a tortilla and cook, turning once, until very lightly colored, about 1 minute. Transfer to a serving dish and cover with a towel. Fry the remaining tortillas.

6. Transfer the duck pieces to a serving dish. Serve with the tortillas, cilantro, cheese, and salsa.

Venison Summer Sausage

This isn't a classic summer sausage because it isn't fermented or finished by smoking (or drying), characteristics that distinguish a true summer sausage. It's written for venison, but you can substitute bison or grass-fed beef. This recipe uses curing salt, which improves the safety of the finished product and helps create the characteristic color and texture of summer sausage. (See the note on page 161 for more information.) I use a food processor for the first chopping, because it's easier to clean and more convenient than my hand-crank meat grinder. The meat grinder fitted with a 4.5 mm plate works best for the final processing; although you can chop the meat in a food processor, it's difficult to get an even texture. **Note:** The seasoned meat must be refrigerated for 2 days before it is baked in the oven.

3 SAUSAGE ROLLS

1½ pounds lean, well-trimmed venison, cut into 1-inch cubes

¾ pound boneless pork shoulder, cut into 1-inch cubes

1 tablespoon Morton Tender Quick

2 teaspoons coarse kosher salt

1 teaspoon sugar

½ teaspoon garlic powder

⅛ teaspoon ground nutmeg

1 teaspoon mustard seeds

1 teaspoon coarsely ground black pepper

1. Combine the venison and pork cubes with the Tender Quick, salt, sugar, garlic powder, and nutmeg in a large bowl. Mix well with your hands. Chop very coarsely in a food processor (or grind through the large plate of a meat grinder). Pack into a ceramic or glass bowl. Cover tightly with plastic wrap and refrigerate for 2 days.

2. Grind the meat through the fine plate of a meat grinder (or chop finely in a food processor; see headnote). Place in a large bowl and add the mustard seeds and pepper. Mix well with your hands, kneading and squeezing for several minutes. Divide the mixture into three equal portions. Roll one portion into a log about 6½ inches long and 2 inches thick, packing firmly to eliminate air pockets. Cut a 1-foot length of cheesecloth and open it up so there are two layers (most cheesecloth is folded into four layers). Wrap the log tightly in the cheesecloth, twisting the cheesecloth tightly at the ends and tying with kitchen string. Repeat with the remaining two portions of meat mixture. Refrigerate the wrapped rolls while you heat the oven to 325°F.

3. Place the wrapped rolls on a broiler pan and bake for about 1¼ hours, or until the centers reach 160°F. Let the rolls cool, then wrap in foil and refrigerate for at least 12 hours before sampling; peel away the cheese-cloth before slicing. The cooked sausage will keep in the refrigerator for about 1 week; freeze for longer storage.

Grilled Venison Loin with Honey, Juniper, and Black Pepper Glaze

The loin is a long, boneless muscle that runs along either side of the backbone; it's also called the backstrap. For this dish, use a venison loin portion that's 10 to 12 inches long, which will weigh about 1¼ pounds. You can also use thick venison round steaks, or thick-cut steaks from an elk or moose loin; grass-fed beef steaks are delicious for this recipe as well. For more information about juniper berries, see the headnote for Juniper Bitters on page 84.

2 OR 3 SERVINGS

1 (10- to 12-inch-long) strip venison loin, or 1¼ pounds boneless thick-cut steaks (see headnote)

¼ teaspoon salt

¼ teaspoon dried juniper berries

¼ teaspoon whole black peppercorns

3 tablespoons honey

2 tablespoons unsalted butter

Sea salt or coarse kosher salt, for garnish

1. Cut the loin into two or three shorter pieces; this makes it easier to handle. Ensure that all silverskin or other connective tissue has been removed. Sprinkle the meat on both sides with the salt and set aside at room temperature while you prepare the grill.

2. **For a gas grill:** Preheat a two-burner gas grill on high for 15 minutes. **For a charcoal grill:** Prepare a medium-hot fire on half of the coal grate, leaving the other half free of coals.

3. While the grill is heating, prepare the glaze. Crush the juniper berries and peppercorns with a mortar and pestle until medium-coarse. (Alternately, place the spices in a heavyweight plastic bag and crush with the back side of a cast-iron skillet.) Combine the crushed mixture with the honey and butter in a very small saucepan. Cook over low heat, stirring occasionally, for about 5 minutes.

4. When the grill is ready, turn off one of the burners of the gas grill, or spread out the coals of the charcoal grill, keeping half of the coal grate free of coals. Place the meat over the hot part of the grill. Cook until nicely marked on both sides. Move the meat to the cool area of the grill and brush with the honey glaze. Flip and brush the second side with the glaze. Cover the grill and cook, flipping and brushing the meat with the glaze every few minutes, until it reaches the desired doneness. Total cooking time will be 15 to 20 minutes; near the end, you may want to put the meat back over the hot area to give it a nice color. Venison is best when still somewhat rare; for best results, don't cook it beyond 135°F (medium-rare), as the temperature will rise a bit during the resting period.

5. When the venison is a few degrees below the desired doneness, transfer to a serving plate. Sprinkle with sea salt. Cover loosely and let rest for 5 minutes. Slice thickly and serve.

Venison Liver Pâté

Make this with the liver from deer, elk, moose, or antelope. It's a nice change from the usual bacon-and-onion fried treatment that is the most common preparation for venison liver. Serve this with crackers, toasted baguette slices, or small squares of coarse, dark pumpernickel bread. Some coarse mustard might be welcome also.

10 tablespoons plus 1 teaspoon butter, softened

3 tablespoons olive oil

1 pound well-trimmed venison liver (see headnote), cut into ½-inch chunks

1 cup chopped onion

½ cup chopped carrot

2 teaspoons salt

¼ teaspoon crumbled dried thyme

¼ teaspoon freshly ground black pepper

⅛ teaspoon ground nutmeg

2 teaspoons Cognac or good-quality whiskey

2 tablespoons chopped fresh parsley

Cornichons, for serving

Pickled onions, for serving

1. Coat a 4- by 8-inch loaf pan with the 1 teaspoon butter; set aside.

2. Heat the oil in a large skillet over medium heat. Add the liver. Cook, stirring frequently, until the liver is golden brown outside and just cooked through, about 5 minutes. Transfer the liver to a food processor.

3. Melt 2 tablespoons of the butter over medium heat in the skillet used to cook the liver. Add the onion, carrot, salt, thyme, pepper, and nutmeg to the skillet. Cook, stirring occasionally, until the vegetables are tender, 5 to 7 minutes. Scrape the onion mixture into the food processor with the liver. Add the Cognac and parsley to the food processor.

4. Pulse the food processor a few times, until the liver is chopped to a medium texture. Add the remaining 8 tablespoons butter, 2 tablespoons at a time, pulsing between additions. Process until the mixture is smooth.

5. Scrape the liver mixture into the prepared loaf pan. Cover with plastic wrap, pressing the plastic against the surface of the liver mixture. Refrigerate for at least 8 hours, and up to 24 hours.

6. To unmold, uncover the pâté and immerse the bottom half of the loaf pan in a sink full of very hot water for about a minute. Place a serving plate over the loaf pan, and flip the plate and loaf pan together to unmold the pâté onto the plate. Surround the pâté with cornichons and pickled onions.

Tater Tot Hotdish Goes Wild

You betcha, Minnesotans really *do* eat Tater Tot Hotdish . . . it's a fixture at church-hall suppers, after-funeral lunches, potlucks, family reunions, and card parties. If you took a poll of Minnesotans to ask what their favorite hotdish is, I think a version of this ground-beef-and-tater-tot dish would come out on top; variations of this recipe can be found in most church- or community-published cookbooks, and it's usually the first to disappear at a potluck supper. When this dish is prepared in families that include a hunter, ground venison is often used in place of ground beef. Don't fight the use of the canned cream soups here; they are integral to the dish, and attempts to substitute homemade mixtures in this dish generally fall flat.

8 SERVINGS

1½ pounds ground venison

1 cup diced onion

⅓ cup diced celery

½ teaspoon salt

Freshly ground black pepper

1 (10-ounce) package frozen mixed corn, peas, and carrots, thawed

1 (10¾-ounce) can condensed golden mushroom soup

1 (10¾-ounce) can condensed cream of chicken soup

¾ cup milk

1 (2-pound) bag frozen tater tots (you won't use it all)

1. Preheat the oven to 350°F. Coat a 9- by 13-inch baking dish with cooking spray.

2. Cook the venison in a large skillet over medium heat, stirring frequently to break it up, until the meat has lost its pink color, 8 to 10 minutes. Spoon out and discard excess grease, leaving enough to continue frying. Add the onion and celery. Continue cooking, stirring frequently, until the vegetables are tender-crisp, about 5 minutes longer. Sprinkle with the salt, and season with pepper to taste. Add the mixed vegetables, stirring to mix. Spread evenly in the prepared baking dish.

3. Stir together the soups and milk in a mixing bowl. Spread evenly over the ground meat mixture. Arrange a layer of the tater tots on top, using enough to make a fairly solid layer. Bake for 50 minutes to 1 hour, until the tater tots are golden brown and crisp on top and the mixture is bubbly. Remove from the oven and let stand for 5 minutes before serving.

Variation: Tater Tot Hotdish with Cheese

Assemble the hotdish as described, and bake for 50 minutes. Sprinkle 1½ cups shredded cheddar or Colby cheese over the tater tots. Bake for 5 minutes longer, or until the cheese melts.

Juniper Bitters

Common juniper shrubs (*Juniperus communis*) grow in the wild throughout much of Minnesota, and they are also a common landscape planting in yards and parks. Their dusty-looking bright blue berries smell like gin when crushed; indeed, they are the primary flavoring used in gin. Fresh juniper berries can be harvested in Minnesota from late summer through early winter, to be used fresh or to be dried for later use. Dried juniper berries are also found in the spice aisle; they're used in meat marinades and sausage making. Tammy Kimbler (page 167) uses both dried and fresh berries, harvested from the shrubs in her South Minneapolis yard, in combination with fresh herbs and peppercorns to prepare this recipe for wonderful, intense bitters that give a special flavor to cocktails. She's also provided two go-along recipes to make a festive cocktail. **Note:** This recipe requires a 2-month infusion time.

ABOUT 1 PINT

2 cups vodka

2 tablespoons fresh juniper berries

2 teaspoons whole black peppercorns

2 (4-inch) sprigs rosemary

2 (4-inch) sprigs thyme

¼ cup dried juniper berries

1. Combine the vodka, fresh juniper berries, peppercorns, rosemary, and thyme in a pint glass jar. Cover and store in a cool, dark place for 1 month.

2. Strain the vodka, discarding the solid materials. Return the vodka to the jar. Add the dried juniper berries. Cover and store in a cool, dark place for 1 month longer.

3. Strain the vodka, discarding the juniper berries. Store the finished bitters in a tightly sealed glass jar. Use about ½ teaspoon of the bitters per cocktail, or to taste.

Recipe from TAMMY KIMBLER

Cranberry-Ginger Simple Syrup

This is combined with the Juniper Bitters (facing page) to make a festive cocktail (below). It also makes a refreshing nonalcoholic beverage when stirred into sparkling water.

ABOUT 1¾ CUPS

1¼ cups water
1 cup fresh cranberries
3 thick slices fresh gingerroot
1 cup sugar

Simmer the water, cranberries, and gingerroot in a saucepan over medium heat for 5 minutes. Strain, discarding the cranberries and gingerroot. Stir in the sugar and simmer over medium heat, stirring constantly, until the sugar dissolves. Let cool completely and store in the refrigerator; it will keep for a month or longer.

Recipe from TAMMY KIMBLER

Cranberry Juniper Twist Cocktail

This uses the Juniper Bitters (facing page) and Cranberry-Ginger Simple Syrup (above) to make a cocktail that is perfect for the holidays.

1 COCKTAIL

½ teaspoon Juniper Bitters
1 orange slice
1 thin slice peeled fresh gingerroot
1½ ounces gin
2 tablespoons Cranberry-Ginger Simple Syrup
Juice of half a lime
Ice cubes
Soda water, as needed
1 lime slice

Combine the bitters, orange slice, and gingerroot in a tall glass. Muddle until well crushed. Add the gin, simple syrup, and lime juice. Stir well, then add ice. Fill with soda water and garnish with the lime slice.

CHAPTER 3

Co-ops, CSAs, and Farmers' Market Finds

MINNESOTA IS ONE OF THE TOP FIVE STATES when ranked by crop value and cash receipts. Farming takes up a lot of room, though, so more than 60 percent of the state's total population lives in cities — primarily the Twin Cities of Minneapolis and St. Paul. The Twin Cities rank at or near the top in listings of America's healthiest cities, and part of the reason for that is the availability of fresh, healthy foods from co-ops, community-supported agriculture (CSA) programs, and farmers' markets.

These options are great for consumers who are looking for something beyond typical supermarket fare. Unprocessed foods, those that are locally grown or produced, organic choices, and offerings from small farms and producers satisfy the demands of food-aware consumers. Co-ops also give consumers a chance to join with others who share the vision of a healthy food stream that is environmentally sound and fits with the concept of fair trade and food justice.

Many shoppers rely on co-ops to research vendors, effectively vetting the products sold. This includes visiting farms to check on animal treatment and farming practices, meeting with producers from butchers to bakers to tortilla-chip makers, and cutting through marketing hype. CSA programs, in contrast, put consumers solely in charge of vendor selection, while still allowing them to put their food dollars to work supporting small, local producers whose ideals align with their own.

Farmers' markets also put the consumer in direct contact with growers and producers, and there's no months-long commitment, as there is with CSA shares. Many people enjoy visiting a farmers' market as much for the experience as for the escarole. The atmosphere is festive, and there are often musical performances, food trucks, and cooking or other demonstrations.

Following are about two dozen recipes that feature the best and freshest produce from co-ops, CSAs, and farmers' markets.

Garlic Scape Pesto

Garlic scapes are the flower stalks that come up from planted garlic in early summer. Growers trim the scapes off before the flowers open, to increase the size of the bulb below. The first time I made garlic scape pesto was when I got a bunch of scapes in my CSA box from Driftless Organics in Soldier's Grove, Wisconsin, just over the southeastern border with Minnesota. The fine folks at Driftless provided not only the scapes but also a recipe, which I have been tinkering with over the years. This pesto is great on pasta and works well to dollop on grilled chicken or fish. It also makes a terrific smear on bruschetta. Unlike basil pesto, it stays bright green.

ABOUT 1 CUP

¼ cup slivered blanched almonds

¾ cup sliced garlic scapes (¼-inch pieces)

½ cup freshly grated Parmesan cheese

¼ cup packed fresh basil leaves

1 tablespoon lemon juice

¼ teaspoon coarse kosher salt

⅔ cup extra-virgin olive oil, or as needed

1. Toast the slivered almonds in a skillet over medium-high heat, stirring constantly, until golden brown, about 3 minutes. Transfer the toasted nuts immediately to a food processor.

2. Add the garlic scapes, Parmesan, basil, lemon juice, and salt to the food processor. Pulse on and off until chopped fairly fine. With the machine running, pour the oil through the feed tube, adding enough to produce the consistency you like. The pesto is now ready to use. You can store it in the refrigerator for a week or two if you pour a little additional oil over the top to seal it.

Asparagus Guacamole

One thing is certain: Avocados don't thrive in Minnesota. If you like guacamole but want to prepare a version with fewer food miles (not to mention less fat), try this easy recipe with fresh, locally grown asparagus. You won't miss the avocado at all — and as an added bonus, this guac won't darken like the traditional version.

ABOUT 2 CUPS

½ pound asparagus, cut into 1-inch lengths

3 tablespoons plain Greek-style yogurt or sour cream

2 tablespoons chopped white onion

1 tablespoon lime juice

1 teaspoon pressed or finely minced garlic

½ teaspoon ground cumin

½ teaspoon dried oregano

¼–½ teaspoon hot pepper sauce

¼ teaspoon salt

⅓ cup canned diced tomatoes, drained before measuring

1. Bring a saucepan of salted water to a boil. Add the asparagus and cook until just tender, about 2 minutes. Drain and rinse with plenty of cold water. Pat dry and let stand until completely cool.

2. Transfer the cooled asparagus to a food processor. Add the yogurt, onion, lime juice, garlic, cumin, oregano, hot pepper sauce, and salt. Pulse a few times, until the asparagus is finely chopped but not puréed. Add the tomatoes and pulse a few times to blend. Transfer to a bowl. Taste, and adjust the seasoning if necessary. Chill before serving.

MINNEAPOLIS FARMERS' MARKET, MINNEAPOLIS

Farmers' markets in Minnesota are blossoming and expanding across the state, for many reasons. Of course, they're great places to buy just-picked produce, baked goods, homemade preserves and pickles, farm-fresh meats and eggs, flowers, maple syrup and honey, wild rice, cheese, and so on. But to the thousands who visit them each season, they offer more than just a shopping trip. For many families, it's a festive outing and an adventure for the kids. Others come to munch on ready-to-eat foods sold at various booths or food trucks while listening to live music. Serious cooks come looking for hard-to-find produce and to get tips on its preparation from the people who grew it. In city areas, concrete-weary apartment dwellers come simply to stroll among artfully arranged piles of produce, a treat for the eyes as well as the soul.

Minnesota is home to over 180 farmers' markets, 30 of which are within 10 miles of downtown Minneapolis or St. Paul. The largest of these is the Lyndale market in near-north Minneapolis, close to the Minnesota Twins' home at Target Field; it's so well established that it is typically referred to simply as "the Minneapolis farmers' market."

THE LYNDALE MARKET is the largest open-air market in the Upper Midwest, and it has been in its current location since 1937. Produce offerings have changed quite a bit since then, enriched in part by an influx of Hmong farmers who have made Minnesota their new home after being forced out of their mountain villages in Southeast Asia after the Vietnam War. Bitter melon, tatsoi, gai lan, and lemongrass sit alongside more familiar offerings such as onions, carrots, and herbs.

Unlike many markets that allow only locally grown produce, the Lyndale market has a small number of vendors who are resellers or importers. If you see bananas and avocados, for example, look for the sign above the booth that lists the vendor as a reseller. It's easy enough to avoid resellers if you want strictly local produce. On the other hand, if you need a bell pepper in May to go along with the fresh, locally grown salad greens you just bought, you can pick it up without stopping at the supermarket on the way home.

The Lyndale market is open 7 days a week from mid-April to mid-November. Free cooking and other demonstrations are offered on Saturdays from May through October. The Central Minnesota Vegetable Growers Association, the nonprofit group that manages the Lyndale market, also runs a farmers' market on Nicollet Mall, a mostly pedestrian mall that is the heart of downtown Minneapolis. That market occupies seven blocks of the mall and operates every Thursday from May to October, giving downtown workers an opportunity to pick up fresh produce, flowers, and other market items during their lunch break.

ANOTHER OPTION IS the St. Paul Downtown Farmers' Market across the river, which offers Minnesota's largest selection of strictly locally grown fruits and vegetables (no resellers or importers are allowed). The Twin Cities metro area also has many outstanding neighborhood and suburban farmers' markets that are worth a visit, and if you're outside the metro area, check out Minnesota Grown (see Resources on page 270 for website address) for a list of farmers' markets throughout the state.

Icebox Pickles

These pickles are super-easy to make because they're not canned; the process also ensures crisp, fresh-tasting pickles. This is a very adaptable recipe. The brine can be used with a variety of vegetables; see the variations, opposite, for some ideas. Seasonings are also flexible and can be adjusted to personal preference. If you prefer a smaller (or larger) batch of pickles, simply adjust the brine ingredients proportionally. You will need 10 widemouthed pint canning jars, with bands and lids. I always sterilize the jars by boiling for 5 minutes in a large pot of water, but many cooks skip that step, simply using squeaky-clean jars.

10 PINTS (EASILY ADJUSTED)

BRINE

- 2 quarts water
- 3¼ cups distilled white vinegar
- ¾ cup canning/pickling salt, or ¾ cup plus 3 tablespoons coarse kosher salt
- 3 tablespoons sugar
- 20 garlic cloves, peeled

PICKLES

- 5½ pounds pickling cucumbers
- 10 fresh cayenne chile peppers
- 1 large bunch dill (fronds, not seed heads)
- 2½ teaspoons mustard seeds

1. **Make the brine:** Combine the water, vinegar, salt, and sugar in a nonreactive soup pot or large saucepan. Place over high heat and stir until the salt and sugar dissolve. Continue cooking until the liquid comes to a full boil. Remove from the heat and add the garlic. Set aside until cooled to room temperature.

2. **Prepare the pickles:** Wash the cucumbers, chile peppers, and dill thoroughly. Place a frond of dill and ¼ teaspoon of the mustard seeds in the bottom of a canning jar. Add one garlic clove from the brine. Cut the cucumbers vertically into halves or quarters, standing them upright in the jar as you go (cut the ends off any that are too long to fit comfortably in the jar). Slip a whole cayenne pepper into the jar alongside the cucumbers. Continue adding cucumbers until the jar is comfortably full; the pickles should be fairly tightly packed but not tight enough to be crushed. Place another dill frond on top of the cucumbers, and add another garlic clove. Set the jar in the empty sink and continue until all the jars are filled.

3. Pour the cooled brine into the jars, filling almost to the top. Seal each jar with a clean lid and a band, turning the band finger-tight. Flip each jar over and gently shake, then stand upright again. Open each jar and check the level of the brine, adding a little more if needed to cover the vegetables. Reseal and rinse each jar, then let stand in the sink until the jars have dried off.

4. Refrigerate the jars for at least 2 days before serving. The pickles will keep in the refrigerator for up to 3 months.

Variations

Here's where you can really have some fun with your pickles. Use the same brine and technique for all of these variations. Feel free to combine the variations; for example, you could use different spices with various vegetable mixes.

- For more dill flavor, use dill with developed seed heads rather than fronds. Choose dill with seeds that are still greenish rather than brown, and use one small head (or half of a large head) per jar.

- Use Thai chile peppers or other fresh hot chile peppers in place of the cayenne peppers. You could also substitute ⅛ teaspoon red pepper flakes for the fresh peppers, or omit the hot peppers altogether.

- Add ¼ teaspoon dried fennel seeds or ⅛ teaspoon dried celery seeds per jar.

- Cut the cucumbers into thick chunks rather than spears. As an additional option, alternate layers of cucumber chunks with bite-size cauliflower florets and ¼-inch-thick carrot slices.

- Replace some of the cucumbers with carrots. Use peeled whole baby carrots that are no thicker than your little finger; you can leave a bit of the stems attached at the top for a pretty look (scrub the base of the stems very well). You can also use larger carrots, peeled and cut into spears about ⅜ inch thick.

- Try a jar of mixed vegetables, including bite-size cauliflower florets, carrot slices, halved Brussels sprouts, and chunks of red bell pepper; add some cucumber chunks if you like, or omit the cucumber completely.

- You don't have to use cucumbers at all! Pack a jar full of green beans or thin asparagus, adding a little extra dill and a few slices of white onion. Snow peas also make a wonderful pickle that works great on sandwiches.

Marinated Cucumbers with Dill

Use garden-fresh cucumbers for this easy salad. Grocery store cucumbers that have been shipped long distances are often bitter and disappointing in flavor, with tough skins.

5 OR 6 SERVINGS

1 cucumber (about ¾ pound)

1 small red onion

1 bunch dill (fronds, not seed heads)

½ cup unseasoned rice vinegar or white wine vinegar

¼ cup cold water

2 tablespoons honey

½ teaspoon salt

Pinch of ground white pepper

1. Before deciding how to proceed, cut off a thin slice of the unpeeled cucumber and taste it. If the skins are tough or taste even slightly bitter, peel the cucumber. If the taste is mellow and fresh and the skins are tender, score the skin by raking lengthwise with a fork to create an even pattern of lines. European-style seedless cucumbers don't need to be peeled; you may score the cucumber if you like, or simply proceed with slicing.

2. Slice the cucumber very thinly. Cut a few very thin slices of onion, then cut them across the rings into 1-inch pieces; you will need about ⅓ cup onion pieces. Pull small dill fronds away from the larger stems, measuring as you go; you will need about ⅔ cup loosely packed small fronds. Arrange a layer of cucumbers in a wide, shallow serving dish. Top with a scattering of sliced onion. Scatter some dill fronds over the onion. Repeat the layers until all of the cucumbers, onion, and dill have been used; the top layer should be dill fronds.

3. Combine the vinegar, water, honey, salt, and pepper in a measuring cup or small bowl, stirring until the honey is dissolved. Pour the vinegar mixture over the cucumbers. Cover and refrigerate for at least 4 hours, or as long as overnight. Spoon off a little of the liquid before serving, if necessary, so the cucumbers are not swimming in the dish.

Shredded Brussels Sprouts with Buttery Crumb Topping

Use top-quality Romano or Parmesan cheese, and grate it by hand on the fine holes of a box grater (or use a rotary cheese grater) just before starting preparation of this dish.

4 SERVINGS

¾ pound Brussels sprouts, ends trimmed and loose outer leaves removed before weighing

1 tablespoon unsalted butter

1 garlic clove, pressed or very finely minced

⅔ cup fresh breadcrumbs (see Note)

1 tablespoon plus 1 teaspoon hazelnut oil, walnut oil, or olive oil

½ teaspoon salt

⅛ teaspoon freshly ground black pepper

2 tablespoons finely grated Romano or Parmesan cheese

1. Cut each Brussels sprout in half lengthwise, then lay the halves flat on the cutting board and slice lengthwise, a bit over ⅛ inch thick. Fluff with your hands a few times to loosen and separate the slices somewhat. Set aside.

2. Melt the butter in a large skillet over medium heat. Add the garlic and cook, stirring constantly, for about 45 seconds. Stir in the breadcrumbs and continue to cook, stirring constantly, until the crumbs are golden brown, about 2½ minutes longer. Transfer the crumb mixture to a small bowl. Let the skillet cool until it is comfortable to handle, then wipe out the crumbs with a paper towel.

3. Heat the oil in the wiped-out skillet over medium heat until shimmering. Add the sliced Brussels sprouts, stirring to coat evenly with the oil. Sprinkle with the salt and pepper. Cook, stirring frequently, until the sprouts are tender-crisp and beginning to brown in spots but are still bright green, 4 to 5 minutes. Meanwhile, stir the Romano into the breadcrumb mixture.

4. Transfer the cooked Brussels sprouts to a serving dish. Sprinkle the breadcrumb mixture evenly over, and serve immediately.

Note: **To make the fresh breadcrumbs,** cut day-old French bread (or other hearty bread) into ¾-inch cubes; 1 cup bread cubes will yield about ⅔ cup fresh breadcrumbs. Start a blender on medium speed (if possible; otherwise, use high), then drop the cubes, a few at a time and in rapid succession, through the hole in the lid. The cubes will bounce vigorously in the blender jar, so be sure to re-cover the hole in the lid as soon as all the cubes are added. Increase the speed to high and process until the crumbs are medium-fine and fairly even in texture, about 45 seconds.

Sauce Verte: Herb and Caper Sauce
with Homemade Mayonnaise and Crème Fraîche

This classic French sauce features homemade mayonnaise, which is easy to make in a food processor. Use a pasteurized egg (available at most large supermarkets) to eliminate the possibility of salmonella. Look for crème fraîche in the dairy case, or make your own following the instructions below. This vibrant green sauce is lovely served with steamed vegetables, grilled chicken, or poached fish. It also makes a tasty dip for crusty bread or breadsticks, and elevates a simple omelet or scrambled eggs to new heights. It's a key component of the Salmon or Trout Mousse on page 18.

ABOUT 2 CUPS

1 pasteurized egg, room temperature

¼ cup coarsely chopped fresh parsley

2 tablespoons coarsely chopped fresh chervil or tarragon

2 tablespoons lemon juice

1 teaspoon Dijon mustard

Dash of hot pepper sauce

Half of a small shallot, cut into chunks

¾ cup top-quality extra-virgin olive oil, or as needed

½ cup crème fraîche (see box below) or sour cream

¼ cup sliced scallions

¼ cup drained brined capers

Salt and freshly ground black pepper

1. Combine the egg, parsley, chervil, lemon juice, mustard, hot pepper sauce, shallot, and 1 tablespoon of the oil in a food processor. Process for 15 to 20 seconds. With the machine still running, start pouring the remaining oil in a very thin stream through the feed tube; as the mayonnaise begins to thicken, you can pour more quickly. Stop adding oil when the mayonnaise becomes thick.

2. Add the crème fraîche, scallions, and capers to the mayonnaise. Pulse a few times to mix the ingredients. Transfer to a bowl, and stir in salt and pepper to taste. Chill thoroughly before serving.

Tip: Omit the herbs, capers, and scallions to make delicious plain mayonnaise that is way better than the purchased stuff.

HOMEMADE CRÈME FRAÎCHE

Combine 2 cups heavy cream and ⅓ cup sour cream in a widemouthed quart jar. Stir until thoroughly mixed. Partially cover the jar. Let the mixture stand at room temperature until it has thickened; it should have the consistency of slightly loose sour cream. Depending on the temperature in your kitchen, this could take from 5 hours to overnight. When the mixture has thickened, shake or stir to mix thoroughly, and then store in the refrigerator for up to a week. Use it in place of sour cream; it doesn't separate when cooked.

Roasted Peppers (and What to Do with Them)

I've loved roasted bell peppers most of my life and have tried every technique in the book to make them. After charring peppers on a grill, blistering them on my gas range, and even attacking them with a handheld kitchen torch, I've finally settled on broiling as the easiest, most foolproof method. This method works equally well for cone-shaped peppers such as Italian frying peppers and for meaty, cone-shaped chile peppers such as serranos, jalapeños, and Anaheims.

VARIABLE SERVINGS

Bell peppers or cone-shaped peppers

Ways to Use Roasted Bell Peppers

- Slice vertically into strips. Toss with a little olive oil, vinegar, minced garlic, and salt and pepper to taste. Let marinate at room temperature for 20 minutes or up to 4 hours. Serve at room temperature, with crusty bread if you like.

- Cut into chunks or strips and add to salads.

- Dice and add to egg salad or tuna salad.

- Spread with seasoned cream cheese, then roll up and serve as an appetizer.

- Use in any recipe calling for roasted bell peppers; these are way tastier than the ones you buy in a jar!

1. Position an oven rack at the top of the oven and preheat the broiler. Line a heavy baking sheet with foil (to make cleanup easier).

2. **For bell peppers:** Stand each pepper upright on a cutting board. Starting a short distance from the stem, cut the sides off into slabs, as though cutting a cube. Discard the stem section, which should have most of the seedy ribs still attached. Flip the pepper slabs over and pull off any rib remnants; scrape off any clinging seeds. Place the pepper slabs, cut side down, on the foil-lined baking sheet. Refrigerate the dimpled bottom portion for other uses. **For cone-shaped peppers:** Cut the top off. Slice each pepper in half vertically. Use a serrated-tip grapefruit spoon or a paring knife to scrape out the ribs and seeds. Place the pepper halves, cut side down, on the foil-lined baking sheet.

3. Place the baking sheet under the broiler. Broil until the skins are completely blackened, checking their progress every few minutes and removing pepper pieces with tongs as they become blackened. The timing will range from 5 to 15 minutes, depending on your oven and the peppers themselves.

4. Transfer the blackened peppers to a bowl. Cover with a plate and let steam for 10 minutes. Pull off the blackened skin with your fingertips; you can also lay the pepper pieces flat and gently scrape the skin off with a knife.

Tomato and Mozzarella Salad with *Frico*

When tomatoes are perfectly ripe and gorgeous, put together this simple knife-and-fork salad. You can make the *frico* — baked Parmesan wafers with a delicate, lacy texture — an hour or so in advance, then hold them until you're ready to assemble the salad. Look for the freshest and milkiest mozzarella you can find. I love the hand-pulled mozz sold at Broder's Cucina Italiana deli in southwestern Minneapolis; they are also a great source for top-quality extra-virgin Italian olive oil.

3 OR 4 SERVINGS

½ cup freshly grated Parmesan cheese

2–3 vine-ripened tomatoes, preferably different colors

1 tablespoon top-quality extra-virgin olive oil, or as needed

Sea salt or coarse kosher salt and freshly ground black pepper

1 (8-ounce) ball fresh mozzarella cheese

2 leafy sprigs basil

1. Preheat the oven to 375°F. Line two baking sheets with parchment paper or, better still, silicone baking liners. Heap four piles of Parmesan, 1 tablespoon each, on one of the baking sheets, spacing them as far apart as you can. Pat down each one into a flat circle a bit over 3 inches across; there should be at least 1 inch between each circle. Repeat with the remaining 4 tablespoons Parmesan on the second baking sheet; if you are using a silicone liner and have only one, prepare the *frico* in two batches, letting the first cool for about 10 minutes before shaping and baking the second.

2. Bake for 6 to 8 minutes, until the cheese is bubbling and has melted into a cohesive but lacy disk and is just starting to turn golden brown; don't overbrown them. Remove the baking sheet from the oven and let cool for 5 minutes before lifting the *frico* off the baking sheet with a spatula.

3. When you are ready to assemble the salad, slice the tomatoes crosswise, a little thicker than ¼ inch. Refrigerate the end slices for other uses (or eat them); for the salad, you want just perfect, even slices. Sprinkle one side of each slice with a little oil, and dust very lightly with salt and pepper. Slice the mozzarella ¼ inch thick.

4. Arrange the tomatoes, mozzarella, and *frico* attractively on a serving platter, alternating colors of the tomatoes as you lay them out and slipping pieces of mozzarella between the tomato slices. Break the basil into short sprigs and arrange them around the platter. Sprinkle a little salt over the tomatoes and mozzarella. Serve immediately.

Carrot Risotto

Take advantage of flavorful fresh, in-season carrots to make a batch of this carrot-themed risotto. This makes a beautiful side dish with grilled fish or chicken. Begin preparing the Roasted Carrot Batons (opposite) before you start cooking the risotto.

4 SERVINGS

1 quart reduced-sodium chicken broth

1 (2- by 2- by ¼-inch) chunk Parmesan rind, optional

A few threads saffron, or a pinch of ground saffron or turmeric

1 tablespoon olive oil

1 cup finely diced carrots (⅛-inch dice)

2 tablespoons unsalted butter

1 cup Arborio rice

2 tablespoons finely minced shallots

½ cup dry white wine

⅛ teaspoon nutmeg, preferably freshly grated

¼ cup freshly grated Parmesan cheese

2 tablespoons snipped fresh chives

Roasted Carrot Batons (see recipe opposite)

1. Combine the broth, Parmesan rind, and saffron in a medium saucepan. Bring to a simmer over medium heat. Adjust the heat so the broth simmers but isn't boiling, and maintain the simmer throughout cooking. **Note:** You will be discarding the Parmesan rind when the rice is fully cooked; it's just there to add flavor to the broth.

2. Heat the oil in a heavy-bottomed saucepan over medium heat. Add the diced carrots. Cook, stirring occasionally, for 5 minutes. Transfer the diced carrots to a small bowl.

3. Melt 1 tablespoon of the butter in the same saucepan over medium heat. Add the rice and shallots. Cook, stirring constantly with a wooden spoon, for 2 minutes. Add the wine and continue cooking, stirring constantly, until the liquid is mostly cooked away. Add ½ cup broth and cook, stirring frequently, until the liquid is mostly cooked away; adjust the heat so the mixture bubbles gently, not furiously, and be sure to stir into the corners of the saucepan. Add another ½-cup portion of broth, and continue cooking in this manner until the rice is almost tender but still a bit underdone; this will take perhaps 15 minutes total. (If you run out of broth before the rice is fully cooked, add some water to the saucepan and heat to simmering before adding to the rice.)

4. When the rice is almost tender but still a bit underdone, stir the diced carrots and nutmeg into the rice. Continue adding broth in ½-cup portions and cooking until the rice is just tender to the bite, with a pleasant chew in the center. Add the remaining 1 tablespoon butter and a bit of additional broth if necessary so the mixture is creamy but not soupy. Stir in the grated Parmesan.

5. To serve, mound one-quarter of the rice on each serving plate. Tuck five or six carrot batons next to the rice. Scatter the chives over the rice.

Roasted Carrot Batons

These are used as an accent for the Carrot Risotto (opposite). If possible, use two different colors of carrots; one red and one yellow make a lovely contrast.

2 medium-large carrots, peeled

1½ tablespoons olive oil

1 tablespoon honey

⅛ teaspoon ground cumin

⅛ teaspoon Sriracha, optional

Coarse kosher salt and freshly ground black pepper

1. Preheat the oven to 400°F. Line a square baking dish with heavy foil.

2. Cut the carrots into 2½- to 3-inch lengths. Cut each length into ¼-inch planks, then cut each plank lengthwise into ¼-inch batons. You should have at least 20 batons.

3. Stir together the oil, honey, cumin, Sriracha (if desired), a pinch of salt, and a few grindings of pepper in a mixing bowl. Add the carrots, stirring to coat.

4. Transfer the mixture to the prepared baking dish, spreading the carrots in a single layer. Place in the oven and roast until they are nicely browned and beginning to shrivel, 30 to 40 minutes. Remove from the oven and keep warm until needed.

Grill-Roasted Tomatoes

Roasting amplifies the naturally sweet notes of vine-ripened tomatoes. If you don't want to heat up your kitchen during the dog days of summer, try this grill-roasting method. Roasted tomatoes can be chopped coarsely and tossed, along with the oil and juices from the roasting pan, with hot pasta for a quick but delicious meal. They also make a nice topping for crusty bread or bruschetta and are wonderful set on a charcuterie plate or on a composed salad.

VARIABLE SERVINGS

2 pounds vine-ripened tomatoes, cored

3 tablespoons olive oil or sunflower oil

2 tablespoons chopped fresh basil

2 tablespoons chopped fresh parsley

1 teaspoon chopped fresh thyme or marjoram, optional

5 garlic cloves, sliced ⅛ inch thick

Coarse kosher salt or sea salt and freshly ground black pepper

1. Prepare a grill for indirect grilling with a hot bed of charcoal, or high heat if using a gas grill.

2. If you're roasting Roma tomatoes, grape tomatoes, or others less than 1¼ inches across, cut them in half, cutting Romas vertically and others crosswise. Tomatoes up to 2½ inches across should be cut into quarters; cut larger tomatoes into 1½-inch chunks. Remove the seedy portions of larger tomatoes, if you like. Place the tomatoes in a 9- by 13-inch foil or other grill-safe pan. Add the oil, basil, parsley, thyme (if desired), and garlic. Stir to coat the tomatoes and mix well. Sprinkle with salt and pepper to taste.

3. Place the pan on the grill grate, away from the coals. Cover the grill and roast, stirring every 45 minutes, until the tomatoes are roasted as much as you like. They should be somewhat puckered and shrunken, and smell very tomatoey; depending on your grill setup and your preference, this will take 2 to 4 hours. Use immediately, or cool and store in the refrigerator for up to 3 days. The roasted tomatoes will keep in the freezer for several months.

Mediterranean Shepherd's Salad

Prepare this in mid- to late summer, when tomatoes are ripe and plump and bell peppers and cucumbers are crisp and juicy. Serve it as a simple lunch, with pita bread or a crusty loaf of rustic bread. It also totes well in a picnic cooler, and it makes a fine starter to a casual dinner.

5 OR 6 SERVINGS

1 small red onion

1 pound ripe tomatoes, diced

1 cucumber, seeded and diced

1 green bell pepper, diced

12 kalamata olives, pitted and quartered

¼ cup coarsely chopped fresh flat-leaf parsley

8–10 fresh basil leaves, halved lengthwise and cut crosswise into strips

3 tablespoons extra-virgin olive oil

2 tablespoons lemon juice

2 tablespoons red wine vinegar

1 teaspoon minced fresh oregano or ½ teaspoon dried

¼ teaspoon salt

Freshly ground black pepper

½–¾ cup crumbled feta cheese, such as Stickney Hill Dairy goat feta

1. Cut the onion in half vertically, then cut one half vertically into 4 wedges; refrigerate the remaining half for other uses. Slice each wedge crosswise, about ⅛ inch thick. Soak in a bowl of very cold water for about 10 minutes. Drain well. Place in a large mixing bowl, and add the tomatoes, cucumber, bell pepper, olives, parsley, and basil to the bowl.

2. Whisk together the oil, lemon juice, vinegar, oregano, salt, and pepper to taste in a small bowl. Add to the bowl with the vegetables and toss gently. Cover and refrigerate for about 1 hour. Serve the feta on the side; if you don't anticipate leftovers, you may also scatter it over the top just before serving.

White Bean Salad with Grill-Roasted Tomatoes

4 SERVINGS

1½ cups cooked white beans, such as cannellini, Great Northern, or navy beans, rinsed and drained if canned

½–⅔ cup diced Grill-Roasted Tomatoes (facing page), diced before measuring

2 tablespoons finely diced red onion

1 tablespoon extra-virgin olive oil, or as needed

2 teaspoons white balsamic vinegar or sherry vinegar, or as needed

Salt and freshly ground black pepper

Combine the beans, tomatoes, red onion, 1 tablespoon oil, and 2 teaspoons vinegar in a mixing bowl; sprinkle with salt and pepper. Stir and taste. Adjust with additional oil, vinegar, salt, and/or pepper as needed. Serve at room temperature.

YOUNG FARMERS

To paraphrase an old saying, "Give people food and you feed them for a day; teach them to farm and you feed them for a lifetime." That's exactly what's going on with Dream of Wild Health and Urban Roots, two programs that are teaching young people from the Twin Cities to farm — and showing them the value of what they grow.

DREAM OF WILD HEALTH (DWH) began in 1998 to connect Native Americans with the food, medicine, and traditions of their ancestors. DWH is committed to providing access to indigenous foods for the Native community through farmers' markets, food donations, and their Community Harvest, a farm-to-table event providing indigenous lunches and produce. DWH owns and operates a 10-acre organic farm (including a collection of heirloom seeds) in Hugo, about 25 miles from Minneapolis.

During summer, the farm's Garden Warriors Apprenticeship program brings Native teens from the Twin Cities to the farm, where they learn to plant, grow, harvest, and cook fresh vegetables; they also learn cultural traditions. Workdays begin with a prayer circle and discussion. After that, some head to the fields to work, while others focus on learning about healthy cooking. Other activities include gathering wild chokecherries, practicing archery, and making traditional birch-bark baskets.

Harvests are sold by the teens at Minneapolis's Midtown Farmers' Market and St. Paul's Market on the Bluff, where the young people hone their social skills and learn about the business world. There's also a CSA-style food-sharing program that provides weekly deliveries of indigenous foods to over 30 families. DWH holds workshops throughout the year on topics such as food preservation, healthy cooking, and how to prepare traditional foods such as hominy.

URBAN ROOTS is a 46-year-old organization based in East St. Paul whose stated mission is "to build vibrant and healthy communities through food, conservation, and youth development." One way they do this is to provide paid internships for area teens. In their Market Garden Program, Urban Roots operates multiple urban gardens where the youth plant, maintain, and harvest fruits and vegetables including some, such as shiso and

lemongrass, that are used in foods traditional to the Hmong and other varied cultures of area residents. The teens also run a CSA program, sell their produce at Minneapolis's Mill City Farmers' Market, and contribute food to area food pantries.

Interns also work in the Cooking & Wellness Program, where they teach classes in cooking and nutrition to area families. The program's emphasis on making healthy food choices is a boon to residents of St. Paul's East Side, where some neighborhoods are dotted with fast-food restaurants and mini-marts. As part of the Conservation Program, the youth install rain and pollinator gardens, assist in renovating local parks, and help remove invasive species from public land.

ROOTS FOR THE HOME TEAM partners with the young farmers of both Urban Roots and Dream of Wild Health. Roots for the Home Team sells fresh, healthy, exciting salads at Target Field during Minnesota Twins baseball games. (See page 244 for more information about Roots for the Home Team.)

Susan Moores, creator and director of Roots for the Home Team, recalled a time when the youth brought beets from their gardens to Izzy's Ice Cream in St. Paul. "When they watched their beets being used to make ice cream, and had a chance to talk with the Izzy's team, they realized that their experience might lead to something later on. They could work as a chef, or start a restaurant. These programs give them the poise to work with adults, and the confidence and sense of self-worth that allows them to dream and to see possibilities." Those are seeds well worth planting.

Iron Skillet Pizza Dough

This dough recipe makes enough for two skillet pizzas, each serving two or three people. The second half of the dough can be refrigerated for up to 3 days; let stand at room temperature for an hour or two, then proceed as directed.

2 CRUSTS

1 cup water, warmed to 105 to 110°F

2 teaspoons active dry yeast (not quick-rise or instant yeast)

1 teaspoon sugar

4½ teaspoons olive oil

1¾ cups bread flour, plus more for handling dough

¼ cup semolina flour

1 teaspoon salt

1. Stir together the water, yeast, and sugar in a small bowl. Set aside until foamy, about 10 minutes. Stir in 2 teaspoons of the oil. Whisk the bread flour, semolina flour, and salt in a large mixing bowl. Add the yeast mixture. Stir well, then mix with your hands until the dough comes together, adding a bit more flour if needed. Knead the dough on a lightly floured work surface for 5 minutes, adding a little more flour if necessary to prevent sticking. Lightly coat a clean mixing bowl with 1 teaspoon oil. Add the dough, turning to coat. Cover and let rise until doubled, about 1½ hours.

2. When the dough has risen, punch it down and divide into two equal portions. Refrigerate one portion if not using immediately (see headnote). Place the remaining portion on a lightly floured work surface and knead a few times. Roll into a 7-inch circle, and let rest for 10 minutes. Roll the rested dough into a 12-inch circle.

3. Brush the remaining 1½ teaspoons oil on the inside of a 10-inch cast-iron skillet. Add the crust dough, rolling the edges over.

Iron Skillet Pizza with Roasted Tomato, Pesto, and Mozzarella

Here's a delicious topping option for the Iron Skillet Pizza Dough. If you want to prepare two pizzas at once, you'll need two skillets and double the amount of toppings.

2 OR 3 SERVINGS

1 crust (facing page)

1½ tablespoons prepared pesto

3 tablespoons shredded Parmesan cheese

½ cup coarsely chopped Grill-Roasted Tomatoes (page 102)

¼ cup thinly sliced onion

⅓ cup cooked, crumbled Italian sausage, optional

4 ounces fresh mozzarella cheese, sliced ¼ inch thick

1. Preheat the oven to 425°F.

2. Spread the pesto over the center of the dough, up to the rolled edge. Sprinkle the Parmesan over the dough. Arrange the tomatoes over the Parmesan. Scatter the onion over the tomatoes. Distribute the sausage, if desired, over the onion. Arrange the mozzarella slices on top.

3. Place the skillet on the stovetop over medium-high heat and cook for 3 minutes, moving the pan frequently to ensure even cooking. Transfer to the oven and bake for 20 minutes, or until the cheese is lightly golden in spots and the crust is nicely browned. Remove from the oven and let stand for 5 minutes. Use a spatula to transfer the pizza from the skillet to a cutting board. Cut into eight wedges. Serve immediately.

Iron Skillet Pizza with Sweet Peppers, Red Onions, and Salami

The toppings listed below are for a single pizza.

2 OR 3 SERVINGS

1 garlic clove, pressed or very finely minced

1 tablespoon olive oil

1 crust (facing page)

¼ cup shredded Parmesan cheese

3 thin slices from a red onion, cut into 1-inch lengths

⅔ cup bell pepper strips (¼ by 1½ inches), preferably a mix of colors

6 very thin slices Genoa salami (about 1 ounce), cut into ¼-inch ribbons and separated

½–¾ cup shredded low-moisture mozzarella cheese (2–3 ounces)

1. Preheat the oven to 425°F.

2. Stir the garlic into the oil in a small dish. Brush the garlic oil over the dough, including the rolled edge. Sprinkle the Parmesan over the dough, up to the edge. Scatter the onion, pepper strips, and salami ribbons over the Parmesan. Scatter the mozzarella cheese over the top.

3. Place the skillet on the stovetop over medium-high heat and cook for 3 minutes, moving the pan frequently to ensure even cooking. Transfer to the oven and bake for 20 minutes, or until the cheese is lightly golden in spots and the crust is nicely browned. Remove from the oven and let stand for 5 minutes. Use a spatula to transfer the pizza from the skillet to a cutting board. Cut into eight wedges. Serve immediately.

Farmers' Market Chopped Salad

This is a marvelous lunch when served with a loaf of good crusty bread. Depending on what's available and in season, you could substitute local blueberries or raspberries for the strawberries.

VINAIGRETTE

¼ cup extra-virgin olive oil

2 tablespoons apple cider vinegar

1 teaspoon Dijon mustard

1 teaspoon honey

1 garlic clove, pressed or very finely minced

Salt and freshly ground black pepper

4 cups sturdy salad greens, such as sliced romaine or Buttercrunch

Kernels cut from 1 ear cooked sweet corn, preferably roasted

1 cup halved grape tomatoes

¾ cup cooked chickpeas, rinsed and drained if canned

1 cup small fresh strawberries, halved before measuring

½ small cucumber, diced

1 cup diced Genoa salami or other salami

½ cup diced Roasted Peppers (page 97), preferably red, yellow, or orange bell peppers

¾ cup crumbled feta cheese, such as Stickney Hill Dairy goat feta

4 scallions, sliced

10 large leaves fresh basil

1. **Make the vinaigrette:** Combine the oil, vinegar, mustard, honey, and garlic in a small jar. Cover tightly and shake well to blend. Season with salt and pepper to taste.

2. Spread the salad greens in a wide serving bowl. Arrange the corn, tomatoes, chickpeas, strawberries, cucumber, salami, and roasted peppers in separate wedges around the edge, in the order listed. Mound the feta cheese in the center. Sprinkle the scallions over the entire salad.

3. Immediately before serving, stack half of the basil leaves together, then roll up tightly, parallel to the main vein. Slice thinly across the roll. Repeat with the remaining basil. Fluff the basil strips with your fingers, and scatter on top of the salad.

4. Present the arranged salad to the table of diners. Shake the vinaigrette again and drizzle over the salad. Toss gently with salad tongs and divide among shallow soup plates or individual salad bowls. Serve immediately.

Buttermilk-Herb Dressing

Prepare this easy dressing at the height of summer, when fresh herbs are plentiful and full of flavor.

⅔ cup buttermilk

1 tablespoon extra-virgin olive oil

3 tablespoons mayonnaise

1½ tablespoons seasoned rice vinegar

1 tablespoon Dijon mustard

1 tablespoon finely chopped fresh basil

1 tablespoon finely chopped fresh parsley

1 tablespoon snipped fresh dill fronds

2 teaspoons snipped fresh chives

1 teaspoon finely minced shallots

Combine the buttermilk, oil, mayonnaise, vinegar, mustard, basil, parsley, dill, chives, and shallots in a pint jar. Seal tightly and shake to blend. Refrigerate for at least 30 minutes before serving, to allow the flavors to blend. The dressing will keep in the refrigerator for up to 2 weeks.

COMMUNITY-SUPPORTED AGRICULTURE

February is generally a pretty bleak month in Minnesota, with piles of snow and below-freezing temperatures. National CSA Sign-Up Day, which typically takes place at the end of February, is a reminder that winter's white will soon give way to green fields — and, for those who sign up for a CSA share, bountiful boxes of just-picked, locally grown vegetables and other farm produce.

The CSA concept was developed in the late 1980s as a way to help small farms by providing them with literal "seed money" to pay for the front-end seasonal costs of farming. CSA customers buy shares and, in exchange, receive a portion of the farm's produce over the growing season. They also share the risk inherent in farming, namely, that the harvest bounty might be lessened by poor weather or other events.

Finding a CSA is easy: Local Harvest, Land Stewardship Project, and Minnesota Grown all have searchable online links to CSAs that deliver either to the Twin Cities area or other locations across the state (see Resources on page 270 for website addresses). Some co-ops, including Seward Community Co-op in Southeast Minneapolis (page 124),

host CSA fairs, where potential customers can meet a number of farmers to discuss the farm's philosophy, learn about what can be expected in each weekly box, and simply get to know the farmers.

Some farms also support other programs, giving CSA shareholders a chance to effectively vote with their dollars. Amador Hill Farm and Orchard in North Branch, 65 miles north of the Twin Cities, is a CSA farm with a bigger mission. It's part of the Women's Environmental Institute (WEI), a nonprofit organization that is "committed to teaching and promoting organic and sustainable agriculture in relationship to environmental and social justice" (see Resources on page 270 for website address). In addition to its mission to strengthen the sustainable agriculture movement, WEI operates as a demonstration and education farm. Visitors learn about organic farming principles and best practices, agricultural justice, crop rotation and cover cropping, and cultural heritage projects. WEI also holds workshops and area hikes where participants learn about ecology, land stewardship, and water quality. Weekly CSA shares can be picked up at the North Branch farm or at several locations in the Twin Cities.

Beets and Apples with Goat Cheese and Tarragon

Beets cooked this way have an intense, deep color and rich flavor. The goat cheese adds a nice tang and color contrast, which is accented by the tarragon. **Note:** When slicing the raw beets, I use a flexible plastic cutting board rather than a rigid polypropylene or wooden board, both of which stain very easily. The flexible board seems to release the stains more readily. Be very careful when cutting up the raw beets; they are quite hard and somewhat slippery, so a knife slip could cause injury.

4 SERVINGS

¾ pound beets

½ cup apple juice

1 tablespoon unsalted butter

¼ teaspoon salt

Freshly ground black pepper

1 crisp, tart apple, such as Honeycrisp or Braeburn

1 sprig tarragon

½ cup crumbled goat cheese, such as Singing Hills Dairy goat feta

1. Cut off the tops and root ends of the beets. Peel the beets with a swivel-bladed peeler. Slice ¼ inch thick, then cut the slices lengthwise into ¼-inch-wide sticks. Transfer to a large skillet. Add the apple juice, butter, salt, and pepper to taste. Bring to a gentle boil. Cover and adjust the heat so the liquid boils very gently, and cook for 10 minutes.

2. Meanwhile, peel the apple. Slice vertically into pieces ¼ inch thick, cutting around the core so you have a square core segment. Discard the core. Cut the slices lengthwise into ¼-inch-wide sticks. When the beets have cooked for 10 minutes, add the apple sticks, stirring gently. Increase the heat so the mixture bubbles gently and continue to cook, uncovered, until the beets are tender and the liquid has cooked away, 8 to 10 minutes longer.

3. Meanwhile, pull 15 to 20 leaves off the tarragon sprig. Cut each leaf crosswise into ½-inch lengths. When the beets are tender, transfer the beets and apples to a wide serving bowl. Scatter the goat cheese over the beets. Sprinkle with the tarragon. Serve immediately.

Ground-Cherry Custard Bars

In Minnesota, bars are probably the most common dessert item on the table at potlucks, card parties, group picnics, church-basement suppers, and other events where everyone brings "a dish to share." Keep your neighbors guessing with these bars; although ground cherries are often found at farmers' markets in late summer (and also grow in the wild in most of Minnesota), they are unfamiliar to many people. Here, the custard filling plays nicely with the ground cherries, which have a flavor that is slightly tropical yet dusky.

16 BAR COOKIES

CRUST

5 tablespoons unsalted butter, melted

1¼ cups graham cracker crumbs

¼ cup granulated sugar

CUSTARD FILLING

⅔ cup whole milk

2 tablespoons lemon juice

1 teaspoon vanilla extract

3 egg yolks

½ cup granulated sugar

3 tablespoons all-purpose flour

¼ teaspoon salt

½ pound ground cherries, husked, rinsed, and quartered vertically

2 tablespoons confectioners' sugar

1. **Make the crust:** Preheat the oven to 350°F. Use a pastry brush to lightly coat the inside of an 8-inch square baking dish with some of the melted butter. Stir the graham cracker crumbs and sugar together in a mixing bowl. Stir in the remaining melted butter. Press into the bottom and ½ inch up the sides of the baking dish. Bake for 8 minutes. Remove from the oven and set aside.

2. **Make the custard filling:** Whisk the milk, lemon juice, vanilla, and egg yolks together in a mixing bowl. Add the granulated sugar, flour, and salt to the milk mixture and whisk until smooth. Pour into a heavy-bottomed nonreactive saucepan. Cook over medium heat, stirring frequently with a wooden spoon, until the mixture thickens, about 4 minutes; be sure to get the spoon around the edges of the saucepan, and be careful not to overcook the custard or the eggs will form curds. Remove from the heat and stir in the ground cherries.

3. Scrape the custard mixture into the crust, spreading evenly. Bake for 33 to 38 minutes, until the custard is just set when touched lightly with a fingertip. Let cool completely on a wire rack. Just before serving, place the confectioners' sugar in a fine-mesh sieve and shake it over the bars to lightly dust. Cut into 2-inch squares. Refrigerate leftovers.

Kale, Bacon, and Ricotta Dumplings

This is my riff on an old Italian recipe for spinach dumplings, recently resurrected by the good folks at Food52.com. I've changed it over to kale, which makes for a heartier dumpling, and added chopped crisp-fried bacon. Serve these simply, with a side of rice or crusty bread.

¾–1 pound kale, thick stems trimmed

4 tablespoons unsalted butter

1 tablespoon extra-virgin olive oil

¼ cup finely minced onion

2 garlic cloves, pressed or very finely minced

⅔ cup ricotta cheese

4 thick-cut bacon strips, cooked crisp and finely chopped

2 eggs

⅓ cup all-purpose flour, plus more for shaping dumplings

⅔ cup freshly grated Pecorino Romano cheese

½ teaspoon freshly ground black pepper

Pinch of ground nutmeg

1. Bring a large pot of salted water to a boil. Cook the kale in the boiling water until tender, 5 to 7 minutes. Drain well and squeeze dry; you should have about 2 cups after squeezing. Chop the kale very finely in a food processor.

2. Heat 1 tablespoon of the butter and the oil in a large skillet over medium heat. Add the onion and cook, stirring frequently, for 3 minutes. Add the chopped kale and garlic and cook, stirring constantly, until any moisture cooks away and the mixture starts to stick to the skillet, about 3 minutes. Add the ricotta and cook, stirring constantly, until the mixture is dry and begins to cling to the skillet, 4 to 5 minutes longer. Remove from the heat and stir in the bacon. Let cool slightly.

3. Whisk the eggs and flour in a large bowl. Add the kale mixture, ⅓ cup of the Romano cheese, the pepper, and nutmeg. Stir well. Cover and refrigerate for at least 1 hour, or up to 4 hours.

4. Position an oven rack in the top third of the oven and preheat the broiler. Bring a large pot of salted water to a boil. Flour your hands and shape the kale mixture into eight balls, each about 2 inches across, arranging them on a plate until all of the mixture has been shaped. Dust each ball lightly with flour, shaking off excess. Slip them into the boiling water. Cook until the dumplings float and have firmed up, about 5 minutes. Use a slotted spoon to transfer them to paper towels, and let dry for a few minutes.

5. Melt the remaining 3 tablespoons butter in a small saucepan over medium-low heat. Pour half of the melted butter into a shallow casserole. Arrange the dumplings in a single layer in the casserole. Drizzle with the remaining butter. Sprinkle with the remaining ⅓ cup Romano cheese. Broil until the cheese is golden brown and bubbly, about 4 minutes. Serve immediately.

Recipe from SUSAN WAUGHTAL, SQUASH BLOSSOM FARM

Tomato-Onion Tart

To make this knockout tart, Susan Waughtal says, "I use farm tomatoes, of course, selecting from a blend of whatever cherry, grape, pear, or heritage tomatoes are ripe, in an assortment of colors (red, yellow, indigo, green, purple)," noting that you can vary the appearance by cutting the tomatoes and olives into wedges, halves, or slices, depending on the design you want and the tomatoes you have. The instructions below will produce a tart similar to the one in the photo, but feel free to make your own variation, as Susan suggests. Serve this as a main course, or cut it into smaller wedges for an appetizer. Susan also makes mini tarts, and she sells them alongside full-size tarts during tomato season at the Squash Blossom Farm booth at the Rochester Downtown Farmers' Market. See page 252 for information about Squash Blossom Farm.

6–8 SERVINGS

2 tablespoons olive oil

2 large red onions, thinly sliced

Salt

Pastry for a single 10-inch piecrust

¼ pound Gruyère cheese, shredded (about 1 cup)

¼ pound cheddar cheese, shredded (about 1 cup)

½–¾ pound cherry tomatoes, grape tomatoes, or pear tomatoes, preferably a mix of colors

¼–½ cup pitted olives, such as kalamata or Castelvetrano, preferably a mix of black and green

2 plum tomatoes, quartered vertically

Freshly ground black pepper

1. Heat the oil in a large skillet over medium heat. Add the onions and sprinkle with salt. Cover and cook, stirring occasionally, until softened, 15 to 20 minutes. Remove the cover and cook, stirring occasionally, until any liquid evaporates and the onions are golden, about 5 minutes. Set aside to cool for about 15 minutes.

2. While the onions are cooling, begin preheating the oven to 375°F. Fit the pastry into a 10-inch tart pan with a removable rim (or a quiche pan), doubling the edge to make it sturdier. Refrigerate until needed.

3. Spread the cooled onions over the bottom of the crust. Sprinkle evenly with the Gruyère and cheddar. Begin cutting the cherry tomatoes (or other small tomatoes) in half, arranging them around the outer edge of the tart as you go. Continue until you have a complete ring. Cut more small tomatoes, preferably of a different color, making a second concentric ring. Make a third ring, alternating halved small tomatoes with some of the olives (whole or halved). Make a fourth ring with the quartered plum tomatoes, standing them on one cut edge with the cut sides facing inward. Make a fifth ring of sliced olives. Fill in the center with a few more small tomato halves. Sprinkle with the pepper and salt to taste.

4. Bake in the center of the oven for 1 hour, or until the pastry is golden and the tomatoes look slightly puckered. Cool for at least 30 minutes. Serve warm or at room temperature.

Dry-Fried Sugar Snap Peas

Green beans — or Chinese long beans, in traditional renditions — are generally the star of this classic Szechuan dish. Sugar snap peas are a nice change, and this method leaves them crisp on the outside with tender insides. This works best in a cast-iron skillet, which provides a large area of high heat. For the tenderest pods, pinch the blossom end off, using it to "peel" the string away from the outside of the pod. Make sure that the pea pods are completely dry; any moisture will cause extra spattering in the oil.

4 SERVINGS

1½ teaspoons dry sherry

1½ teaspoons chile-garlic sauce, such as Tuong Ot Toi brand

½ teaspoon toasted sesame oil

1 teaspoon sugar

½ teaspoon salt

¼ cup peanut oil

¾ pound sugar snap peas

2–6 small dried hot chile peppers, optional

2 ounces ground pork

3 scallions, white and light green parts only, thinly sliced

1 tablespoon minced garlic

2 teaspoons minced fresh gingerroot

Freshly ground black pepper

1. Stir together the sherry, chile-garlic sauce, sesame oil, sugar, and salt in a small bowl; set aside. Line a plate with several layers of paper towels.

2. Heat the peanut oil in a 10- to 12-inch cast-iron skillet or other heavy skillet over high heat until shimmering. Add the sugar snap peas and chile peppers, if desired. Stir to coat, then let cook without stirring for 1 minute. Stir again, and let cook for another minute. Start stirring every 15 to 20 seconds, flipping over individual pea pods as needed to prevent burning, until the pea pods are browned, blistered, and wilted, about 5 minutes total. Remove the skillet from the heat and use a slotted spoon to transfer the pea pods and chile peppers to the paper towel–lined plate.

3. Drain off all but a film of oil from the skillet. Add the pork and cook over medium heat, stirring constantly and breaking up, until the pork is browned, about 2 minutes. Add the scallions, garlic, and gingerroot, and cook, stirring constantly, for about 30 seconds. Add the sherry mixture and cook, stirring constantly, for about 1 minute longer. Return the pea pods to the skillet and cook, stirring constantly, until the pea pods are hot, about 1 minute. Season with black pepper to taste. Serve immediately.

Cauliflower Steaks with Capers, Olives, and Rosemary

Recipes for roasted cauliflower steaks have been cropping up all over the place recently, with versions ranging from plain to curry-dusted to chimichurri-topped cauliflower. They're all excellent, turning the humble vegetable into a center-of-the-plate star. Mine has a Mediterranean twist, which makes a nice vegetarian entrée when paired with a well-seasoned rice pilaf. This recipe works best in the late days of summer, when cauliflower heads are large, fresh, and pristine. Another variation below gives you an idea of other possibilities.

CAULIFLOWER STEAKS

1 tablespoon extra-virgin olive oil, or as needed

1 large head white or golden cauliflower, outer leaves and knobby base removed

Coarse kosher salt

OLIVE TOPPING

8 oil-cured black olives, pitted

2 strips orange zest (colored part only, with none of the white pith), each about 1 by 2 inches

1½ tablespoons extra-virgin olive oil

1½ teaspoons drained brined capers

¼ teaspoon broken dried rosemary

Variation: Parmesan-Herb Cauliflower Steaks

Omit the olive topping. Combine ¾ cup coarse dry breadcrumbs, 3 tablespoons finely grated Parmesan cheese, 1 tablespoon melted butter, and ½ teaspoon mixed dried herbs in a small bowl. Sprinkle over the cauliflower during the last 5 minutes of roasting.

1. **Make the cauliflower steaks:** Position an oven rack in the lowest position of the oven and preheat the oven to 400°F. Line a large rimmed baking sheet with foil. Brush 1½ teaspoons of the oil over the foil.

2. Stand the cauliflower head on a cutting board with the stem side down. Cut straight down through the center to make two halves. Working in from the sliced edge, cut two slabs, each about ¾ inch thick, from each half, for a total of four slabs. Refrigerate the remaining cauliflower for another use.

3. Place the cauliflower steaks on the prepared baking sheet, with the prettiest sides down. Drizzle the remaining 1½ teaspoons oil over the steaks, then brush it evenly over the cut surface and edges. Sprinkle with salt to taste. Place on the lowest oven rack and bake for 30 minutes, carefully turning over midway through.

4. **Meanwhile, make the olive topping:** Coarsely chop the olives. Finely mince one of the strips of orange zest. Combine the olives, minced orange zest, oil, capers, and rosemary in a small bowl. Stir well. Slice the remaining strip of orange zest lengthwise into strips that are as thin as you can make them.

5. When the cauliflower has baked for 30 minutes and is nicely colored, remove from the oven. Transfer the steaks to a serving platter. Spoon the olive mixture over the top. Scatter the zest strips over the top.

Roasted Pumpkin Soup with Curry Oil and Microgreens

People tend to forget about cooking with pumpkins after Thanksgiving. That's a shame, because pie pumpkins store well and can bring the sunny taste of the harvest to a dreary February night. Be sure to use a pie pumpkin (also called a sugar pumpkin), not a jack-o'-lantern-type pumpkin, for this soup. Refrigerate leftover curry oil for up to a month; use it as a garnish for vegetables, rice, or eggs.

6 SERVINGS

CURRY OIL

⅓ cup sunflower oil or olive oil

1 tablespoon toasted sesame oil

1 tablespoon curry powder blend (Madras is a good choice)

SOUP

1 yellow onion, cut into 1-inch chunks

4 garlic cloves, peeled

1½ tablespoons sunflower oil or olive oil

½ teaspoon crumbled dried thyme

1 small pie pumpkin (about 3 pounds), halved and seeded

¼ teaspoon ground nutmeg

Salt and freshly ground black pepper

1 quart chicken broth or vegetable broth

1 cup microgreens or watercress

1. **Make the curry oil:** Warm the sunflower oil and sesame oil together in a small saucepan over medium heat until shimmering. Stir in the curry powder and remove from the heat. Let stand until cool. Strain through a fine-mesh strainer into a small bowl.

2. **Make the soup:** Position an oven rack in the center of the oven and preheat the oven to 400°F. Line a large rimmed baking sheet with foil. Divide the onions into two mounds on the baking sheet. Add two garlic cloves to each mound. Drizzle each mound with 1½ teaspoons of the sunflower oil, then sprinkle with the thyme. Rub the remaining 1 tablespoon oil over the insides and skin of the pumpkin halves. Sprinkle the pumpkin flesh with the nutmeg, and season with salt and pepper to taste. Place the pumpkin halves, cut side down, over the onion mounds.

3. Bake for 30 minutes. Remove from the oven and turn the pumpkin halves so the cut sides are up. Stir the onions, distributing them around the pumpkin halves. Return the baking sheet to the oven and bake for 30 to 45 minutes longer, until the pumpkin flesh is tender when pierced with a fork. Remove from the oven and let cool for about 15 minutes.

4. Use a metal spoon to scoop the flesh from one of the pumpkin halves, transferring it to a blender. Add half of the broth and about half of the onions and garlic. Process until smooth. Pour into a 1-gallon soup pot. Repeat with the remaining pumpkin half, broth, onions, and garlic. Cook over medium heat until hot but not boiling. Taste for seasoning and add additional salt and pepper if needed. Divide among soup plates. Drizzle about 2 teaspoons of the curry oil over each portion in a spiral pattern, and place a small pile of microgreens in the center. Serve immediately.

SEWARD COMMUNITY CO-OP, SOUTHEAST MINNEAPOLIS

According to Cooperative Network, Minnesota has more food co-ops per capita than any other state. Although co-ops are scattered throughout the state, the highest concentration is in the Twin Cities area. Seward Community Co-op in Southeast Minneapolis is one of the area's largest — and it continues to grow.

Since its founding in 1972, Seward Co-op has outgrown its locations twice; it now occupies a 25,600-square-foot facility on East Franklin Avenue that includes a classroom. Recent courses included planting a pollinator garden, an introduction to Cambodian cooking, and how to make sausage and kombucha. Two blocks away, Seward's Co-op Creamery building houses a café, staff offices, and space for baking and meat processing. A second full-service grocery, the Friendship Store, opened in late 2015 about 4 miles from the Franklin Avenue store.

Seward Co-op is one of the developers of Principle Six, a cooperative trade movement created in concert with fair-trade promoter Equal Exchange and five major food co-ops. According to the P6 website (see Resources on page 270), the program "exemplifies just and equitable trade relationships between farmers, producers, retailers and consumers." Tags throughout the store identify products that meet at least two of the three key P6 principles: cooperative, small, and local.

Seward's meat department is a good example of the standards practiced throughout the store. They work directly with local farmers who follow the principles of natural, humane animal husbandry; whole carcasses are processed at the Co-op. Alongside house-made sausages, Seward's meat cases feature products from local vendors including Red Table Meat, a Minneapolis processor that specializes in dry-cured *salumi*. Seafood comes from Coastal Seafoods, a Twin Cities company known for procuring fresh, sustainably fished seafood, including Lake Superior fish from Dockside Fish Market (page 26) in Grand Marais.

Seward Co-op is a member of the National Co+Op Grocers association and is affiliated with other area co-ops. You don't have to be a member to enjoy shopping at Seward Co-op; everyone is welcome.

Warm Winter Market Salad

Late fall and winter in Minnesota can be pretty dreary in the produce department. Happily, we still have sturdy root vegetables to enjoy; escarole, red cabbage, radicchio, and kale can be found in good markets all winter long. Here's a lovely warm salad that is guaranteed to take the winter chill off.

**4 APPETIZER SERVINGS OR
2 MAIN-COURSE SERVINGS**

1½–2 cups butternut squash slices, about 1 inch square and ¼ inch thick

2½ tablespoons sunflower oil or extra-virgin olive oil

2 small beets, peeled, quartered, and sliced a bit under ¼ inch thick (see headnote on page 114 for tips on cutting up raw beets)

Coarse kosher salt and coarsely ground or cracked black pepper

4 thick-cut bacon strips, cut crosswise into ½-inch pieces

1 large shallot, chopped

2 tablespoons dried cranberries

1 tablespoon pure maple syrup

One-quarter of an orange, peeled (a Sumo mandarin is particularly good, if in season)

2 cups coarsely shredded red cabbage or sliced radicchio

4 cups firmly packed coarsely chopped escarole or baby kale

¼ cup walnut pieces, toasted

2 ounces feta cheese, such as Stickney Hill Dairy goat feta

1. Preheat the oven to 425°F. Toss the squash with 1 tablespoon of the oil in a large bowl. Transfer to a rimmed baking sheet, keeping the pieces on one half of the baking sheet. In the same bowl, toss the beets with 1½ teaspoons of the oil, then transfer the beets to the other half of the baking sheet. Sprinkle with salt and pepper to taste. Bake for 30 minutes, or until the vegetables are tender and the edges are beginning to brown; stir the vegetables twice, keeping them separated.

2. While the vegetables are roasting, heat the remaining 1 tablespoon oil in a wok or very large skillet over medium-low heat. Add the bacon and cook, stirring frequently, until the bacon is cooked but not too crisp, 7 to 8 minutes. Add the shallot and cranberries. Cook for about 1 minute longer. Remove from the heat and stir in the maple syrup. Set aside until the squash and beets are ready.

3. Break up the segments from the orange quarter into a small bowl; they should be in pieces that are ½ inch or less across. Press with a spoon to start the juices flowing.

4. Set the wok with the bacon mixture over medium heat. Add the cabbage to the wok. Cook, tossing frequently with tongs, for about 2 minutes (about 1 minute if using radicchio). Add the escarole and continue to cook until the escarole is wilting but not mushy, 2 to 4 minutes longer. Add the orange segments and their juices and cook for about 1 minute longer.

5. Divide the escarole mixture evenly among serving plates. Divide the squash and beets evenly on top of the escarole. Sprinkle evenly with the walnuts and feta. Serve immediately.

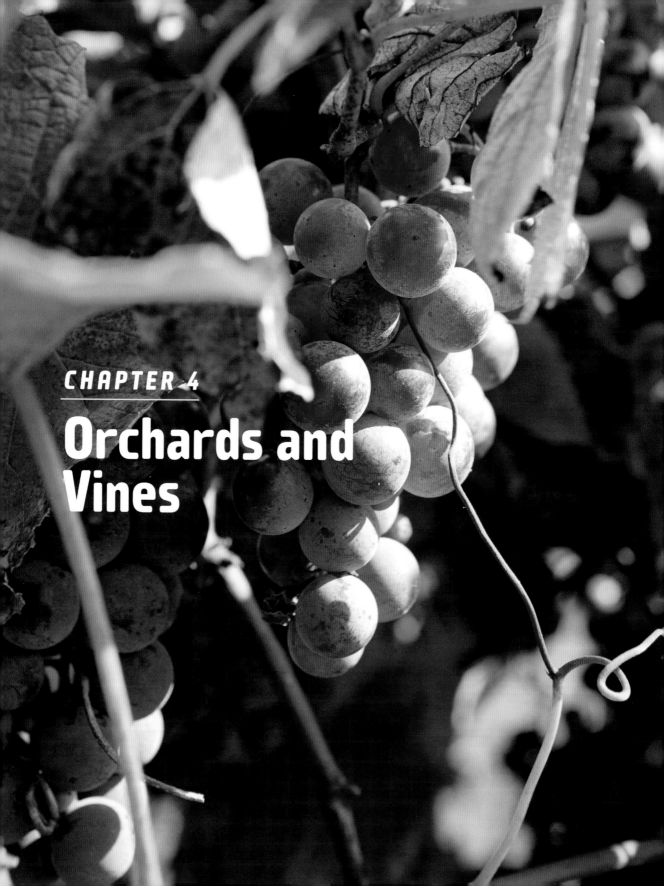

CHAPTER 4

Orchards and Vines

LATE SUMMER CAN BE A BITTERSWEET PERIOD for Minnesotans. It's time to lock up the cabin, send the kids back to school, and think about digging out the snow shovels. But it's also time to bite into a cracking-crisp Honeycrisp apple and to visit a local vineyard where they're harvesting grapes to make the season's wine.

The fruit-breeding program at the University of Minnesota has developed many of the nation's best-loved apples, including Honeycrisp, Haralson, and Beacon, as well as the cold-hardy wine grapes Marquette, La Crescent, and Frontenac. Lesser-known cold-climate fruit introductions include the Summercrisp pear, an early-season variety; Chippewa, Superior, and Polaris blueberries; Mesabi, Itasca, and Winona strawberries; the North Star cherry; and several plum cultivars.

Hops are another frequently used fruit of the vine — well, actually, hops are a bine, meaning that although they twine around their supports in vinelike fashion, they don't use suckers or tendrils to hang on (your fun fact for today). Hops are, of course, one of the starring players in beer, which is enjoying a boom that shows no sign of slowing down. The Minnesota Hop Growers Association (see Resources on page 270 for website address) is a networking and research group that's working to find hop varieties and cultivation methods appropriate to Minnesota's harsh climate.

Minnesota is also home to Rahr Brewing, a powerhouse in the brewing industry that is headquartered in Shakopee, about 30 miles southwest of Minneapolis. The Shakopee plant produces about 25 million bushels of malt annually, making it one of the largest single-site malt production facilities in the world. Barley, primarily from Canada and North Dakota, is steeped, germinated, and kiln-dried in a weeklong process to produce several malt styles, including smoked, pilsner, and 2- and 6-row barley malt; they also produce white or red wheat malt. Rahr also runs the Brewers Supply Group, a subsidiary that provides ingredients and supplies for beer and wine homebrewers, as well as specialty malts, yeasts, spices and botanicals, oak products, and equipment for craft distilleries.

Following are some recipes featuring Minnesota's fruits of the vine — and bine.

Strawberry Flats: Shortbread Rounds with Glazed Strawberries

Prepare this during strawberry season, when you can pick your own berries or get small, home-grown berries from the farmers' market; don't use sad, giant, white-hearted strawberries that have been shipped in from afar. To prepare the shortbread rounds, you'll need a drinking glass with a flat, thick bottom that is about 2¼ inches across, such as a 1-pint beer glass. The shortbread rounds can be prepared earlier in the day and set aside at room temperature; do the final assembly just before serving.

11 OR 12 SERVINGS

SHORTBREAD ROUNDS

- 10 tablespoons (1¼ sticks) unsalted butter, softened
- ¼ cup granulated sugar
- ¼ cup confectioners' sugar
- ¼ teaspoon salt
- 1 egg yolk
- 1½ teaspoons vanilla extract
- 1⅓ cups unbleached all-purpose flour, plus more for handling dough

GLAZED STRAWBERRIES

- 3 cups small to medium top-quality fresh strawberries (see headnote), hulled and cut in half vertically
- ⅓ cup currant jelly or other red jelly
- 1 teaspoon balsamic vinegar
- Mascarpone or whipped cream, for serving, optional

1. **Make the shortbread rounds:** In a large mixing bowl, beat the butter with an electric mixer on medium speed for about 15 seconds, just until smooth and creamy. Add the granulated sugar, confectioners' sugar, and salt. Beat for about 30 seconds. Scrape the bowl, then add the egg yolk and vanilla and beat for about 30 seconds longer. Add the flour and beat on low speed just until incorporated. Transfer to a lightly floured work surface and roll the dough into a log about 6 inches long and 2½ inches in diameter. Pat the ends in so they are fairly smooth. Wrap in waxed paper and refrigerate for at least 3 hours, or as long as overnight.

2. When you're ready to bake, preheat the oven to 350°F. Line two baking sheets with parchment paper. Slice the chilled dough into ½-inch-thick rounds. Transfer to the baking sheets, leaving 2 inches between rounds. Let stand at room temperature for 10 minutes to soften slightly.

3. Moisten the bottom of the drinking glass (see headnote) with a little water, then dip in a small dish of flour. Press the glass gently onto a dough circle to flatten the center, creating a shallow rim about ¼ inch wide. Press together any large cracks with your fingertips. Repeat with the remaining rounds, dipping the glass into the flour each time. Bake for 10 minutes. Remove from the oven and, working quickly, press the floured bottom of the drinking glass gently into the center of each shortbread to flatten the center, which will have puffed up a bit. Return to the oven and bake for 8 to 10 minutes longer, until the edges are golden brown. Cool on the sheets for a few minutes, then transfer to a wire rack to cool completely.

Recipe continues on page 130

4. **Make the glazed strawberries:** Shortly before you're ready to serve, place the strawberries in a heatproof bowl. Heat the jelly and vinegar in a small nonreactive saucepan over low heat, stirring constantly until the jelly melts. Pour over the strawberries, then toss gently to coat. Let marinate for about 5 minutes. Meanwhile, arrange the shortbread rounds in a single layer on a serving platter.

5. Divide the strawberries evenly among the shortbread rounds. Drizzle any remaining jelly mixture from the pan evenly over the strawberries. Top each with a dollop of mascarpone, if desired. Serve immediately.

Red-Red Strawberry Vinegar

For the best results, choose small, fragrant strawberries that are red throughout for this lovely, bright red vinegar. Use it in vinaigrettes or in any recipe that calls for red wine vinegar. Also see page 132 for a quick and easy vinaigrette that uses the finished vinegar.

Also see page 132 for a quick and easy vinaigrette that uses the finished vinegar.

ABOUT 3 CUPS

½ pound fresh or frozen strawberries (about 2 cups small berries; do not thaw if frozen)

2 cups red wine vinegar

1 cup white wine vinegar

1–2 tablespoons sugar, optional

1. Combine the strawberries with the red wine vinegar and white wine vinegar in a 1-quart canning jar. Seal tightly and shake gently. Set aside in a cool, dark spot for 1 week, shaking the jar gently once each day.

2. Strain the mixture through a fine-mesh strainer lined with a double layer of cheesecloth into a 1-quart glass measuring cup. Let the fruit drip for about 30 minutes, but don't press on the fruit or stir it; doing so will make the vinegar cloudy. Meanwhile, rinse the canning jar. After 30 minutes, discard the fruit in the strainer.

3. Dampen a paper coffee filter and place it in a funnel set into the cleaned canning jar. Pour the strained vinegar through the filter, changing to a fresh, dampened filter if the dripping slows too much. Taste the strained vinegar, and add sugar if you think it needs it; if your strawberries were fresh and sweet, sugar usually isn't needed unless you prefer a really sweet vinegar.

4. Pour the strained vinegar into one or two bottles. Cap tightly and store in a cool place for up to 6 months; it will keep a bit better and retain its color better if refrigerated, but this is not strictly necessary.

Strawberry–Poppy Seed Dressing

This tangy-sweet dressing is particularly good on spinach salad, especially one decorated with fresh strawberries and crumbled feta cheese.

½ cup sunflower oil or extra-virgin olive oil

¼ cup Red-Red Strawberry Vinegar (page 131)

2 tablespoons honey

2 teaspoons Dijon mustard

½ teaspoon poppy seeds

½ teaspoon pressed or finely minced garlic

Coarse kosher salt and freshly ground black pepper

Combine the oil, vinegar, honey, mustard, poppy seeds, and garlic in a half-pint jar. Seal tightly and shake to blend. Taste, and add salt and pepper as desired. Store in the refrigerator; it keeps for several weeks.

U-PICK FARMS

Unless you have your own patch, there's no better way to get fresh strawberries than at a U-pick farm. You'll also find farms that offer blueberries, cherries, and raspberries for picking. It's a great family activity; kids love it, and they have an easier time than adults when it comes to crouching down for low-growing fruit.

Always call the farm you're planning to visit right before you go, to check current conditions; ripe fruit gets picked out quickly, especially on weekends. Remember that you'll be in a field, so dress accordingly. Wear sturdy shoes, and clothes you don't mind getting dirty or muddy. Most farms provide baskets or boxes to hold your harvest, but you might want to bring an ice cream pail with a handle, which is easier to carry and set on the ground. Finally, be sure you have a plan for your harvest, as it's easy to pick more than you'll know what to do with.

Check the Minnesota Grown website (see Resources on page 270) for a current listing of U-pick farms, which are found throughout the state.

Stewed Pears with Port

Whole pears simmered in port are a well-known dessert, but preparing it requires picture-perfect pears and, often, a whole bottle of port. Here's a version for cut-up pears that's easier to make, more versatile for serving, and really maximizes a small amount of port. It's outstanding when prepared with the excellent, award-winning port from Carlos Creek Winery (page 134). If you can find Minnesota-grown Summercrisp pears — one of the cold-hardy fruits developed by the University of Minnesota's fruit-breeding program (page 142) — so much the better. Serve the pears and juice over ice cream or dense, rich chocolate cake. You could also serve them in a bowl, topped with whipped cream or lightly sweetened mascarpone cheese, perhaps garnished with chocolate curls. Leftovers are fabulous on top of waffles for a lazy Sunday brunch.

4 SERVINGS

¾ cup port

3 tablespoons sugar

2 strips orange zest, each about ½ inch by 2 inches

2 whole cloves

¼ teaspoon vanilla extract

1 pound pears, just ripe but not overripe, peeled, quartered, and cored

1 tablespoon unsalted butter

1. Stir together the port, sugar, orange zest, and cloves in a small nonreactive saucepan. Bring to a boil, then reduce the heat and simmer for 5 minutes. Remove from the heat and stir in the vanilla.

2. Slice the pear quarters crosswise, about ⅜ inch thick. Melt the butter in a large skillet over medium-high heat. Add the pear slices and cook, stirring occasionally, for about 5 minutes; the pears should be lightly colored. Pick out and discard the orange zest and cloves from the port mixture. Add the port to the skillet. Adjust the heat so the liquid is simmering and cook, stirring occasionally, until the pears are very tender but not falling apart, 3 to 5 minutes depending on the ripeness of the pears.

3. Use a slotted spoon to transfer the pears to serving bowls. Cook the liquid in the skillet over medium-high heat until reduced to a medium-thick syrup, about 3 minutes. Pour the syrup over the pears. Serve warm or chilled.

CARLOS CREEK WINERY, ALEXANDRIA

The 45th parallel, midway between the Equator and the North Pole, passes through some of the world's best wine regions, including France's Rhône Valley and the Piedmont in Italy. In Minnesota, the 45th goes through Alexandria, a town of about 12,000 on the western edge of Minnesota's Lakes Region that is home to Carlos Creek Winery, voted Minnesota's Best Winery in a recent poll.

Kim and Tami Bredeson purchased the winery in 2008 and have been racking up awards ever since. They came to the world of wine making in a roundabout way when Kim, a woodworker, was commissioned to craft a mantelpiece for the Robert Mondavi Corporation in California. As a bonus to thank him for the exceptional work, Mondavi sent the Bredesons a $180 bottle of Opus One wine, which touched off their interest in serious wine.

Like all Minnesota winemakers, the Bredesons have some challenges to overcome — as do the grapes they grow, which have it a lot tougher than their French cousins. Latitude notwithstanding, Minnesota's winters are unsuitable for vinifera grape cultivars. The cold-climate grapes grown by Carlos Creek tend to be higher in acid and lower in tannin than vinifera grapes, making them suited for semisweet wine styles. For dry styles, the Bredesons blend California grapes with cold-climate grapes to increase the wine's tannin content.

Hospitality comes naturally to Minnesotans, and Carlos Creek Winery wants to be sure its visitors have a "Minnesota nice" experience. The charming tasting room, which showcases Kim's woodworking, is open year-round, and during the summer the MN Nice Grill serves snacks and light meals. Special events include Murder Mystery Dinners and the Bootlegger's Bash. The Grape Stomp is a three-day party in September featuring art and food competitions, a logging camp show, and the signatory event, when over 300 two-person teams stomp 10,000 pounds of grapes. Hot Dish Day is held at the end of September; visitors can sample a variety of hotdishes as they enjoy sipping on Carlos Creek's Hot Dish Red . . . a perfect end-of-summer celebration.

Oatmeal Stout Latte

These are great for a relaxed weekend brunch or a nice after-dinner drink in place of a coffee beverage. The first time I had a drink like this was at the Minneapolis restaurant Victory 44, where it was prepared with porter. I knew right away that I wanted to learn to make this at home. It took a few tries (and some problems with curdling milk; see suggestions below to avoid this problem) to get it right, but I think the formula here is just about perfect. There are also a few variations, in case you want to make your own custom latte. **Note:** You need an espresso machine with a steamer wand to prepare this.

½ cup oatmeal stout, such as Brau Brothers Moo Joos Oatmeal Milk Stout or Lake Superior Sir Duluth Oatmeal Stout, room temperature

1½ teaspoons vanilla syrup, preferably Torani brand

½ cup whole milk

1. Pour the stout and vanilla syrup into a large (12-ounce) coffee mug. Stir to mix well.

2. Pour the milk into a metal steaming pitcher. Bring the espresso machine up to temperature. Steam and froth the milk with the wand until the milk reaches 160 to 165°F and has a rich head of froth. Hold back the froth with a spoon and pour the milk into the mug. Spoon the froth into the mug. Serve immediately.

Variations

- Use porter, such as Summit Great Northern Porter, instead of the oatmeal stout. You could also try a coffee porter, or coffee-infused ale such as Bent Paddle Cold-Press Black Ale.

- Substitute pure maple syrup for the vanilla syrup; delicious!

- Use up to ⅔ cup stout (or porter) per drink, for a more beery flavor; be aware that this may cause slight curdling.

- For a sweeter drink, increase the vanilla syrup (or maple syrup) to 2 teaspoons per drink.

- Drizzle a little caramel sauce over the froth just before serving.

Keys to Avoid Curdling

Acids cause milk to curdle. Since half of this beverage consists of beer, which is fairly acidic, you need to do a few things differently than you would when preparing steamed milk for a coffee beverage.

- Use whole milk rather than reduced-fat milk, which curdles more easily.

- Buy the freshest milk you can find; older milk tends to curdle more easily.

- Steam the milk to 160 to 165°F; this may be hotter than what you normally use for lattes, but it needs to be hot enough to warm up a relatively large volume of room-temperature beer. Do not steam the milk above 170°F or it will curdle.

- Beers that are higher in alcohol may cause more curdling.

THE MINNESOTA BEER SCENE

The year before the start of Prohibition, Minnesota had over 40 breweries, many in business for more than 40 years. Most folded when Prohibition was enacted in 1919; the few survivors spent the next 14 years producing nonalcoholic beverages. Indeed, Minnesota is home to one of the Midwest's most highly regarded craft root beers: 1919 Root Beer, manufactured for the New Ulm Brewing & Beverage Company by Schell's Brewing and sold only on draft.

In 1986, Mark Stutrud, a South Dakota native, opened Summit Brewing in St. Paul — the first new brewery in the state since the end of Prohibition. Summit joined August Schell, Cold Spring, Jacob Schmidt (which later became Pfeiffer and then Heileman), and Hamm's (taken over by Stroh's in 1983), the only four pre-Prohibition breweries still operating in Minnesota.

Minnesota has fully embraced the craft-beer movement and now boasts over 100 commercial brewing operations. Styles include standards such as IPAs and stouts, as well as sour beers, unusual infusions, and everything in between. Compared to other states with a similar brewery explosion, Minnesota has laws that are challenging for breweries and confusing for hopheads. It comes down to distribution, a hotly contested topic among beer advocates.

Companies defined as breweries can package their products to sell to distributors, so you can find their beer in bottles or cans at liquor stores, as well as on tap at bars and restaurants. Breweries smaller than a certain size can also sell their beer on draft at taprooms at the brewery, as well as in growlers to take home. Each brewery is limited to one taproom and can sell only its own products.

Brewpubs, in contrast, make small-batch brews for consumption on-site; they can also sell growlers to take home. Brewpubs can serve wine and products from other breweries, and hard liquor if appropriately licensed. However, brewpubs can't sell beer to wholesalers, so it's not available in liquor stores, other bars, or restaurants; you need to go to the source to enjoy the beer. A tour of Minnesota brewpubs is a lot of fun and gives you a chance to try unique microbrews that can't be found anywhere else. Check the website for *The Growler* magazine (see Resources on page 270 for the website address) for locations of brewpubs and breweries across the state.

Home brewing is also enjoying a renaissance in Minnesota, with numerous specialty stores. The Minnesota beer scene is really hopping these days. For a fascinating read, check out *Land of Amber Waters: The History of Brewing in Minnesota*, by Doug Hoverson.

Porter and Spice Cake with Porter Icing

The Bundt pan is the brainchild of Minnesotan H. David Dalquist, a metallurgical engineer who created this fluted tube pan in the early 1950s based on the design of a German *kugelhopf* pan. David was a cofounder of Nordic Ware, a specialty cookware company that has been headquartered in Minneapolis suburb St. Louis Park since 1949. The pan rocketed to fame in 1966, when it was used to create the "Tunnel of Fudge" cake that took second place in the Pillsbury Bake-Off. This recipe uses rich, dark porter to create a moist, not-too-sweet Bundt cake with an intriguing spice blend.

10–12 SERVINGS

CAKE

- 1 (12-ounce) bottle porter, such as Summit Great Northern Porter
- 2 cups all-purpose flour, plus more for coating the pan
- 2 tablespoons unsweetened cocoa powder
- 1 teaspoon baking soda
- ½ teaspoon salt
- ½ teaspoon ground nutmeg
- ½ teaspoon ground cardamom
- ¼ teaspoon ground ginger
- ¼ teaspoon five-spice powder
- ¼ teaspoon ground coriander
- 1 cup (2 sticks) unsalted butter, softened
- 2 eggs
- 1¼ cups granulated sugar
- 1 teaspoon vanilla extract

GLAZE

- 1½ tablespoons unsalted butter, melted
- 2 tablespoons porter (left over from making the cake batter)
- 1⅓ cups confectioners' sugar, or as needed

1. **Make the cake:** Pour the porter into a 2-cup measuring cup and let it stand at room temperature for about 30 minutes, stirring occasionally to reduce the foam (this makes measuring easier). Near the end of the 30 minutes, preheat the oven to 350°F. Thoroughly coat a 12-cup Bundt pan with cooking spray and dust it with a liberal amount of flour, tapping out excess.

2. Whisk the flour, cocoa powder, baking soda, salt, nutmeg, cardamom, ginger, five-spice powder, and coriander together in a medium bowl. Beat the butter in a large mixing bowl with an electric mixer on medium-high speed until light and creamy. Beat in the eggs and granulated sugar until well blended. Add the vanilla and beat for 2 minutes longer. Stir in ¾ cup of the porter with a wooden spoon, then stir in half the flour mixture. Stir in ½ cup additional porter, then add the remaining flour mixture, stirring until just moistened. Spoon evenly into the Bundt pan.

3. Bake for 55 minutes to 1 hour, until a toothpick inserted into the center of the cake comes out clean and the cake feels somewhat firm (not too tender). Transfer the pan to a wire rack and let the cake cool in the pan for 30 minutes. Tap the outside of the Bundt pan all over with a wooden spoon, then invert the cake onto a large plate.

4. **Make the glaze:** Stir together the melted butter and porter in a small mixing bowl. Add the confectioners' sugar, whisking until smooth. Add additional confectioners' sugar if needed to make a glaze that is fairly thick but still pourable (it will thicken upon standing); if the glaze is too thick, thin it with a little additional porter. Drizzle the glaze over the cake with a spoon. Store leftovers at room temperature for up to 5 days.

Beer-Cheese Soup

I first had beer-cheese soup in Fergus Falls, Minnesota. I'd stopped at a roadside restaurant and was chuckling at the misspellings on the menu, including "soup de jour" and "deserts" that included "rasberry pie." My waitress, who reminded me of my German grandmother, asked if I had any questions about the menu, so I asked what the soup du jour was. Leaning over and touching my arm in grandmotherly fashion, she said, "Oh, that's the soup of the day, honey!" Beer-cheese soup is common fare at many Minnesota restaurants, cafés, and bars, but it's generally made with bad beer and processed cheese food from a jar. Here, this simple dish is elevated with a good, malty ale and high-quality shredded cheese; diced vegetables add texture.

5 OR 6 SERVINGS

4 tablespoons unsalted butter

½ cup diced onion

⅓ cup diced red bell pepper

¼ cup finely diced carrot

¼ cup finely diced celery

¼ teaspoon crumbled dried thyme

⅓ cup all-purpose flour

2 cups chicken broth

1 (12-ounce) bottle or can malty ale, such as Finnegan's Irish Amber

1 cup half-and-half

½ teaspoon dry mustard

½ teaspoon hot pepper sauce

1 cup shredded sharp cheddar cheese (4 ounces), room temperature

1 cup shredded Gruyère or young Swiss cheese (4 ounces), room temperature

Popcorn, for garnish

1. Melt the butter over medium heat in a 1-gallon soup pot. Add the onion, bell pepper, carrot, celery, and thyme. Cook, stirring frequently, until the vegetables are just tender, 5 to 7 minutes. Sprinkle the flour into the pot, stirring constantly, then cook for about 3 minutes, stirring constantly.

2. Stir in the broth and beer and bring to a boil, stirring frequently. Add the half-and-half, dry mustard, and hot pepper sauce. Reduce the heat to low and cook, stirring frequently, for about 5 minutes. Sprinkle the cheddar and Gruyère into the pot, stirring constantly. Cook until the cheese melts and the mixture is smooth, 1 to 2 minutes. Spoon into warm bowls, and top each serving with a scattering of popcorn.

Hard Apple Cider Golden Sangria

Here's an unusual version of sangria made with white wine and hard apple cider. Since the word *sangria* is from the Spanish word for "blood," this golden-colored drink probably shouldn't be called sangria at all, but it is in the same style as the fruit-spiked red wine drink of the same name. **Note:** The infusion in the refrigerator allows the juices from the fruit to blend with the wine, making the drink smoother. It can infuse for up to 8 hours before serving.

1 small orange

1 Honeycrisp or other sweet, crisp apple

1 (750 ml) bottle Chenin Blanc or other fruity, off-dry white wine

⅔ cup apple juice

2–3 tablespoons honey

1 teaspoon grenadine, optional

1 (22-ounce) bottle chilled semidry hard apple cider, such as Sapsucker Farms Yellow Belly

1. Wash the orange well, since you will not be peeling it. Slice the orange crosswise about ¼ inch thick, then cut each slice into quarters. Pick out the seeds. Place the orange quarters in a pitcher. Cut the apple into ½-inch cubes, discarding the core. Add to the pitcher. Add the wine. Stir together the apple juice, honey, and grenadine, if desired, in the measuring cup holding the apple juice, ensuring that the honey is well mixed. Add to the pitcher with the wine. Stir well. Cover and refrigerate for at least 1 hour or up to 8 hours.

2. Just before serving, add the chilled hard apple cider and stir well. Serve in chilled glasses, or over ice if you prefer, adding some of the fruit to each glass.

MINNESOTA-BRED APPLES

Well over a century ago, horticultural scientists at the University of Minnesota began amassing a collection of apple trees, both wild and cultivated, in order to work on developing varieties that would thrive in the harsh climate of the Upper Midwest and, equally important, produce great-tasting apples. Over the ensuing years, the university research facility, now known as the Horticultural Research Center, has produced some of the best-loved apples in the country, including relative old-timers such as Haralson, Fireside, Beacon, and Regent, and recent superstars Honeycrisp (the official Minnesota state fruit), Zestar! (Minnewashta), SnowSweet (Wildung), and SweeTango (Minneiska).

Apple breeding is a decades-long project. The breeder selects two apple varieties with good characteristics — the explosively crisp, sweet, juicy Honeycrisp and the sweet-tart, juicy Zestar!, for example — and introduces pollen from one to the blossoms of the other. Seeds from the resulting fruit are planted, and when those trees bear fruit (generally 5 to 8 years later), it is tested for desirable characteristics. If it passes muster (which most don't), cuttings are grafted onto dwarf rootstock and further testing begins. It can take 5 to 15 years of production to determine if the apple variety is commercially viable, with no undesirable characteristics or cultivation problems. The SweeTango apple, which hit supermarkets in 2009, is the child of Honeycrisp and Zestar!; it has a crunch similar to the Honeycrisp and the juiciness of both parents, but boasts its own unique flavor: sweet-tart and zesty, with a hint of brown sugar.

Habitat also comes into play with apples; although something like a Honeycrisp can be grown in, for example, North Carolina, the fruit won't have the same characteristics as that of a Honeycrisp grown in the Upper Midwest. The University of Minnesota is managing production of some varieties, including SweeTango, allowing SweeTango to be planted only in areas where the fruit will have the "correct" taste, crunch, and other characteristics.

During apple season, the AppleHouse at the University of Minnesota's Landscape Arboretum in Chanhassen sells a large selection of apples developed at the HRC, including as-yet-unnamed apples that are identified with a number and a tag listing its genetic parents. There's also a small orchard to visit, and, behind deer-inhibiting fences (and off-limits to visitors), you can see row after row of young apple trees in the breeding program — the potential parent stock of the next great apple variety to be bred in Minnesota.

Blue Cheese with Quick-Pickle Apples
and Honey-and-Cream Butter

This simple, delicious appetizer goes together in minutes, once you have the honey butter and pickled apples prepared. The apples can be stored in the fridge for up to a week. Cut-up leftover apples make a lovely addition to green salads.

6 APPETIZER SERVINGS

1¼ cups water

1 cup white wine vinegar

¼ cup honey

2 tablespoons salt

½ teaspoon whole fennel seeds

1 bay leaf, broken up

2 crisp apples, such as Honeycrisp, Sweet 16, or Zestar!

1 (8-ounce) wedge top-quality blue cheese, such as Shepherd's Way Big Woods Blue or Caves of Faribault St. Pete's Select

Honey-and-Cream Butter (page 181), as needed

1 baguette, thinly sliced

1. Combine the water, vinegar, honey, salt, fennel seeds, and bay leaf in a small nonreactive saucepan. Bring to a boil, stirring until the honey and salt dissolve. Remove from the heat and let cool.

2. Quarter and core the apples, then slice vertically to about ⅛ inch thick, transferring to a glass bowl as you go. Pour the cooled pickling liquid over the apples. Weight with a small plate to keep the apples submerged. Let stand at room temperature for at least 1 hour and up to 2 hours. For longer storage, transfer to a jar and refrigerate for up to 1 week.

3. To serve, place the blue cheese in the center of a serving platter. Spoon about ¼ cup of the honey butter next to the cheese. Drain the apples (save the liquid in case you have leftovers) and pat them with paper towels to remove excess moisture. Arrange around the edge of the platter. Place the sliced baguette in a basket and serve alongside.

Apple Dessert Hotdish

A dessert hotdish . . . why not? The typical main-course hotdish is a combination of starch, meat, vegetables, and a creamy sauce. Here, fruit replaces the meat and vegetables, and a lightly sweetened cream cheese imitates the cream soups that bind and moisten many hotdishes. The result is a sort of cross between a bread pudding and an apple–cream cheese pie.

6–8 SERVINGS

3 cups unseasoned croutons

½ cup orange juice

3 apples of your choice, peeled, quartered, and cored

¾ cup apple juice

¼ cup raisins, dried blueberries, or dried cranberries

2 tablespoons firmly packed light brown sugar

½ teaspoon ground cinnamon

¼ teaspoon salt

1 tablespoon cornstarch mixed with 2 tablespoons cold water

8 ounces cream cheese, softened

¼ cup honey

3 tablespoons heavy cream or half-and-half

½ teaspoon vanilla extract

1 cup granola

1½ tablespoons unsalted butter, melted

1. Preheat the oven to 350°F. Coat a 9-inch square baking pan with cooking spray. Add the croutons and orange juice to the pan, stirring briefly to moisten the croutons.

2. Slice the apple quarters crosswise, ¼ inch thick. Combine the apple slices, apple juice, dried fruit, brown sugar, cinnamon, and salt in a large skillet. Bring to a gentle boil over medium-high heat. Adjust the heat so the liquid bubbles gently and cook, stirring occasionally, for 5 minutes. Stir in the cornstarch mixture and cook, stirring constantly, for 1 minute; the mixture should be thickened and glossy. Spoon evenly over the croutons in the baking pan.

3. Combine the cream cheese, honey, cream, and vanilla in a mixing bowl. Beat with a handheld electric mixer until smooth. Spoon over the apples, then spread evenly with the back of the spoon. Sprinkle the granola evenly over the cream cheese. Drizzle the melted butter over the granola. Bake for 35 minutes. Cool on a wire rack for at least 45 minutes before serving. Serve warm, at room temperature, or cold.

Recipe from JOAN DONATELLE

Pork Loin Roast Braised with Apples and Hard Cider

Apples and apple cider pair nicely with pork in this easy but delicious recipe from Joan Donatelle, who has a long history in the food business. She commented, "It's a favorite Sunday dinner for us. We like to serve it with polenta." Joan also teaches cooking classes and is the author of *Astonishing Apples*. She is a lifelong student of Italian cooking; in October 2014, Joan and her husband, David, guided their first culinary tour to Tuscany.

6–8 SERVINGS

1½–2 tablespoons chopped fresh rosemary

1 tablespoon sea salt

1 teaspoon freshly ground black pepper

3 garlic cloves, minced

1 (2- to 2½-pound) pork loin roast

1½ tablespoons olive oil

3 Honeycrisp, Haralson, or other firm, tart apples, cored and cut into wedges

1 large yellow onion, cut into 8 wedges

2 (12-ounce) bottles or 1 (22-ounce) bottle dry hard cider, such as Four Daughters Vineyard Loon Juice

1. Preheat the oven to 325°F. Mix together the rosemary, salt, pepper, and garlic in a small bowl. Rub the rosemary mixture all over the pork roast.

2. Heat the oil in a Dutch oven over medium-high heat. Add the roast and sear on all sides, about 4 minutes per side. Remove from the heat and position the roast with the fat side up. Add the apples, onion, and hard cider to the Dutch oven. Cover and roast in the oven for 1 to 1½ hours, until the center reads 145°F on an instant-read thermometer.

3. Transfer the roast, apples, and onion to a deep platter. Cover with foil to keep warm. Place the Dutch oven over high heat and cook until the liquid reduces by a bit more than one-half, about 18 minutes. Spoon enough of the sauce over the roast to moisten it; pass the remainder in a small pitcher.

Variation

Substitute fresh, nonalcoholic apple cider (from the refrigerated case, not the kind sold unrefrigerated in bottles on the shelf) for the hard cider.

Sliced Pumpkin and Apple Pie with Crumble Topping

Instead of the usual pumpkin pie made with puréed pumpkin, this version features slices of fresh pie pumpkin mixed with sliced apples. It's a delightful combination.

Pastry for single 9-inch piecrust

FILLING

- ½ cup granulated sugar
- 1½ tablespoons cornstarch
- ½ teaspoon ground cinnamon
- ½ teaspoon salt
- ¼ teaspoon ground cardamom
- ¼ teaspoon ground nutmeg
- 1 (2¼- to 2½-pound) pie pumpkin, (you won't use it all)
- 2 Honeycrisp or other apples, peeled, quartered, and cored
- 1 tablespoon chilled unsalted butter, cut into thin slices

TOPPING

- ¾ cup all-purpose flour
- ⅓ cup granulated sugar
- ¼ cup firmly packed light brown sugar
- ½ teaspoon ground cinnamon
- ⅛ teaspoon salt
- 5 tablespoons chilled unsalted butter, cut into ½-inch cubes

1. Fit the pastry into a 9-inch pie plate. Flute the edges, and refrigerate for at least 30 minutes. When you are ready to prepare the pie, preheat the oven to 375°F.

2. **Make the filling:** Mix the granulated sugar, cornstarch, cinnamon, salt, cardamom, and nutmeg together in a large bowl. Cut the pumpkin in half, then remove the seeds and stringy material from the center of one half; a serrated grapefruit spoon works well to remove the stringy material. Wrap the remaining half and refrigerate for other uses. Peel the cleaned pumpkin half and cut into 1-inch-wide wedges. Cut each wedge crosswise into ¼-inch slices; you should have 3 to 3½ cups. Slice the apple quarters crosswise, ¼ inch thick. Toss the pumpkin slices and apple slices in the sugar mixture. Arrange the pumpkin mixture in the chilled pie shell; scatter the sliced butter over the filling. Place the pie on a rimmed baking sheet.

3. **Make the topping:** Stir together the flour, granulated sugar, brown sugar, cinnamon, and salt in a mixing bowl. Add the cubed butter. Rub the mixture together with your fingertips until the mixture resembles very coarse sand with a few pea-size lumps. Sprinkle the topping evenly over the pumpkin-apple filling, spreading it to the edge of the crust. Gently pinch strips of foil around the exposed crust, leaving the topping exposed.

4. Bake the pie for 30 minutes. Remove the foil strips and reduce the oven temperature to 350°F. Bake about 45 minutes longer, or until the filling is bubbly around the edges and the topping is golden brown. Cool for at least 1 hour before serving.

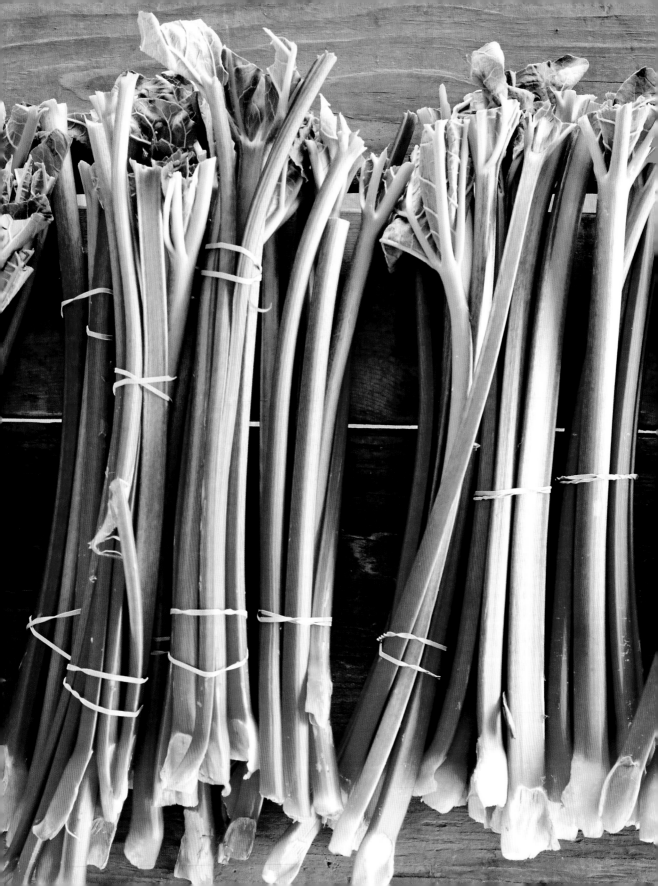

Rhubarb and Apple Cobbler with Candied Ginger

Sweet-tart rhubarb is mellowed and complemented by apples, while tangy candied ginger kicks the flavor up a notch. The cobbler topping is a nice change from the usual rhubarb pie. This is a great way to welcome spring.

6 SERVINGS

FILLING

- 2 apples of your choice, peeled, quartered, and cored
- 3 cups sliced rhubarb, sliced about ½ inch thick
- ½ cup sugar
- 2 tablespoons chopped candied ginger (also called crystallized ginger)
- 2 tablespoons all-purpose flour
- 1 teaspoon vanilla extract
- ½ teaspoon ground cinnamon
- ¼ teaspoon salt

TOPPING

- 1 cup all-purpose flour
- ¼ cup sugar
- 1½ teaspoons baking powder
- ¼ teaspoon salt
- 4 tablespoons chilled butter, cut into 4 slices
- ¼ cup milk
- 1 egg

1. Preheat the oven to 375°F. Coat a 1½-quart baking dish with cooking spray.

2. **Make the filling:** Cut the apple quarters in half vertically, then slice the pieces crosswise, ¼ inch thick. Place in a large mixing bowl. Add the rhubarb, sugar, candied ginger, flour, vanilla, cinnamon, and salt to the bowl. Stir well, and set aside to macerate while you prepare the topping.

3. **Make the topping:** Stir together the flour, 2 tablespoons of the sugar, the baking powder, and salt in a medium bowl. Cut in the butter with a pastry blender or two forks until crumbly. Beat the milk and egg together in the measuring cup used to measure the milk, then add to the flour mixture. Stir with a fork until the flour is just moistened; the batter should be crumbly and lumpy. Don't overmix.

4. Stir the rhubarb mixture, then scrape into the prepared baking dish. Pick up heaping tablespoons of the topping, packing it just slightly, and place on top of the rhubarb; it will look clumpy and uneven, and that's okay. Sprinkle with the remaining 2 tablespoons sugar.

5. Bake for about 40 minutes, or until the filling is bubbling and the topping is crisp and nicely browned. Cool for at least 30 minutes before serving. Serve warm or at room temperature.

CHAPTER 5

Pastures and Prairies

MINNESOTA CAN BE SPLIT INTO TWO DISTINCT ZONES by drawing an arc from Wild River State Park, on the eastern border about halfway up the state, to the Northwest Angle, the rectangular bump that juts out along our border with Canada. The pie-shaped half to the northeast is a land of forests, lakes, and glacial rock. The land to the south and west of the arc is a domain of agriculture, grassland, and prairie.

Corn and soybeans are the top crops grown in Minnesota, followed by spring wheat; together they comprise about 40 percent of the state's agricultural output. Hogs and dairy products account for another 30 percent. We're the nation's number one producer of sugar beets and turkeys; products from Jennie-O, the turkey division of Minnesota megacorporation Hormel Foods, are available nationwide and are distributed in 70 countries.

Numerous farms in Minnesota specialize in pastured beef and hogs, giving consumers an alternative to factory-farmed meats. Some offer pastured or free-range bison, lamb, elk, and deer, or game birds such as pheasants and ducks. Farmers' markets include products from small local farmers who sell free-range chickens as well as eggs from free-roaming hens. We also have a great farmstead dairy industry, including award-winning cheeses made not only from cow's milk but from sheep's or goat's milk as well.

Vestiges of the running grass country can still be found, but most of the land is now under cultivation. This chapter provides a look into some of Minnesota's best agricultural products, along with more than 20 recipes featuring the bounty of our pastures and prairies.

"As I looked about me I felt that the grass was the country, as the water is the sea. The red of the grass made all the great prairie the colour of winestains. . . . And there was so much motion in it; the whole country seemed, somehow, to be running."
— Willa Cather, *My Ántonia*

Molten Cheeseburger with Grass-Fed Beef

The genesis for this dish is the locally famous "Jucy Lucy" (or "Juicy Lucy," depending on the establishment serving it), which first appeared in South Minneapolis neighborhood beer joints in the 1950s. Many say the original is from Matt's Bar at 35th and Cedar; Matt's is certainly the source of the peculiar spelling, which is attributed to an error on a menu or handwritten menu board. The 5-8 Club at 58th and Cedar, and Adrian's Tavern at 48th and Chicago, have also been serving Lucys since the '50s. In recent years, gussied-up Lucys have appeared at more-upscale venues, even jumping the river to some St. Paul restaurants.

Wherever it is served, the premise is the same: Two thin burger patties are sealed around cheese (sliced American cheese, classically), then grilled until nicely charred with a core of molten cheese. Fried onions are a traditional topping. President Barack Obama — a known burger aficionado — had a Jucy Lucy at Matt's during his summer 2014 visit to the Twin Cities.

4 SERVINGS

1–1¼ pounds ground beef, preferably grass-fed

¾ teaspoon salt

¼ teaspoon garlic powder

¼ teaspoon paprika, optional

¼ teaspoon freshly ground black pepper

4 (¾-ounce) sandwich-style slices American cheese

2 tablespoons butter, softened

1 tablespoon plus 1 teaspoon grapeseed oil, sunflower oil, or vegetable oil, or as needed

1 medium onion, diced

4 split hamburger buns

Sliced pickles, for serving

Ketchup, for serving

1. Mix the ground beef, ½ teaspoon of the salt, the garlic powder, paprika (if desired), and pepper together with your hands. Divide the meat into four portions. Divide one portion in half, then shape each half into a thin, circular patty about 5 inches across. (**Tip:** Use a rolling pin to roll the patties between squares of waxed paper.) Cut one slice of cheese into quarters. Stack in the center of one patty, fanning them out slightly but staying an inch from the edge. Top with the second patty. Seal the edges thoroughly with your fingertips (very important!). Cup and push the edges with your hands so the patty is circular and about 4½ inches across. Repeat with the remaining ingredients to make three more patties. Refrigerate the patties while you prepare the fried onions.

2. Melt 1 tablespoon of the butter with 1 tablespoon of the oil in a large skillet over medium-low heat. Add the onion. Sprinkle with the remaining ¼ teaspoon salt. Cook, stirring frequently, until golden brown with a few dark edges, about 15 minutes. Remove from the heat and keep warm.

Recipe continues on page 154

3. Heat a flat griddle (or two large cast-iron skillets) over medium heat for about 5 minutes. Spread the cut sides of the buns with the remaining 1 tablespoon butter. Toast on the griddle until golden. Transfer the buns to a plate. Grease the griddle with the remaining 1 teaspoon oil. Cook the burgers for 4 to 5 minutes on the first side, or until very well browned; move them around as needed to heat evenly, but don't press on the burgers. Flip the burgers and jab the centers with the tip of a knife, going all the way through both patties. (As the cook at Matt's told me, "If you don't poke a vent hole in 'em, the edges will blow out!") Top each with fried onions. Cook until the centers reach 160°F on an instant-read thermometer, 4 to 5 minutes longer. Transfer the burgers to a plate. Cover loosely with foil and let rest for about 3 minutes. Serve the burgers in the toasted buns, with pickles and ketchup on the side — and warn diners to beware of the molten cheese.

Grass-Fed Steak with Blue Cheese Butter

Grass-fed beef steaks lack the internal marbling found in corn-fed beef cuts. They are best when cooked at a lower heat and not beyond medium-rare to medium doneness. A tiny bit of sugar sprinkled on the steaks before browning encourages a nice crust.

2 SERVINGS; EASILY INCREASED

2 (6-ounce) boneless grass-fed top sirloin or strip loin steaks, about ¾ inch thick, patted dry

2 teaspoons sunflower oil or olive oil

Freshly ground black pepper

¼ teaspoon sugar, or as needed

2 teaspoons unsalted butter

2 tablespoons Blue Cheese Butter (below)

1. Rub each surface of the steaks with the oil; sprinkle generously with pepper. Let the steaks stand at room temperature for about 30 minutes. Preheat the oven to 325°F.

2. When you're ready to cook, sprinkle the steaks on both sides with the sugar. Heat a cast-iron skillet large enough to hold the steaks over medium-high heat until a drop of water sizzles and evaporates immediately. Add the steaks. Cook without moving for 3 minutes for medium or slightly medium-rare or 2 minutes for rare, then use tongs to turn the steaks and cook for 2 minutes longer. Place 1 teaspoon butter on each steak. Place the skillet in the oven and bake for 5 minutes. Transfer the steaks to a plate; pour the pan juices over. Cover loosely with foil and let stand for 5 minutes. Top each steak with 1 tablespoon Blue Cheese Butter; serve immediately.

Blue Cheese Butter

This compound butter is very simple and relies on the quality of the ingredients.

ABOUT ¼ CUP

2 tablespoons unsalted butter, cut into 4 chunks

1 ounce top-quality blue cheese, such as Shepherd's Way Big Woods Blue or Caves of Faribault St. Pete's Select, crumbled

1 small garlic clove

1. Place the butter chunks in a flat dish. Let stand at room temperature until just soft enough to mash, 15 to 20 minutes; don't let it soften too much or the texture will be wrong. Add the blue cheese. Use a garlic press to squeeze the garlic over the butter and cheese (or mince very finely). Mash everything together with a fork until the pieces of butter and cheese are fairly small; if you mash it too much the whole thing will turn blue and look somewhat unappealing. Scrape the mixture onto a piece of waxed paper and wrap it up to shape it into a rough log; refrigerate for at least 1 hour.

2. Slice off as needed. Refrigerate for up to 1 week; for longer storage, wrap tightly in foil and freeze.

SNAKE RIVER FARM, BECKER

Before the colonization of America, massive herds of bison roamed the Great Plains, providing food and hides to the Native peoples who inhabited the area. Well adapted to cold winters, bison have coats that are heavy enough to prevent snow from melting, even when it covers their backs. They seem impervious to the cold, and will face a winter storm head-on. Using their huge heads as a plow, they can uncover forage buried under deep snow. In summer, their thick hides provide protection from biting insects.

Minnesota's shallow hills and rolling prairies no longer resonate with the thunder of bison hooves. Cars, trucks, and tractors have replaced the bison as cities, housing developments, and farms now cover the bison's original range. Native grasses that provided forage for the bison have been replaced by row crops (or pavement) throughout much of the state.

TOM BARTHEL AND GAIL WILKINSON are working to restore the native prairie on their 225-acre farm in Becker, a small town in central Minnesota. The Indian grass, switchgrass, bluestem, and other plants provide natural forage for the fully pastured bison, cattle, and hogs they raise. The meat is sold direct to consumers who order, for example, a half-pig or quarter-beef in late winter, for delivery later in the year. Tom and Gail limit the number of animals they raise for sale each year, based on the amount of pasture they have.

Talking with Tom and Gail about their farming practices is like getting a short course in enlightened land stewardship and animal husbandry. Soil health and plant diversity are maintained — and improved — by their methods. In late fall, for example, Tom examines the pastures where the small herd of bison that live year-round at the farm will be wintered. He puts bales of grass hay on poor spots, so that the chaff remaining after the bison eat the hay during winter will enrich the soil in spring; the bison dung left in the area will also return nutrients to the soil. The next season, Tom seeds that pasture with native grasses and legumes. When a group of young pigs is let into the pasture to eat the fresh growth, they will root in the area where the hay had been, turning the soil and mixing in the nutrients.

THERE ARE NO HANDLING PENS or electric cattle prods at Snake River Farm. The animals never live on concrete, something Tom says is common at many livestock farms — even some organic farms — that allow their stock to move about. "Pigs need to root and dig in the soil; it's their nature, and without this activity, they are not happy," he says. "We raise our animals as humanely and naturally as possible. The bison can splash in the creek, which they love to do on hot days. And when the pigs are in a pasture next to the driveway, they'll run along the fence opposite an approaching car, like an excited dog. Folks bring garden scraps to feed the pigs, and the pigs are excited at the prospect of a treat."

Tom and Gail encourage their customers to come to the farm to visit; several special Farm Days are set aside for this each year, and during

Tom Barthel

the winter Farm Day, Tom enjoys giving visitors rides on their horse-drawn sleigh. Tom and Gail also enjoy showing visitors around while explaining their farming practices. "The best way to know how your food is raised is to know your farmer. We give our animals the best life possible and a stress-free death. We're lucky, because we can farm the way we prefer," says Tom, and Gail nods in agreement. The nearly 400 families that are customers of Snake River Farm are also lucky to have such a wonderful source for top-quality, humanely raised meats.

Recipe from GAIL WILKINSON, SNAKE RIVER FARM

Bison, Bacon, and Cheddar Meatballs

Gail Wilkinson, of Snake River Farm in Becker, says this is her favorite bison meatball recipe. "I like it for many reasons. It is virtually a no-fail recipe. Everybody of all ages enjoys eating them, and they freeze good for later use. I use our bison, our bacon, and our eggs from the farm." Gail also notes that she uses home-rendered lard in place of the olive oil.

4 OR 5 MAIN-COURSE SERVINGS

1 tablespoon plus 1 teaspoon olive oil

½ cup minced onion

¼ pound bacon strips, diced

1 pound ground bison

3 ounces cheddar cheese, grated (about ¾ cup)

¼ cup dry breadcrumbs

1 egg, lightly beaten

¾ teaspoon kosher salt

1. Preheat the oven to 450°F. Brush a 7- by 10-inch baking dish with 1 tablespoon of the oil.

2. Warm the remaining 1 teaspoon oil in a large skillet over medium heat. Add the onion and bacon and cook, stirring frequently, until they are light golden brown, about 10 minutes. Transfer with a slotted spoon to a plate and let cool.

3. Combine the ground bison, cheese, breadcrumbs, egg, salt, and bacon mixture in a large mixing bowl. Mix thoroughly by hand. Roll the mixture into golf ball–size meatballs. (Gail uses a small cookie scoop.) Transfer the meatballs to the baking dish. Bake for 15 to 18 minutes, or until just cooked through; Gail notes that it is best not to overcook bison meat.

Lamb and Pork Breakfast Sausage

This is a nice way to use ground lamb. Be sure to use ground lamb and pork that has some fat in it, so that it's similar to 85 percent lean hamburger blend. This sausage is great formed into patties and fried for breakfast, and it also works in any recipe that calls for bulk breakfast-type sausage, such as the Scotch Eggs on page 168.

ABOUT 1½ POUNDS

1 tablespoon pure maple syrup

1 tablespoon ice water

2 teaspoons rubbed dried sage

1 teaspoon salt

½ teaspoon dried marjoram

½ teaspoon finely ground black pepper

¼ teaspoon dried thyme

⅛–¼ teaspoon hot pepper sauce

⅛ teaspoon nutmeg, preferably freshly grated

1 pound ground lamb

½ pound ground pork (unseasoned)

Vegetable oil, for frying

1. Combine the maple syrup, ice water, sage, salt, marjoram, black pepper, thyme, hot pepper sauce, and nutmeg in a medium mixing bowl. Stir until well combined. Add the lamb and pork. Mix very well with your hands.

2. If you plan to cook the sausage the same day, cover the bowl and refrigerate for at least 1 hour before proceeding. Otherwise, pack ½-pound portions into quart-size freezer-weight ziplock bags, pressing the mixture flat so the packages are easy to store. Overwrap with freezer paper and freeze until needed; it keeps for about a month.

3. To serve, shape the sausage mixture (thawed if previously frozen) into 2- to 3-inch-wide patties. Heat a little oil in a skillet over medium heat and cook until browned on both sides and cooked through, about 5 minutes.

Home-Cured Maple Bacon

Homemade maple-kissed bacon is surprisingly easy to prepare. This recipe explains how to use a covered charcoal grill for smoking, but the bacon can also be prepared in a smoker that can be held at 225°F. Look for slabs of uncooked pork belly or side bacon (a meatier cut, slightly higher on the hog than the belly) at full-service butchers; many co-ops and Asian markets also carry it, and if you buy a half-hog from a farm such as Snake River Farm (page 156), you'll have a beautiful piece of pork belly to work with. Cold weather makes it easier to control the temperature of the charcoal grill, so this is a good recipe to prepare in Minnesota during late fall or early winter. **Note:** This recipe is easy to adjust for the exact weight of pork belly you have. Three pounds of bacon is about as much as you can prepare at one time in a kettle grill; however, if you have a smoker, you can scale the ingredients and prepare as much as your smoker will hold.

For this recipe, you will also need 4 quarts of natural-lump charcoal (less than half of a 20-pound bag; do not use charcoal briquettes), or as needed, and apple wood or other fruitwood chunks, 1 to 2 inches across, as needed.

---

2 TO 3 POUNDS

2–3 pounds skinless pork belly or side bacon (see headnote)

2–3 tablespoons Morton Tender Quick (see Note, opposite), or as needed

4–6 tablespoons pure maple syrup, or as needed

1. Cut the pork belly into 1- to 1½-pound pieces to make it easier to handle and slice. Weigh each piece separately, and place each in a separate gallon-size freezer-weight ziplock bag, making note of the weight for each piece.

2. For *each piece* of pork belly, measure 1 tablespoon Tender Quick and 2 tablespoons maple syrup *per pound,* preparing a separate measured batch of salt mixture for each piece. For example, if you've got a 1-pound piece and a 1¼-pound piece, make one batch of cure using 1 tablespoon salt and 2 tablespoons syrup for the 1-pound piece, then make another batch, using 1¼ tablespoons salt (1 tablespoon plus ¾ teaspoon) and 2½ tablespoons maple syrup for the 1¼-pound piece. Stir together the salt and maple syrup in a small bowl; the mixture will be pastelike. Scrape the syrup mixture into the bag, and rub with your fingertips into all surfaces of the meat. Seal the bag, pressing out as much air as possible. Place the bag(s) in a 9- by 13-inch baking dish.

3. Refrigerate the meat, turning the bag(s) daily and redistributing the liquid, until the meat feels firm to the touch; a 1-inch-thick piece will be ready in about 5 days, but a thicker piece may take up to 7 days.

4. Rinse the meat very well in cold water and gently pat dry. Refrigerate, uncovered, on a rack set over a baking sheet, overnight or for as long as 24 hours.

5. When you are ready to smoke, open the vents on the grill lid and the bottom of the grill bowl. Use about 2 cups of charcoal to prepare a small fire on one side of your grill, using newspaper rather than lighter fluid (a chimney starter is ideal). When the coals are lightly ashed, add a few chunks of wood to the coals and insert the grill grate. Place an oven thermometer on the side of the grill grate away from the coals, then cover the grill so the vent in the grill lid is over the thermometer. Check the temperature after 10 minutes. If it is close to 225°F, you're ready to add the meat. If it is much hotter, spread out the coals (or remove a few) and close the vents most of the way, then check again after another 10 minutes; if it is cooler than 225°F, add another chunk or two of charcoal and check again in 15 minutes.

6. When the grill temperature is stable and as close to 225°F as possible, place the meat on the grate, on the side away from the coals. Maintain a temperature between 175 and 225°F for about 2 hours, checking the temperature every 20 minutes or so and adding a few additional lumps of charcoal (unstarted) when the temperature begins to drop below 200°F;

if the temperature gets too high, close the bottom vents partway, or spread out the coals more widely to dissipate some heat. Also add another chunk or two of wood every 30 minutes, or as needed to maintain a light smoke.

7. After 2 hours, check the internal temperature of the meat with an instant-read thermometer. It needs to reach at least 150°F at the thickest part. If it is too low, either continue cooking on the grill or transfer it to a 250°F oven and bake until it reaches 150°F at the thickest part. Let the bacon cool, then wrap and refrigerate for up to 2 weeks; freeze for longer storage (up to 3 months).

Note: This recipe calls for Morton Tender Quick, a curing salt that contains a small percentage of sodium nitrate and sodium nitrite. These help prevent botulism, a deadly bacteria that grows in low-temperature, low-acid anaerobic environments. Nitrates and nitrites are somewhat controversial due to potential health issues, although recent studies published by McGill University in Montreal suggest that concerns about nitrates/nitrites in the diet may be overblown. Most experts agree that curing salt is important for safety when home smoking at the temperatures used for homemade bacon. The curing salt also helps provide bacon's special taste, as well as its typical pinkish color. If you wish to prepare unsmoked, uncured bacon, use an equal measurement of canning/pickling salt in place of the curing salt and simply roast the brined pork belly in a 200°F oven until the internal temperature reaches 150°F.

ABOUT *SOUS VIDE* COOKING

Sous vide means "under vacuum," and that's one of the key points in this unusual cooking method: Foods are sealed in vacuum bags and then submerged in hot water, which slowly heats the food. The vacuum seal prevents air pockets, allowing the hot water to evenly surround the food. The other key is that in most cases, the water is the exact temperature you want to serve the food at, so the food will never overcook, even if it's left in the water for a while after it has reached the serving temperature.

CONVENIENCE ISN'T THE ONLY ADVANTAGE offered by *sous vide* cooking. Meat, poultry, or fish cooked this way are evenly done throughout; a thick steak won't have a darker edge of overdone meat on the outside, something that's common when thick steaks are grilled, broiled, or pan-fried. The result is juicy, flavorful meat that is perfectly and evenly cooked throughout.

If you look behind the scenes at top restaurants, you'll often find a state-of-the-art thermal immersion circulator, or *sous vide* machine — sometimes more than one, each set at a different temperature. Few home cooks have one, though; prices start at several hundred dollars and escalate into the stratosphere quickly.

In 2010, J. Kenji López-Alt wrote a piece for the food blog *Serious Eats,* explaining how to use an insulated beer cooler to prepare *sous vide* meats. A 2013 article in *Fine Cooking* magazine elaborated on the technique and also reported research on the safety of cooking in plastic bags. *Fine Cooking* recommended Ziploc bags specifically, because they are made to withstand boiling and don't contain BPAs, harmful compounds that are released from some types of plastic when heated. Regular-weight storage bags and freezer-weight bags both work; thinner sandwich-weight bags are too flimsy. Use ziplock bags that have two rows of push-together, locking "zipper" strips, which provide a better seal than a single strip. Don't use slider-style or gusseted bags.

TO SET UP A MEDIUM-SIZE PICNIC COOLER (the kind that holds about 20 beverage cans) for *sous vide* cooking, fill it two-thirds full with hot tap water.

Adjust the temperature with boiling water until it is 3 to 5 degrees hotter than the final serving temperature you want, or at least 138°F; the water temperature will drop a few degrees when you add the cold food.

Place the food in the ziplock bag, using one bag per item or placing smaller pieces side by side without overlapping. Seal the bag most of the way, then lower one bag at a time into the hot water, completing the seal when the bag is almost fully submerged and the air has been squeezed out (make sure the bag is sealed *very* well). Close the cooler. Check the water temperature in about 10 minutes, adjusting it if needed so the water is at the target serving temperature. Ensure that there is space between bags, if using more than one. If a bag is floating, weight it down with a plate. Check foods at the times directed in individual recipes in this book.

A NOTE ABOUT FOOD SAFETY: Bacteria such as salmonella can multiply rapidly at temperatures below 120°F, and certain pathogens found in fish may not be destroyed at temperatures below 135°F. Out of an abundance of caution, I recommend a minimum water temperature of 135°F for your *sous vide* cooking. This means that if you want steak cooked to 125°F or 130°F, you must monitor it more closely to prevent overcooking. Once these lower-temperature foods have reached your desired target temperature, remove from the cooler and do any final preparations promptly. Steak that is intended to be served at 135°F or above will be cooked at the serving temperature, so the food can remain in the water bath for a while, even after it reaches the desired temperature, since it can't overcook.

SERVING TEMPERATURES FOR BEEF, BISON, VENISON, OR LAMB	
Rare	125°F
Medium-rare	130–135°F
Medium	135–140°F
Medium-well	140–150°F
Well done	155°F
Ground	160°F

Grass-Fed Beef or Bison Steaks, *Sous Vide*

Slow, gentle *sous vide* cooking is perfect for grass-fed beef and bison steaks, which lack the marbling found in grain-fed beef and may become tough if cooked like a well-marbled steak. A quick sear in a hot skillet just before serving provides a beautiful crust. Thick steaks, ¾ to 1 pound each, work best for this method; each steak serves two diners. Before starting, please read About *Sous Vide* Cooking on the opposite page.

You will need a small insulated cooler and one or two 1-gallon ziplock bags for this recipe.

2–4 SERVINGS

1–2 tablespoons olive oil

1–2 garlic cloves, finely minced

½–1 teaspoon chopped fresh rosemary

1–2 (¾- to 1-pound) grass-fed beef or bison steaks, about 1 inch thick

Coarse kosher salt and freshly ground black pepper

1 tablespoon grapeseed oil or sunflower oil, or as needed

1. Begin heating about 1½ gallons of water to a boil in a large pot. Meanwhile, prepare the seasoning oil, using 1 tablespoon olive oil, 1 garlic clove, and ½ teaspoon rosemary per steak. Heat the oil in a small skillet over medium heat. Add the garlic and rosemary. Cook, stirring frequently, until fragrant, about 2 minutes. Remove from the heat and let cool for a few minutes.

2. Place the steak in a gallon-size ziplock bag, using a separate bag for each steak. Add the oil mixture, dividing equally if preparing two steaks. Rub the oil evenly over both sides of the meat.

3. Set up the cooler as directed in About *Sous Vide* Cooking, using the boiling water as needed to adjust the temperature so it is 3 to 5 degrees warmer than your target serving temperature, or at least 138°F. Seal the bag(s) as described, then close the cooler. Check and adjust the water temperature as described. Close the cooler and let it stand for 45 minutes if you want rare steak, 1 hour if you want medium-rare steak, or 1¼ hours if you want medium steak. Open a bag and check the internal temperature of the steak at the thickest part with an instant-read thermometer. If the internal temperature is what you want, the steaks are ready for final preparation; if not, reseal the bag and return it to the water until the desired temperature is reached.

4. When you are ready for the final preparation, turn on the vent fan. Heat a cast-iron skillet over high heat until it is very hot. Remove the steak(s) from the bag(s) and season with salt and pepper. Add the grapeseed oil to the skillet and heat for about 30 seconds. Add the steak(s). Cook until well browned, 1 to 2 minutes per side; also brown the edges (hold the steak upright with tongs while you sear the edges). Serve immediately.

Corn Flour Waffles (little Gluten-Free)

This is adapted from a pancake recipe supplied by Lin Hilgendorf at Whole Grain Milling. These waffles are much lighter than traditional waffles, with a delicious, sweet flavor from the corn. **Note:** Because they are gluten-free, they have a tendency to pull apart if the waffle iron is opened too soon, so have patience; a little extra browning is better than a torn waffle!

4 SERVINGS

1 cup plus 1 tablespoon Whole Grain Milling corn flour (yellow or blue)

1 teaspoon baking powder

¼ teaspoon salt

1 cup nonfat buttermilk, or as needed

1½ tablespoons sunflower oil, plus more as needed for the waffle iron

1 teaspoon honey

1 egg, preferably extra-large

Unsalted butter, for serving

Pure maple syrup, for serving

1. Preheat the oven to 300°F; also preheat a waffle iron. Whisk the flour, baking powder, and salt together in a mixing bowl. In another bowl, whisk together the buttermilk, oil, honey, and egg. Make a well in the center of the dry ingredients. Pour in the buttermilk mixture. Whisk until smooth; if the mixture is too stiff, add a little more buttermilk.

2. Brush the waffle iron with a little oil. Bake the waffles one at a time, using ½ cup of batter per waffle and preparing them according to the method you use for your particular waffle iron. Transfer the cooked waffles to a lightly greased baking sheet as you go, and keep them warm in the oven until all have been prepared. Serve with butter and syrup, or whatever toppings you like.

Whole Grain Milling, Welcome

Doug and Lin Hilgendorf believe in working with nature rather than fighting against it. After observing the negative impact that chemical fertilizers and herbicides had on the health of both the soil and livestock, the Hilgendorfs committed to the old ways of farming, receiving their organic certification in 1989.

Doug Hilgendorf

One crop they grow at their farm just north of the Iowa border is a special, non-GMO corn that's high in lysine, an essential amino acid that, among many other health benefits, helps the body synthesize protein. Regular corn has less lysine, and what it does contain is not readily available to the body unless the corn undergoes nixtamalization, a process discovered long ago by indigenous Americans that liberates both lysine and tryptophan. The high-lysine corn grown by Whole Grain Milling has almost twice as much effective protein content as other corn, making it a great choice for vegetarians.

In 2015, Whole Grain Milling added a new facility to make its own organic tortilla chips from its blue and yellow corn. The chips, which had been produced off-site since 2003, are a favorite for many; Dara Moskowitz Grumdahl, senior food editor at *Minnesota Monthly* magazine, calls them "the best chips in the USA."

Doug and Lin process their own oats, rye, spelt, buckwheat, soybeans, and popcorn, as well as other beans and grains from small-scale organic farmers in the Midwest. Processing is minimal, retaining as much of the whole grain's nutrition as possible. Their two sons are involved in the business; Jeff is in charge of the mill, while Ross is in charge of the farming and also runs their tortilla chip plant, which he helped build. In addition to simply milled whole grains, they offer numerous healthful mixes, including whole-grain pancake mixes, eight-grain hot cereal, and bread-machine mixes.

Look for Whole Grain Milling products at co-ops and natural food stores in the Twin Cities area and other Minnesota cities; they're also popping up at stores in Wisconsin, Iowa, and South Dakota.

Recipe from TAMMY KIMBLER

Tarragon Pickled Eggs

Faced with a lengthy wait for the tiny cucumbers needed to make her homemade cornichons, food blogger Tammy Kimbler decided to adapt her cornichon recipe to make a batch of pickled eggs. She writes, "Laced with tarragon, chives, mustard seeds, garlic, and chile peppers, these pickled eggs make the perfect complement to a cheese tray, charcuterie plate, or chilled salad . . . [they also] make a marvelous potato salad and an even better egg salad sandwich." As a backyard urban farmer who keeps laying chickens (opposite), Tammy knows whereof she speaks when it comes to eggs. I have adapted Tammy's recipe to prepare 12 eggs rather than 18.

12 EGGS

12 eggs
1 small bunch tarragon
1 small bunch chives
1¼ teaspoons brown mustard seeds
1¼ teaspoons whole black peppercorns
3 garlic cloves, crushed
3 small dried red chiles
1⅓ cups white wine vinegar
1⅓ cups cold water
2 tablespoons kosher salt

1. Place the eggs in a large saucepan and cover them with cold water. Bring to a boil, then remove from the heat, cover, and let stand for 7 minutes. Rinse in cold water until cool, or submerge in an ice bath. Peel the eggs.

2. Combine the peeled eggs, tarragon, chives, mustard seeds, peppercorns, garlic, and chiles in a large, clean jar that holds the eggs comfortably (Tammy uses a half-gallon jar for 18 eggs), standing the tarragon and chives upright along the sides of the jar and layering the remaining ingredients as you go. Combine the vinegar, water, and salt in a mixing bowl, stirring until the salt dissolves. Pour the vinegar brine into the jar, covering the eggs completely; if you need more brine, simply mix equal amounts of vinegar and cold water.

3. Cover the jar and refrigerate for 1 week before serving. The egg whites will become firm, while the yolks will stay creamy and crumbly yellow. The eggs will keep for at least 1 month in the refrigerator, assuming they last that long.

FARMING IN THE CITY

The urban farm movement is growing in the Twin Cities . . . one chicken at a time.

In addition to permitting the conversion of vacant city lots to productive community and for-profit gardens, Minneapolis and St. Paul (along with other cities including Duluth and Rochester) allow homeowners to keep chickens and other poultry in backyard coops, with written permission from near neighbors; beekeeping is also encouraged.

Tammy Kimbler is an urbanite who takes full advantage of the opportunities in the city to produce much of her family's food. Raised on a farm, she brings a rural sensibility to her South Minneapolis home. She and her partner, Christopher Wlaschin, and daughter Claire Weber work two plots at the nearby Dowling Community Gardens, one of the few original World War II–era victory gardens still in use. They also tend a salad and herb garden in their backyard and keep a backyard coop of four heritage-breed laying hens.

Of the chickens, Tammy says, "We chose our chicken breeds for a combination of good laying, foraging, winter tolerance, and personalities. Our Dark Cornish hen, Chickie Boots, is an amazing guard dog, running off every rabbit, squirrel, bird, and cat that enters our yard! Maude and May are our two Black Jersey Giants. Pearline is a gray speckled Dominique, the original colonial chicken; it's America's oldest chicken breed. We named most of our chickens after our great-aunts."

In addition to her backyard farm, Tammy makes cheese, bacon, home brews, and fermented foods; she also forages. As she writes on her blog at www.onetomato-twotomato.com, "There are so many foods we consume that can easily be done at home. This has a huge impact on our heath, our environment, our local community, and oftentimes, our pocketbook. I'm here to demystify many food processes and show how easy, accessible, healthful, and delicious gaining control of your personal food system can be."

Tammy is also a contributor to *Mother Earth News*, as well as to the food and drink section for the local *City Pages* weekly. For some of Tammy's recipes, see Tarragon Pickled Eggs on the opposite page and Juniper Bitters on page 84.

Tammy Kimbler

Scotch Eggs with Horseradish-Mustard Sauce

This classic British pub snack is delicious hot or cold; obviously, it goes great with beer. Chilled Scotch eggs also make delightful picnic fare, with the sauce carried in a separate container. Use pork or turkey breakfast sausage; the Lamb and Pork Breakfast Sausage on page 159 works wonderfully with this recipe.

4 SERVINGS

10 ounces bulk breakfast sausage

1 teaspoon pure maple syrup

½ cup all-purpose flour

4 eggs, hard-boiled, cooled, and shelled

1 egg, lightly beaten

1 cup cornflake crumbs

HORSERADISH-MUSTARD SAUCE

½ cup mayonnaise (do not use salad dressing)

¼ cup Dijon mustard

3 tablespoons prepared horseradish

1 tablespoon coarse or whole-grain mustard, optional

Vegetable oil, for frying

1. **Make the Scotch eggs:** Combine the sausage and maple syrup in a bowl, then mix well with your hands. Divide into four equal portions. Place the flour in another bowl. Working with one egg at a time, roll the egg in the flour, shaking off excess. Moisten your hands lightly. Flatten one portion of sausage into a patty that covers your palm generously. Place the floured egg in the center, and wrap the sausage around the egg. Press and roll the sausage-coated ball with your hands until the sausage is evenly covering the egg, with no gaps or thin spots. Repeat with the remaining sausage and eggs.

2. Roll the sausage-covered eggs in flour, shaking off excess. Dip in the beaten egg, letting excess drip off. Coat evenly with the cornflake crumbs. Place on a plate and refrigerate for at least 1 hour or up to 4 hours.

3. **Meanwhile, make the Horseradish-Mustard Sauce:** Stir the mayonnaise, Dijon mustard, horseradish, and coarse mustard, if desired, together in a small bowl. Cover and refrigerate until needed.

4. When you're ready to finish the eggs, heat oil in a deep fryer to 375°F and line a plate with paper towels. Carefully add one egg to the oil. Fry, turning the egg once or twice, until the coating is a rich brown and the sausage is cooked through, about 3½ minutes. Transfer to the paper towel–lined plate. Return the oil to 375°F if the temperature dropped while the first egg was cooking, and continue frying the eggs, one at a time.

5. Serve the eggs, warm or chilled, with the Horseradish-Mustard Sauce. The eggs are easiest to eat when cut into halves or quarters lengthwise before serving, and they also look very pretty.

LOCALLY LAID EGG COMPANY, WRENSHALL

The 1,800 laying chickens at Lucie and Jason Amundsen's farm outside Duluth all have names. To make it easy, however, the names are all the same: LoLa, a shortening of Locally Laid, the moniker of the Amundsens' egg-farming business, featuring locally marketed eggs from pastured chickens.

The chickens don't care about that name thing; they've got it good compared to most laying hens, which live in cages so small they're unable to turn around. Chickens that produce "cage-free" eggs aren't confined to cages, but most spend their lives in crowded warehouses.

In contrast, Locally Laid chickens spend spring through fall in hoop houses over pasture, pecking for insects and munching on dandelions, clover, and grasses, supplemented by custom-blended non-GMO feed. When a pasture begins to look scrubby, the Amundsens move the hoop houses so the birds have fresh pickings. In late fall, the chickens are moved to roomy barns equipped with roosts, where they spend the winter picking apart nutritious bales of hay and grasses and dreaming of spring dandelions.

The eggs are better for it. The whites are firmer and easier to whip than those from standard supermarket eggs, and hold their shape better for poaching and frying. The deeply colored yolks have more beta-carotene, vitamins, and healthful omega-3 fatty acids, as well as less cholesterol and saturated fat.

The Amundsen farm falls into what is referred to as the agriculture of the middle: farms that are too large to sell all their products directly to consumers, but too small to compete on a price level with commodity producers. Luckily, Lucie and Jason found a receptive market in the Duluth area. As Lucie says, "Stores and co-ops opened their shelves, restaurants opened their kitchens . . . and because Locally Laid eggs are only sold regionally, all that retail income sticks around, stamping down food miles."

To meet increasing demand for their eggs, the Amundsens now partner with several other midsize farms that produce eggs to brand standards and sell them in their own regions under the Locally Laid name. It's good for everyone: consumers, farmers, and a chicken named LoLa.

Lucie Amundsen

Classic Pound Cake with Cardamom

Pound cake is a great vehicle for farm-fresh eggs and sweet butter; with such a simple recipe, the quality of the ingredients really comes through. This version — which is actually a half-pound cake, since it uses 8 ounces each of the principal ingredients — is perked up with the addition of some cardamom and a crackly sugar top. The flavor is even better the next day.

5 large eggs, or as needed, room temperature

1 cup (2 sticks) unsalted butter, softened

½ pound granulated sugar (about 1⅛ cups)

½ teaspoon salt

1 teaspoon vanilla extract

½ teaspoon ground cardamom

½ pound cake flour (about 2 cups)

1 tablespoon coarse sugar, such as demerara

1. Preheat the oven to 325°F. Coat a 5- by 9-inch loaf pan with cooking spray. Line with a strip of parchment paper that extends up the long sides and hangs out by about 1 inch per side.

2. Whisk the eggs in a bowl, then weigh; you should have 8 ounces. Adjust by subtracting some of the beaten egg, or beating in another yolk. (If you don't have a scale, use four whole eggs and one additional egg yolk; it will be close enough.)

3. Combine the butter, granulated sugar, and salt in a large mixing bowl. Beat with an electric mixer on high speed for 5 minutes. Add half of the eggs and beat for about 1 minute, then add the remaining eggs, the vanilla, and cardamom and beat for another minute. Add the flour, and stir with a wooden spoon until just mixed. Scrape into the prepared pan, smoothing the top. Sprinkle the coarse sugar over the top. Bake for 1 hour, or until a toothpick inserted into the center comes out clean. Place the pan on a wire rack and let cool for 10 minutes, then turn the cake out of the pan and let cool completely before serving.

Butter-Fried Pound Cake with Berries

If you've got more pound cake than you can eat in a few days, try this delicious dessert recipe: Fry ¾-inch-thick slices of left-over pound cake in a skillet with ample butter over medium heat until the cake is golden on both sides. Top the warm cake with fresh berries that have been macerated with sugar; add a dollop of whipped cream or a scoop of ice cream, if you like.

Big Woods Blue Cheesecake

Chef Dan Parker took time from working on his own cookbook project to share this recipe featuring Shepherd's Way Big Woods Blue sheep's milk cheese. Having worked in some of the best restaurants across Minnesota and South Dakota, Chef Dan now uses his skills as craft beer and culinary specialist for Original Gravity craft-beer distributors. He has a passion for creating delicious recipes featuring small farms and artisanal producers from both the food and the craft-beer arenas. You can also find his influence in the world of food and beer as an instructor, writer, and judge in the Twin Cities and beyond. A Certified Cicerone, Chef Dan suggests pairing this cheesecake with barley wine, Imperial stout, or port.

10 SERVINGS

2 cups crushed shortbread cookies

4–5 tablespoons unsalted butter, melted

6 ounces Shepherd's Way Big Woods Blue cheese, crumbled

1½ pounds cream cheese, softened

¾ cup sugar

½ cup sour cream

3 eggs

¼ cup all-purpose flour

2 tablespoons dry vermouth

1 teaspoon lemon juice

1 teaspoon vanilla extract

Wild plum preserves, walnuts, or figs (fresh or dried) for serving, optional

1. Preheat the oven to 325°F. Mix the crushed cookies and 4 tablespoons of the melted butter in a medium bowl. Add a little more butter if the mixture seems too dry. Wrap the outside of a 10-inch springform pan with foil. Press the cookie mixture in an even layer into the bottom of the pan. Refrigerate until needed.

2. Add half of the blue cheese, the cream cheese, sugar, and sour cream to the bowl of an electric mixer fitted with the paddle attachment. Blend on medium-low speed until all the ingredients are combined; small lumps are okay. Add the eggs one at a time, blending after each addition until it is fully incorporated. Add the flour, vermouth, lemon juice, and vanilla. Mix until well combined. Fold in the remaining blue cheese with a rubber spatula. Spread the cheese mixture in an even layer over the prepared cookie crust.

3. Place the springform pan inside a larger baking dish and add about 1 inch of hot water to the larger baking dish (this step is optional, but helps prevent cracking). Bake for 40 minutes. Turn the oven off, leaving the cake in the oven to cool gradually for 1 hour. Remove from the oven and take it out of the water bath, if used. Let the cake cool at room temperature for another hour. Cover and refrigerate for 3 hours, or up to overnight.

4. To unmold, run a butter knife around the edge of the cake a few times, then release the outer band of the springform pan. Serve with wild plum preserves, walnuts, or figs, if desired.

SHEPHERD'S WAY FARMS, NERSTRAND

This is the cheese that was made by the farmers who milked the ewes that ate the grass that was made by the sun that shone on the pasture at the beautiful farm in Nerstrand. Sound like a nursery rhyme? The story of Shepherd's Way Farms is more of a fairy tale, with a happy ending involving award-winning artisan cheese.

Shepherd's Way Farms was started in 1994, when Steven Read and Jodi Ohlsen Read, weary of their traditional Twin Cities jobs and wanting to spend more time with their four growing sons, bought a small flock of dairy sheep and became farmers. By 1998, they were marketing their first artisan sheep's milk cheese: Friesago, a semiaged cheese named after their Friesian sheep. Four years later, Friesago took second place in the Aged Sheep's Milk Cheese category at the American Cheese Society's annual competition. In 2007, it was recommended as a "must-try" cheese by *Food & Wine* magazine, which praised it as a "supremely good Manchego-like" cheese.

Jodi Ohlsen Read

Like Friesago, all Shepherd's Way cheeses are handmade in small batches by Jodi, who says she still feels the magic each time a batch of milk begins to set up after she adds the culture. Steven is happy in his role as shepherd, which he says is both avocation and vocation. The couple's sons are still active at the farm and help staff the farm's booth every weekend during market season at Minneapolis's Mill City Farmers' Market and the St. Paul Farmers' Market.

As in most fairy tales, there are both happy and grim chapters. In October 2004, Jodi and Steven traveled to Terra Madre, the international Slow Foods gathering in Milan, Italy, to represent the local Slow Foods convivium. About 3 months later, a devastating arson fire destroyed more than 500 sheep and lambs, also demolishing the animal housing. With perseverance and an outpouring of support from the local community and others, they rebuilt their flock, resuming full production in 2011.

Today, their lineup includes the original Friesago and two more ACS award winners, Big Woods Blue and Shepherd's Hope, along with Hidden Falls, Burr Oak, Morcella (made with morels), and short-production cheeses destined for members of their cheese CSA program. Life is good at the beautiful farm in Nerstrand.

Shepherd's Hope Panzanella Salad

Jodi Ohlsen Read is the cheese maker at Shepherd's Way Farms, and she shared this recipe featuring their award-winning Shepherd's Hope, a mild soft-ripened cheese made with the farm's own sheep's milk. If you've never had panzanella, you'll be surprised that such a simple recipe can produce such a wonderful salad. Serve it as a luncheon, first course, or light supper dish, paired with a crisp Chardonnay to complement the creamy cheese. It's also wonderful for picnics.

4–6 SERVINGS

1 baguette, cut into 1-inch cubes (about 6 cups)

⅓ cup plus 2 tablespoons extra-virgin olive oil

2 garlic cloves, minced

½ teaspoon coarse kosher salt, plus more as needed

3½ tablespoons balsamic vinegar

2 tablespoons drained brined capers, smashed

4 ounces (or more!) Shepherd's Hope sheep's milk cheese, original or garlic-herb

1¾ pounds ripe tomatoes, cored, cut into bite-size pieces

½ red onion, thinly sliced

¾ cup coarsely chopped fresh basil

Freshly ground black pepper

1. Preheat the oven to 375°F. Toss the bread cubes with 2 tablespoons of the oil in a large bowl. Spread in a single layer on a rimmed baking sheet. Bake, stirring once, for 12 to 15 minutes, until golden. Set aside to cool.

2. Place the garlic in a small bowl with the salt. Mash to a paste. Scrape into a large salad bowl or mixing bowl. Add the vinegar, capers, and remaining ⅓ cup oil. Whisk until well blended.

3. Cut the cheese into ½-inch cubes and add them to the bowl with the dressing mixture. Add the croutons, tomatoes, onion, and basil. Stir gently and set aside at room temperature for 20 minutes. Taste, and add salt and pepper as needed.

Szechuan Spice Honey

This infused honey is really delicious served as a dip with fried chicken and biscuits. It also goes well with grilled meats, especially ribs, and can be used as part of the baste when grilling. Try drizzling it on a sandwich made with a top-quality Brie, or another soft cheese such as Shepherd's Way Hidden Falls. It also works well served in a small bowl on a cheese plate.

1 cup honey

1 tablespoon Szechuan peppercorns

2 thin slices peeled fresh gingerroot

¼ teaspoon red pepper flakes

1 teaspoon unseasoned rice vinegar

1. Stir together the honey, peppercorns, gingerroot, and pepper flakes in a small saucepan. Place over medium-low heat and warm just until small bubbles appear around the edges; don't let it boil. Remove from the heat and set aside to infuse for about 1 hour.

2. Return the saucepan to medium-low heat and warm for a few minutes, just until the honey becomes more fluid. Stir in the vinegar. Strain the honey through a fine-mesh strainer into a small widemouthed jar. Discard the solids in the strainer. Let the honey cool completely before sealing. Store at room temperature; it keeps for months.

Bolognese-Style Pasta with Lamb

The use of cream is somewhat controversial in Bolognese sauce. Some purists say that it has no place in the traditional dish (and they also eschew butter, which is often used in recipes, particularly those written by non-Italians). It does add a lush finish to the sauce and is particularly good with this lamb version, which, in itself, is a departure from the chopped beef used in traditional recipes. If you choose not to use the cream, the sauce will be ready at the end of step 3. Tagliatelle — wide, thin pasta — is the traditional shape to serve with Bolognese sauce. I prefer bucatini (also called perciatelli), a thick spaghetti shape with a center that's hollow, like a straw.

10 GENEROUS SERVINGS

2 tablespoons sunflower oil or olive oil

¼ pound pancetta, thickly sliced and cut into ¼-inch squares

2 small onions, diced

2 carrots, diced

2 celery stalks, diced

3 garlic cloves, minced

1 pound ground lamb

1 cup Chianti or other dry red wine

½ cup beef broth

1 (14.5-ounce) can crushed tomatoes

½ teaspoon salt

2 bay leaves

⅓ cup heavy cream or half-and-half, optional

Hot cooked pasta, such as tagliatelle, bucatini, or linguine

Freshly grated Parmesan cheese, for serving

1. Heat the oil in a 1-gallon soup pot or large saucepan over medium heat. Add the pancetta. Cook, stirring occasionally, until the pancetta is light golden, about 5 minutes. Stir in the onions, carrots, celery, and garlic. Cook, stirring occasionally, for about 5 minutes.

2. Increase the heat to medium-high. Add the lamb. Cook, breaking up and stirring occasionally with a wooden spoon, for about 8 minutes. Stir in the wine and broth. Increase the heat to high and bring to a boil. Cook for 5 minutes; the liquid should reduce a bit during this time.

3. Stir in the tomatoes, salt, and bay leaves. Put a lid on the pot, adjusting it so the pan is only partially covered. Adjust the heat so the mixture is just barely simmering. Cook for 1¼ hours, stirring occasionally. Fish out and discard the bay leaves.

4. Add the cream, if desired, in a slow stream, stirring constantly. Cook for about 15 minutes longer, stirring several times. Serve over hot cooked pasta, using about ½ cup sauce per serving. Pass Parmesan at the table. Leftover sauce will keep in the freezer for up to 3 months.

SMUDE'S SUNFLOWER OIL, PIERZ

Tom and Jenni Smude's story is one of persistence and rising above problems that might put less-determined folks out of business — and also features some good sense about finding a product that hits the sweet spots for today's consumers.

They started farming in 1998, raising Angus cattle and growing corn and soybeans on their 120-acre farm in central Minnesota. A 2007 drought caused them to consider other crops. After some research, they replaced their soybeans with non-GMO high-oleic sunflowers. The seeds are cold-pressed, and the resulting oil is simply filtered, with no chemical refining. This sets it apart from commercially processed vegetable oils that are clarified with high heat and hydrogenated, steps that destroy antioxidants and create dangerous trans fats. Smude's cold-pressed oil has a buttery, slightly nutty taste that carries through to foods prepared with it. (Among other uses, I love it for popcorn, pan-fried fish, vinaigrettes, and homemade mayonnaise.) It's naturally shelf stable and is rich in healthful oleic acid; it also has half the saturated fat of olive oil and more vitamin E than any other vegetable oil.

In 2010, the Smudes had their first batch of oil ready to ship. They had planned to sell it in bulk to distributors for the food industry, but when the bulk-oil market suddenly tanked, they decided to bottle the oil for direct sales.

Their oil found a receptive audience as people discovered the benefits of cold-pressed high-oleic sunflower oil. Chefs and home cooks alike appreciate the oil's sunny taste and cooking properties; its flavor makes it an exciting, local substitute for olive oil, and its high smoke point makes it ideal for frying. Bakers love it because goods prepared with the oil are shelf stable and trans fat–free. Cardiologists recommend it to help patients reduce their cholesterol and triglycerides. As a bonus, cattle thrive on the meal left after the seeds are pressed.

Today, the Smudes produce about 35,000 gallons of oil annually; to keep up with demand, they've contracted with four other local farms, which each grow about 100 acres of sunflowers for them. Their lineup now includes flavored oils and massage oils, and local companies are using Smude oil in lotions and other products. It's clear that more than just flowers are growing and looking sunny at the Smude farm.

Slow-Cooker Pulled Turkey

Minnesota is the largest turkey-producing state in the United States, although it is sometimes neck and neck (wattle and wattle?) with North Carolina. Here's a tasty way to use turkey thighs, which are a good buy compared to turkey breast and which make a pulled barbecue that's as good as pork. Well, almost. Serve this on regular sandwich rolls for a traditional barbecue sandwich or on small buns for turkey sliders. The Pickled Italian Giardiniera on page 224 is a wonderful complement to these sandwiches; sliced pickles or coleslaw also work well.

8–10 SERVINGS

1 large onion, chopped

¼ cup plus 1 tablespoon tomato paste

2 tablespoons hot pepper sauce, such as Valentina or Frank's RedHot

2 tablespoons apple cider vinegar

1 tablespoon Worcestershire sauce

1 tablespoon chopped garlic

1 tablespoon chili powder

1 teaspoon salt

½ teaspoon ground cumin

2 turkey thighs (2½–3 pounds total), skin removed

Split sandwich rolls, for serving

Pickled Italian Giardiniera (page 224), pickles, or coleslaw, for serving

1. Combine the onion, tomato paste, hot pepper sauce, vinegar, Worcestershire, garlic, chili powder, salt, and cumin in the crock of a slow cooker. Stir well. Nestle the turkey thighs into the mixture. Cover and cook on high for 1 hour, then reduce the heat to low and cook for 7 hours longer.

2. Use tongs and a slotted spoon to transfer the thighs to a rectangular baking dish. Skim excess fat from the surface of the sauce in the slow cooker. Transfer the sauce to a large nonreactive saucepan or 1-gallon soup pot. Cook over medium to medium-high heat until the sauce has reduced to a saucelike consistency, 10 to 15 minutes. Meanwhile, use forks to pull the turkey meat into shreds, discarding the bones and any fat or tendons you encounter; once the turkey has cooled a bit, you can use your fingers to pull the meat apart.

3. Add the shredded meat to the reduced sauce, and heat through. Serve immediately, or return to the slow cooker and keep warm until needed. Serve in split rolls, with condiments as desired.

Recipe from DAVID DONATELLE

Honey-Spiced Chicken Tagine

David Donatelle has been a beekeeper hobbyist for the past 12 years. He and his wife, Joan, have been sharing their love of authentic Mediterranean cuisine since the mid-1980s. With three award-winning restaurants, three gourmet delis, and a catering company, they have provided many satisfying and healthful culinary experiences to loyal guests. David has studied in France and Italy and continues to refine his knowledge of nutrition for health, immunity, and longevity. Currently, he is director of dining services at Sunrise Assisted Living in Edina.

4–6 SERVINGS

2 tablespoons extra-virgin olive oil

6 bone-in, skin-on chicken thighs

1 yellow onion, thinly sliced

1 orange-fleshed sweet potato, peeled and cut into ½-inch cubes

2 garlic cloves, minced

1 tablespoon minced fresh gingerroot

½ teaspoon red pepper flakes

½ teaspoon ground turmeric

½ teaspoon sea salt

¼ teaspoon ground cinnamon

1 cup chicken broth

¼ cup honey

2 tablespoons lime juice

1 tablespoon red wine vinegar

1 (10-ounce) package couscous, prepared according to package directions

½ cup chopped fresh cilantro

2 tablespoons chopped almonds

2 tablespoons golden raisins

1 lime, cut into wedges

1. Preheat the oven to 325°F. Heat the oil in a tagine or Dutch oven over medium-high heat. Add the chicken and brown on both sides, about 10 minutes. Transfer to a plate. Add the onion, sweet potato, garlic, and gingerroot to the tagine. Cook, stirring occasionally, for about 5 minutes. Stir the pepper flakes, turmeric, salt, and cinnamon together in a small bowl. Sprinkle over the onion mixture, stirring to combine.

2. Measure the broth in a 2-cup measuring cup. Pour the honey into the measuring cup, and stir in the lime juice and vinegar. Return the chicken to the tagine. Pour the broth mixture over the chicken. Cover and bake for 1 hour.

3. To serve, spread the hot cooked couscous in a wide serving dish. Spoon the chicken and sauce over the couscous. Top with the cilantro, almonds, and raisins, then tuck the lime wedges around the sides. Serve immediately.

Honey-and-Cream Butter

This simple but delicious butter is creamy and spreadable even when cold. It's fabulous on toast, pancakes, waffles, or oatmeal. It's also a major player in the blue cheese appetizer on page 144.

1 HALF-PINT JAR

½ cup (1 stick) unsalted butter, cut into 8 chunks, softened

⅓ cup honey

⅓ cup heavy cream

1 tablespoon sugar

½ teaspoon vanilla extract

1. Place the butter in a large, heatproof mixing bowl. Stir together the honey, cream, and sugar in a small saucepan. Bring to a full boil over high heat, stirring constantly, then reduce the heat so the mixture doesn't boil over. Cook, stirring constantly, for about 1 minute longer. Pour over the butter, then add the vanilla.

2. Beat with a handheld electric mixer on low speed until the butter has been incorporated, then turn the mixer speed to medium and beat for about 1 minute longer. Spoon into a clean half-pint jar. Cover and refrigerate until needed; it keeps for a month or more.

Maple-and-Cream Butter

Here's a maple version of the Honey-and-Cream Butter. Maple syrup has slightly different characteristics, so the cooking instructions are a bit different, but the result is equally delicious.

1 HALF-PINT JAR

½ cup (1 stick) unsalted butter, cut into 8 chunks, softened

½ cup pure maple syrup

2 tablespoons firmly packed light brown sugar

¼ cup heavy cream

½ teaspoon vanilla extract

1. Place the butter in a large, heatproof mixing bowl. Stir together the maple syrup and brown sugar in a small saucepan. Bring to a full boil over high heat, stirring constantly, then reduce the heat so the mixture doesn't boil over. Cook, stirring constantly, for 1 minute. Add the cream. Continue to cook, stirring constantly, until the mixture again comes to a full boil. Cook, stirring constantly, for 1 minute longer. Pour over the butter, then add the vanilla.

2. Beat with a handheld electric mixer on low speed until the butter has been incorporated, then turn the mixer speed to medium and beat for about 1 minute longer. Spoon into a clean half-pint jar. Cover and refrigerate until needed; it keeps for a month or more.

AMES FARM SINGLE-SOURCE HONEY, WATERTOWN

One location, one hive, one time period. That's the mantra of Brian Fredrickson of Ames Farm, and it's apparently unique in the world of commercially produced honey. It's also responsible for the array of flavors, colors, and aromas found in Ames Farm's raw honey.

Unlike most honey producers, Brian doesn't keep his bee colonies in one convenient spot. He has a network of more than a dozen farms, meadowlands, orchards, and other locations that "host" his 400 hive boxes, each located in proximity to a large source of successively flowering plants and trees. At one location, the bees may be bringing in buckwheat nectar; at another, on a different day, they may be harvesting from marsh flowers . . . or dandelions, basswood, linden, alfalfa, or any of a dozen different floral types. Each has its own unique taste, which Brian calls "a floral snapshot."

Brian extracts the honey from each hive at the appropriate time, traveling from one hive location to another over the course of the summer and fall. The honey from each 34-pound hive box is packed raw and unheated ("Just like the bees made it!" as Brian says), and each jar is labeled with the location, hive number, and year. Customers can visit the Ames Farm website (see Resources on page 270) to learn more about the source of the honey they've purchased.

A high percentage of honey sold in the United States comes from sources outside the country; most is blended with a small amount of American honey so that it does not have to be labeled as a foreign product. It is often filtered to remove all pollen, which is unfortunate because pollen is key to identifying the source and also provides the honey with its distinct taste and healthful properties. This "squeeze-bottle" honey has a predictable but generic flavor. In stark contrast, Ames Farm's single-source honey is blended only by the bees themselves. When the bees are pollinating a dominant flower such as buckwheat, the honey will be labeled as such. At other times, the bees are pollinating a variety of flowers, so the honey's name is less specific. But even these bee-blended honeys are unique. Ames Farm's Summer Blossoms honey has a completely different taste, aroma, and appearance than Fall Wildflower honey or Savory Marsh Flowers honey.

Ames Farm is based in Watertown, about 30 miles west of Minneapolis. Look for the honey at various supermarkets, co-ops, natural foods stores, and specialty shops. You can also stop by several farmers' markets — including Minneapolis, Mill City, or the Nicollet Mall market in downtown Minneapolis — to chat with Brian or other Ames Farm folks and choose your own jar of sunshine to bring home.

Brian Fredrickson

Roasted Smashed Red River Potatoes
with Sage and Bacon

These crispy potatoes are prepared in the oven rather than on the stovetop. A built-in garnish of bacon and crispy sage leaves adds great flavor.

1½–2 pounds small red potatoes, 1½ to 2 inches across

Coarse kosher salt

2½ tablespoons olive oil, plus more as needed

12 fresh sage leaves, cut in half crosswise

3 thick-cut bacon strips, cut into 1-inch lengths

Freshly ground black pepper

1. Place the potatoes in a large pot and add cold water to cover; season generously with salt. Bring to a boil and cook until the potatoes are just tender when poked with a paring knife, 14 to 17 minutes. Drain and let cool for about 10 minutes. While the potatoes are cooking, position an oven rack at the bottom of the oven and preheat the oven to 425°F.

2. Pour the oil onto a heavyweight rimmed baking sheet, distributing evenly with a pastry brush; add additional oil if needed to provide a thick coating of oil. Lay the sage leaf halves singly on the sheet, and cover each with a piece of bacon; place any remaining bacon pieces on the baking sheet, keeping some space between them. Place a potato on a work surface and press with a potato masher to flatten the potato to about a ¾-inch thickness; the potato should break apart into large pieces. Transfer the potato pieces to the baking sheet, breaking them apart as necessary so no piece is larger than about 1 inch. Repeat with the remaining potatoes, spreading them evenly on the baking sheet. Drizzle a little oil over the potatoes. Sprinkle lightly with the pepper and salt to taste.

3. Bake for 20 minutes, then remove from the oven. Turn the potatoes, together with the bacon and sage, with a spatula. Return to the oven and bake until the potatoes are golden brown and crisp, about 10 minutes longer.

THE RED RIVER VALLEY OF THE NORTH

I f you're ever in northwestern Minnesota near the North Dakota border, scan the prairie looking west. Chances are, you won't perceive the Red River Valley, even when you're right on its edge. Most of the land is eerily uninhabited and relentlessly flat; in places, you could get within a mile of the Red River and not see any hint of the valley. You also may not realize that you are standing on some of the richest farmland in the Midwest.

THE RED RIVER VALLEY straddles the line between northwestern Minnesota and North Dakota. The river is a remnant of Lake Agassiz, a glacial lake that left behind a thick layer of silt as it drained thousands of years ago. From its headwaters at Breckenridge, Minnesota, the Red River flows north, assimilating numerous smaller waterways before crossing into Canada near Winnipeg. The flat terrain in the valley is prone to periodic flooding that while sometimes destructive, also leaves behind organic matter that enriches the soil. These factors, coupled with a sparse population, make the area ideal for farming.

Wheat was the main crop for nearly a century, but eventually it gave way to other crops. Although you'll see plenty of corn and soybeans, the crop that is most closely associated with the Red River Valley today is sugar beets, which are used to make everyday sugar. About 35 percent of the world's sugar comes from sugar beets, and Minnesota is the nation's leader in their production.

SUGAR BEETS are related to table beets, but they have tan skins and are much larger. Each beet, which looks like a coarse, fattened turnip in need of a shave, weighs 1 to 2 pounds. Beets are harvested in fall and trucked to "beet dumps," where they are heaped in piles about 15 feet high and 50 yards wide, and up to a quarter-mile in length. Dumps, which can consist of dozens of piles holding tons of beets, are located near a railroad or highway so the beets can be transferred onto train cars or trucks that haul them to processing plants where the sugar is extracted by heat and then crystallized. American Crystal Sugar has plants in East Grand Forks, Crookston, and Moorhead, Minnesota, as well as two in North Dakota. The Minn-Dak Farmers Cooperative, a smaller sugar producer, has a plant in Wahpeton, North Dakota; beets come from farmer-members in both states. Another co-op, the Southern Minnesota Beet Sugar Cooperative, has a plant in Renville, Minnesota.

POTATOES — particularly red potatoes — are another signature crop for the Red River Valley, which produces more red potatoes than any other region in the country. The valley's slightly acidic soil is rich, deep, and well drained, allowing area farmers to grow top-quality potatoes without irrigation. Barnesville, a short drive south of Fargo on the Minnesota side of the river, holds an annual Potato Days Festival at the end of August. Events include contests for picking, peeling, and eating potatoes, as well as the National Lefse Contest, in which cooks vie to prepare the best version of this Scandinavian potato-based flatbread.

BEANS FOR TABLE USE are being planted with increasing frequency, though soybeans for animal feed are a much more common crop in the Red River Valley. Navy beans, pinto beans, and kidney beans are more difficult to grow and harvest than soybeans, but they usually garner higher prices than commodity soybeans. Minnesota produces about 70 percent of the dark red kidney beans grown in the nation, with the largest percentage coming from the Red

River Valley. Across the Red River, North Dakota is generally the nation's leading producer of pinto and navy beans, and the bulk of the production comes from the valley.

Mark Twain may have summed up the feeling of the valley best when, in a July 1895 interview with the *Grand Forks Herald*, he said about the Red River Valley: "This country of yours out here astonished me beyond all imagination. Never in my life have I seen such fields of grain extending in all directions to the horizon. This country appears to me to be as it were a mighty ocean; my conception of it is the same as that of a man who has never seen the ocean before, he sees nothing but water as far as the eye can reach; here I see nothing but oceans of wheat fields. Why, it is simply miraculous."

Sugar Beet Tea Bread

This recipe is written for sugar beets, the homely industrial cousin to the garden beets we eat as a vegetable. Regular beets just won't cut it here. Underneath the sugar beet's rough tan exterior, the flesh is ivory colored and crisp. Sugar beets are grown to be processed into granulated sugar and are rarely eaten as a vegetable. That's a shame, since they have an intriguing flavor that is somewhat like a cross between a parsnip and a carrot, with an added dose of sugar. Here, their natural sweetness works well in a delicious tea bread. Sugar beets aren't found in grocery stores; you'll have to beg a few from a farmer if you want to try cooking with them. This recipe requires about half of a medium sugar beet.

1 (9-INCH) LOAF

1 cup all-purpose flour

½ cup white whole wheat flour or additional all-purpose flour

2 teaspoons baking powder

½ teaspoon salt

½ teaspoon ground cinnamon

½ teaspoon ground nutmeg

2 eggs

½ cup whole or 2% milk

½ cup sunflower oil or vegetable oil

1 teaspoon vanilla extract

½ cup firmly packed light brown sugar

1½–2 cups grated sugar beet

½ cup roasted unsalted sunflower seeds

1. Preheat the oven to 350°F. Coat a 5- by 9-inch loaf pan with cooking spray.

2. Whisk both flours, the baking powder, salt, cinnamon, and nutmeg together in a large bowl. Whisk the eggs, milk, oil, and vanilla together in a separate bowl. Stir the brown sugar into the egg mixture.

3. Make a well in the center of the flour mixture. Pour the egg mixture into the well and stir gently with a rubber spatula until the batter is just combined. Gently fold in the sugar beets and sunflower seeds until evenly distributed throughout the batter. Spread the mixture evenly in the loaf pan.

4. Bake the bread for 50 minutes to 1 hour, until a tester stick or skewer inserted into the center comes out clean. Remove from the oven and let cool on a wire rack for 10 minutes before removing the bread from the loaf pan. Let cool completely before slicing.

Navy Bean Hummus with Olive Garnish

Why do chickpeas get all the love when it comes to making hummus? Navy beans, grown in the Red River Valley that straddles the Minnesota–North Dakota border, can also be used to make a very tasty hummus. This version is dolled up with a chopped olive mixture.

ABOUT 2 CUPS

1 cup dried navy beans, picked over and rinsed

7 cups water

1¼ teaspoons coarse kosher salt, or as needed

¾ cup pitted olives, preferably a mix of black and green

2 tablespoons coarsely chopped roasted red bell pepper (purchased or homemade; see instructions on page 97)

½ teaspoon chopped fresh oregano or ¼ teaspoon dried

¼ cup extra-virgin olive oil

2 garlic cloves, smashed

¼ cup tahini (sesame paste)

2 tablespoons lemon juice, or as needed

¼ teaspoon freshly ground black pepper, or as needed

Sweet or smoked paprika, for garnish

Fresh vegetables, such as carrot sticks, bell pepper strips, and cauliflower florets, for serving

Toasted pita bread quarters, for serving

1. Combine the beans and 2½ cups of the water in a saucepan. Bring to a boil, then remove from the heat and let stand for 1 hour. Drain the beans and return to the saucepan. Add the remaining 4½ cups water. Bring to a boil, then reduce the heat so the water simmers and cook until the beans can be bitten through but are not quite tender; this will take from 30 to 45 minutes, depending on the age of the beans. Add ½ teaspoon of the salt and continue cooking until the beans are tender, 30 to 40 minutes longer. Drain the beans, reserving the cooking water. Let the drained beans stand until cool.

2. Chop the olives very coarsely in a food processor. Add the roasted bell pepper and oregano. Pulse a few times until the mixture is an even, medium-coarse texture. Scrape into a small bowl, then stir in 1 tablespoon of the oil. Wipe the food processor bowl and blade with paper towels.

3. With the food processor running, drop the garlic through the feed tube and process until the garlic is minced. Add the cooked beans, tahini, remaining 3 tablespoons oil, lemon juice, remaining ¾ teaspoon salt, and the black pepper. Process until finely chopped. With the machine running, add some of the reserved cooking water as needed until the mixture is smooth and creamy; try using about 2 tablespoons to start. When the mixture is smooth, taste for seasoning, and add additional salt, black pepper, and/or lemon juice as needed.

4. Spoon the bean mixture into a serving bowl. Sprinkle with paprika. Make a well in the center and fill with the olive mixture. Serve cold or at room temperature with fresh vegetables and pita for dipping.

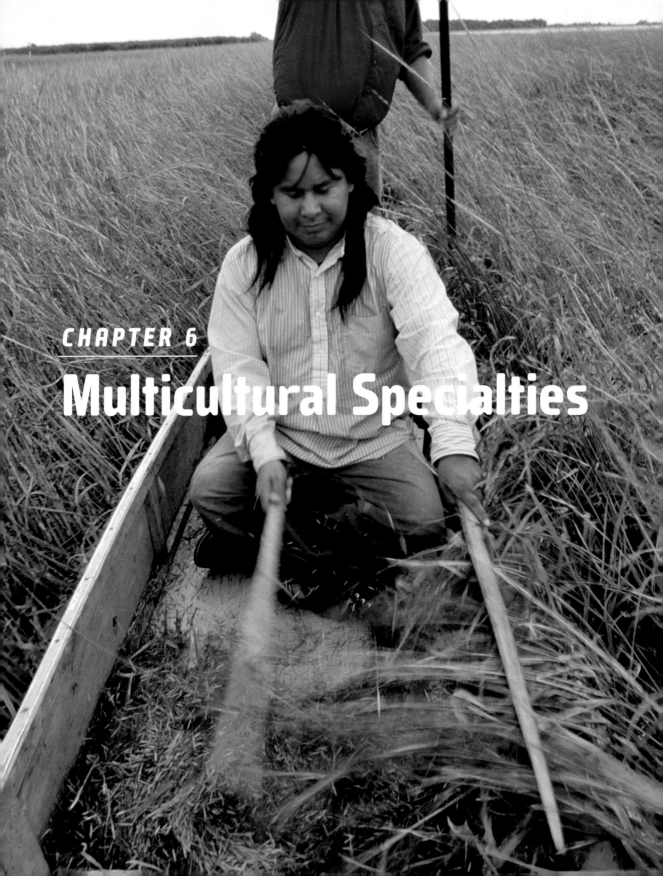

CHAPTER 6

Multicultural Specialties

THE FAMOUS (OR PERHAPS INFAMOUS) Minnesota accent has a decidedly Scandinavian lilt to it. That's not surprising; over one-quarter of the state's residents are of Scandinavian ancestry. The largest group, however, is people of German heritage, who account for over one-third of the state's population.

Some immigrants came to Minnesota simply to start a new life, free of economic difficulties, religious persecution, or political conflicts in their home countries. Others came to fill a need for workers. A mining boom in northeastern Minnesota in the late 1800s brought an influx of mine workers from the British Isles, Italy, Eastern Europe, and Scandinavia. Throughout the twentieth century, people from Mexico, Central America, and South America came to fill jobs in agriculture and other industries. Political and religious refugees also arrived in Minnesota during this time from the Soviet Bloc, Europe, and the Mideast.

From 1975 through 2005, many Hmong immigrated to Minnesota, forced from their homelands in Laos and Vietnam and moving from refugee camps in Thailand. In the early 1990s, numerous Somalis fled a growing civil war in their home country, joining other Somalis who had immigrated to Minnesota earlier to pursue business and educational opportunities. Minnesota also has numerous immigrants from other parts of Africa, particularly Nigeria and Ethiopia.

This chapter starts with a few recipes that celebrate a new interest in foods of the Ojibwe and the Dakota, the original inhabitants of this area who remain a vital part of our culture today. Prior to the arrival of missionaries, trappers, and immigrants from across the globe, indigenous peoples in this area farmed, hunted, and gathered in harmony with the natural world; these activities and foods remain central to the Native cultures of today.

The immigrants who settled in Minnesota brought more than their hopes for a better life; they also brought their culinary traditions. The recipes that follow give a glimpse into the rich and varied dishes that enrich Minnesota's food scene.

Heirloom Beans and Squash with Smoked Fish and Balsam Broth

The inspiration for this came from a dish created by Sean Sherman, the Sioux Chef (page 194). Chef Sean's dish was restaurant-style, much more complex with multiple layers of flavor and texture. It was also elegantly presented, offering a stunning treat for the eyes as well as the palate. My simpler version is easy to prepare at home and incorporates some of the indigenous, local foods that Sean is so adept at using. Any heirloom beans will work here, such as Jacob's cattle beans, runner beans, tepary beans, or yellow-eyed beans. For the balsam fir, snip off 5- to 6-inch-long boughs from the end of a side branch; the few taken for this recipe won't harm the tree. **Note:** The beans must be soaked overnight before cooking.

6 SERVINGS

¾ pound dried Jacob's cattle or other heirloom beans (see headnote), picked over and rinsed

4 short balsam fir boughs (see headnote), well rinsed

1 heaping cup peeled and cubed winter squash or cooking pumpkin (¾-inch cubes)

1 tablespoon pure maple syrup, plus more for serving

½ teaspoon salt

6 ounces boneless, skinless smoked whitefish or lake trout, broken into rough 1-inch chunks (about 2 cups)

1. Soak the beans in water overnight at room temperature.

2. When you're ready to start cooking, drain the beans and place them in a Dutch oven. Add cold water to cover by an inch. Bring to a boil, then reduce the heat so the water simmers and cook until the beans can be bitten through but are not quite tender; this will take from 30 minutes to 1 hour, depending on the variety and age of the beans.

3. Meanwhile, snip the balsam boughs to fit into a 1-gallon soup pot. Add 3 cups water and bring to a boil. Boil gently for 15 minutes, rearranging the boughs occasionally. Remove from the heat and let stand, covered, until needed.

4. Drain the beans through a fine-mesh strainer and return them to the Dutch oven. Strain the balsam broth into the Dutch oven with the beans; discard the balsam remnants. Add the squash, maple syrup, and salt. Simmer until the beans and squash are tender, about 20 minutes. The mixture should be saucy but not soupy.

5. Scatter the smoked fish chunks over the beans and squash. Cover and cook for about 5 minutes longer. Divide the stew between soup plates, including just enough broth for each portion to make it moist but not soupy. Offer additional maple syrup at the table; a little drizzle really adds a special touch to the dish.

Note: The pot used to cook the balsam broth will have sap deposits inside. To remove, scrub with a soapy scouring pad and lots of hot water.

SEAN SHERMAN, THE SIOUX CHEF

"First, we eat with our eyes." The saying is particularly relevant today, as contemporary restaurants emphasize presentation almost as much as preparation. Like many of his peers, Chef Sean Sherman has a keen eye and a deft hand when it comes to plating, and turns out food that is both beautiful and delicious.

There's a major distinction to Sean's works of art, however; he specializes in using indigenous, precontact foods, those that were available to the Ojibwe and Dakota Indians who were Minnesota's first inhabitants. Sean's palette is colored with local foods, among them wild rice and maple products; venison, rabbits, and ducks; bison, once plentiful on the Plains until they were wiped out in campaigns intended to starve Indians off their lands; native fish; wild berries and herbs; corn, beans, and squash, which were cultivated by the Ojibwe and Dakota; and tree products, including sumac berries and boughs from cedar, balsam, and juniper. In addition, Sean uses Native techniques such as smoking and drying in many of his preparations, and doesn't use European ingredients such as butter, flour, and white sugar.

Sean is Oglala Lakota, raised on South Dakota's Pine Ridge Reservation, where diabetes is endemic among his people. He's quick to point out that the traditional foods he's working with are low-glycemic, high in fiber, and very healthful. This contrasts to the commodity foods supplied to Native American tribes by treaty with the U.S. government and the unhealthful food that is too common in the diets of modern-day Natives, whether due to limited availability of fresh, healthy foods or to the pervasiveness of modern fast-food culture.

In addition to doing pop-up dinners and running his Tatanka food truck, Sean is active in outreach to Native communities throughout the region. For example, he's spent time teaching youth at the Little Earth Indian community in Minneapolis about Native foods and showing the young people how to prepare them, while explaining their cultural significance. "I want to inspire young people to take hold of their traditions and heritage, and help make Native American food culture thrive down the road," he says.

Noting the absence of restaurants that serve regional Native foods, he commented, "In the city, you can find any cuisine from around the world, except for the one that came from right under your feet."

Sean Sherman

Bison Jerky with Juniper Berries and Mustard Seeds

Native Ojibwe and Dakota peoples in Minnesota traditionally relied on smoking and drying to preserve food for the lean winter months. This bison jerky, simply seasoned with native juniper berries, mustard seeds, and maple syrup, also uses salt, which some bands had access to through trading. Although it might not have been used by all bands, the salt provides some of the flavor we associate with jerky and also aids in preservation. Because the meat is minimally seasoned here, the taste of the bison really comes through, so top quality is important. **Note:** This recipe requires either a food dehydrator or a smoker.

ABOUT ½ POUND

1 pound bison flank steak or other lean cut, trimmed of exterior fat and connective tissue

6 dried juniper berries (see headnote on page 84)

1 tablespoon plus 1 teaspoon coarse kosher salt

1 teaspoon mustard seeds

2 tablespoons pure maple syrup

1. Cut the bison with the grain into strips that are ¼ inch thick, 3 to 4 inches long, and about ¾ inch wide. Some bison flank steaks are about the right thickness, so you can just cut them into appropriately sized strips; slice thicker cuts into ¼-inch-thick strips. Place the meat in a mixing bowl.

2. Crush the juniper berries and salt together with a mortar and pestle, twisting and grinding the pestle to pulverize the juniper berries until they are fairly fine. Add the mustard seeds, and crush fairly fine. Stir in the maple syrup. Scrape the mixture into the bowl with the bison, stirring to coat. Cover the bowl and refrigerate overnight, stirring once or twice if possible.

3. The next day, blot the pieces lightly with paper towels to dry off excess liquid; the crushed seeds should still be clinging to the meat. Pound lightly on both sides with a meat tenderizer. Arrange the meat in a single layer on dehydrator trays (or smoker racks, if smoking). Dehydrate (or smoke) at 145°F until the meat is dry and dark, 4 to 6 hours; if you bend a piece, it should not ooze any moisture. (If smoking, replenish the wood once or twice, but don't keep a heavy smoke going throughout or the jerky will be too smoky.)

   If you're concerned about the safety of the meat, bake the finished jerky in a 275°F oven for 10 minutes before cooling and storing.

4. Let the jerky cool completely, then wrap and refrigerate for up to 1 month; for longer storage, wrap the jerky very well and freeze it for up to 6 months.

Maple Candy with Walnuts

This confection has been made by Woodland Indian tribes for many generations. The Ojibwe poured the hot mixture into small birch-bark cones or wooden molds, but the only place you'll find those now is in a museum case. Silicone candy molds are a good modern-day substitution — once you become comfortable working with the hot syrup, which goes from liquid to solid in a heartbeat. These instructions call for pouring the syrup into a loaf pan, then cutting it into squares; it's not as pretty as molded candy, but your chances of success are far higher. Once you get a feel for working with the hot syrup, you can graduate to silicone molds, if you like. When you're working with the hot syrup, be aware at all times that it is extremely hot, sticky, and dangerous; guard against spills. **Note:** All recipes in this book that call for maple syrup are referring to the genuine article, not "pancake syrup," which is corn syrup with maple flavoring. For this recipe, in particular, pure maple syrup is required. Do yourself a favor and buy only the real stuff for all your maple syrup needs. You will need a candy thermometer and a silicone spatula for this recipe.

32 PIECES

1½ cups pure maple syrup

3–4 tablespoons chopped walnuts (see Note, opposite), ⅛–¼-inch pieces

1. Draw a 5- by 8-inch rectangle in the center of a foot-long sheet of parchment paper. Turn it over and fold the parchment inward on the lines (with the marked side on the outside), then trim so there is a 2-inch border around the rectangle. Fit into a 5- by 9-inch loaf pan, folding the corners in neatly. Secure the edges of the parchment with freezer tape.

2. Bring a saucepan of water to a full boil. Check the temperature with your candy thermometer. (It may not read 212°F, the official temperature of boiling water at sea level.) Add 23 degrees to the temperature registered on your thermometer; this is the target temperature for boiling the maple syrup. If your thermometer reads 212°F for boiling water, the target temperature is 235°F, which is the lower end of the soft-ball stage.

3. Add the syrup to a 1-gallon soup pot or saucepan at least 5 inches deep (the syrup foams up tremendously during boiling). Clip the thermometer to the pot, ensuring that the bulb doesn't touch the bottom of the pot. Heat to a boil over medium-high heat. Adjust the heat so the syrup continues to boil but does not boil over, and cook until the syrup reaches your target temperature, 6 to 10 minutes. Remove from the heat immediately, and let stand *without disturbing* until the syrup cools to 180°F, 5 to 15 minutes. (You may need to prop up one side of the pot so the syrup pools around the thermometer tip; as an option, use an instant-read thermometer to check the temperature of the syrup as it cools.)

4. While the syrup is cooling, toast the walnuts in a small cast-iron skillet over medium-high heat, stirring constantly, until fragrant and beginning to color, about 5 minutes. Transfer to a bowl.

5. When the syrup cools to 180°F, stir it with a wooden spoon until it is just beginning to look somewhat opaque, 1 to 1½ minutes; if you stir too long, the syrup will harden in the pot. Pour the syrup immediately into the prepared loaf pan, scraping the pot with a silicone spatula. Immediately scatter the nuts over the surface and gently mix with the spatula.

6. After about 30 seconds, the mixture will begin to stiffen and will become paler and opaque. Use the front edge of a thin, flat-bladed metal spatula to score the surface in a 1-inch grid. Clean off the spatula, then push the front edge straight down into the candy on the score lines, using the spatula edge like a knife to cut the candy. Repeat the cleaning and cutting twice more: once about 5 minutes after you pour the mixture into the pan, and again about 5 minutes later. Let the candy cool completely, then remove from the pan by lifting the parchment edges. Break the candy apart and store at room temperature in an airtight container with waxed paper between layers.

Option: For glossier finished candies, place the separated squares in a flat bowl and cover with room-temperature maple syrup. Soak for 2 hours, then remove with a fork and let dry on a piece of parchment, moving once or twice as the syrup pools around the candy. The surface won't be sticky after the candies have dried for an hour or so.

Note: Black walnuts (*Juglans nigra*) grow in the wild in southern Minnesota and taste wonderful, but store-bought English walnuts also work well.

Recipe from HEID ERDRICH

Bering Strait Theory Corn Chowder

The Bering Strait, said to be the migration route for early people of the Western hemisphere, was not a one-way road. This dish combines foods indigenous to the Americas — corn, squash, and Lake Superior fish — with Asian flavors of sesame, ginger, and coconut to create a meeting of the hemispheres. This recipe is based on one in Heid Erdrich's book *Original Local: Indigenous Foods, Stories, and Recipes from the Upper Midwest.* An award-winning poet, Heid is an enrolled member of the Turtle Mountain Band of Chippewa and is coeditor of *Sister Nations: Native American Women Writers on Community.*

4–6 SERVINGS

5 cups vegetable broth

2 cups dry-roasted sweet corn, such as Melissa's, or frozen corn, thawed

½ cup peeled and cubed winter squash (½-inch cubes)

1 medium potato, peeled and cut into ½-inch cubes

1–2 tablespoons toasted sesame oil

4 scallions, white parts chopped, half the green tops chopped and kept separate

1 tablespoon grated fresh gingerroot

1 garlic clove, minced

¼ cup mirin

1 teaspoon Thai or Vietnamese fish sauce

1 egg, lightly beaten

½ cup canned coconut milk

Ground white pepper

1 cup flaked smoked Lake Superior trout

1. Bring the broth to a boil in a large pot. Add the corn, squash, and potato. Adjust the heat so the mixture simmers gently and cook until the potato pieces are tender-firm, 10 to 15 minutes.

2. Warm 1 tablespoon oil in a skillet over medium-high heat. Add the chopped white portions of the scallions, the gingerroot, and garlic, and cook, stirring frequently, until just fragrant, 2 to 3 minutes. Add the scallion mixture to the pot with the broth and stir well. Cook over medium heat for 5 minutes, stirring occasionally, taking care not to overcook the potatoes and squash. Add the mirin and fish sauce, and simmer for a few minutes to blend the flavors.

3. Increase the heat to high and bring to a boil. Use a fork to slowly drop in egg strands, breaking up the strands as they rise to the top of the pot. Stir and reduce the heat to low. When the soup is no longer boiling, stir in the coconut milk, pepper, and up to 1 tablespoon additional oil, to taste. Divide among soup bowls. Top with the flaked smoked trout and reserved scallion greens. Serve immediately.

Egg Coffee

Beloved by Scandinavians and Germans alike, this classic Minnesota coffee can be found in church halls, diners, and cafés throughout the state, particularly in rural areas; it's even available at the Minnesota State Fair. It is known for its smooth taste. The egg binds the grounds together, preventing the bitter sludge often found in percolated coffee; it also provides a subtle, almost malty flavor. Use of the eggshell is optional. It is said to neutralize acids in the coffee, but if you prefer, simply crack the egg into the grounds, discarding the shell.

4¾ cups cold water

¼ cup regular-grind medium-roast coffee

1 egg, well washed if you'll be using the eggshell in the coffee

1. Bring 4 cups of the cold water to a boil in an enamelware coffee pot; you can also use a stainless steel or enameled saucepan, but these are less convenient. While the water is heating, place the ground coffee in a small bowl. Break the egg into the bowl, then toss in the eggshell, if desired. Stir the mixture well with a spoon, breaking the eggshell (if using) into smaller pieces. The mixture should be well blended and somewhat pastelike.

2. When the water has come to a full boil, stir the coffee mixture into the pot. Adjust the heat to prevent the pot from boiling over, and boil gently for 3 minutes.

3. Remove the pot from the heat and immediately stir in the remaining ¾ cup cold water; this helps settle the grounds. Let the coffee stand for 10 minutes. You may wish to pour the coffee through a fine-mesh strainer into serving cups to catch any sediment, or you can simply pour the coffee into the cups slowly, letting any sediment that gets into your cup settle to the bottom.

Note: This coffee is fairly mild, but I recommend you try it and see how you like it. (I tend to drink very strong coffee most of the time, but also really enjoy this mild egg coffee.) For a stronger coffee flavor, increase the amount of ground coffee by a tablespoon or two, adding a little cold water to the egg mixture if it is too dry. You could also use a dark-roast coffee such as a French roast.

Gravlax

Gravlax is a classic Scandinavian dish of fresh salmon that is cured for a few days with salt, sugar, and dill. Its intense color and silky texture make it popular in Danish *smørrebrød,* open-faced sandwiches (page 210), but it also appears on the menu at French and New American restaurants as a starter course. Chef Bill Gregoire says this recipe was one of the most popular starting plates when he was chef at Sophia and Yvette, two related restaurants that were in the St. Anthony Main riverside district of Minneapolis. **Note:** Even after curing, the salmon is perishable and should be eaten within a week. The instructions here are for preparing a whole side of salmon, but you can use half a side (cut in half crosswise, not vertically) and simply halve the remaining ingredients to make a smaller batch.

12–15 APPETIZER SERVINGS

1 (4- to 5-pound) skin-on salmon side (see Note below), rib bones removed

1½ cups sugar

¾ cup coarse kosher salt

1 tablespoon freshly ground black pepper

2 large bunches dill (fronds, not seed heads)

Honey-Mustard Sauce (page 202), for serving

Capers, for serving

Finely chopped onions, for serving

Baguette slices, mini pumpernickel bread, rye crackers, or lefse (page 213), for serving

1. Rinse the fish and pat dry. Use tweezers to remove the pinbones that run up the center of the fillet; you can feel them by running your finger across the midline.

2. Stir together the sugar, salt, and pepper in a mixing bowl. Pack the sugar mixture firmly onto the flesh side of the salmon. Coarsely chop the dill (including the stems) and use it to completely cover the salmon.

3. Wrap the salmon tightly in plastic wrap. Place the salmon, skin side up, on a large rimmed baking sheet. Place another baking sheet on top, and add a few heavy cans of food. Refrigerate for 3 days, changing the plastic wrap each day to drain off the liquid that will accumulate.

4. To serve, scrape off the dill and sugar mixture. Slice the salmon paper-thin with a very sharp chef's knife: Hold the knife almost flat and cut toward the tail, leaving the skin behind. The skin acts like an anchor, making it easier to slice. Discard the first slice, which will have way too much dill.

5. Serve the slices with Honey-Mustard Sauce, capers, chopped onions, and bread or crackers. Refrigerate leftovers and serve within 7 days.

Note: Because this fish is not cooked, ensure that the fish you purchase is sushi grade to avoid problems with microorganisms present in raw fish. Freezing at −10°F for a week will also ensure that the fish is safe to use in this preparation.

Honey-Mustard Sauce

This is a great accompaniment to thinly sliced Gravlax (page 200) or smoked fish.

ABOUT ¾ CUP

½ cup Dijon mustard
2 tablespoons honey
2 tablespoons white wine vinegar
¼ teaspoon ground white pepper
¼ cup sunflower oil or extra-virgin olive oil

Stir together the mustard, honey, vinegar, and pepper in a mixing bowl. Gradually whisk in the oil; whisk until smooth. Refrigerate until ready to serve.

Recipe from CHEF BILL GREGOIRE

Lutefisk

There is probably no dish that has a closer association with Minnesota. Lutefisk (*LOOT-tuh-fisk*) is dried cod that has been rehydrated with lye, and it is a polarizing food: Either you love it or you hate it. It is traditionally served during the Christmas season and often featured at church-hall holiday suppers in communities with heavy Scandinavian populations. The version here comes from Bill Gregoire, whose family tree includes branches in both Sweden and France. The Gregoire family, who settled in Murdock in the late 1800s, has been preparing lutefisk with this recipe for more than 70 years, although Bill notes that they originally used water rather than wine. The Gregoires purchase freshly made lutefisk in bulk, not frozen and prepackaged; Bill looks for pieces from the thicker part of the cod loin, noting that the tail end has more gristle. He cautions that the lutefisk must not be overcooked, because it will fall apart.

2½ pounds lutefisk, skin removed

1 large yellow onion, coarsely chopped

2 cups dry white wine, or as needed

1 cup (2 sticks) unsalted butter, cut into chunks

Salt and freshly ground black pepper

Plenty of melted butter, for serving

Boiled potatoes (peeled), for serving

Lingonberry preserves or cranberry sauce, for serving

"SERVES 4 OR 5 BRAVE SCANDINAVIANS"

1. Preheat the oven to 400°F. Rinse the lutefisk very well and cut into four or five portions.

2. Scatter the onion in the bottom of a glass baking dish (don't use aluminum, which will react with the lye). Arrange the lutefisk on top of the onions in a single layer. Add the wine, using just enough to moisten the bottom of the lutefisk. Scatter the butter chunks over the lutefisk and onions. Sprinkle liberally with salt and pepper.

3. Cover the dish and bake for 10 minutes. Uncover and bake for about 10 minutes longer, monitoring closely. The lutefisk is done when a paring knife inserted in the thickest part of the fish feels hot when removed and touched. Do not overcook; the fish should not go over 150°F. Serve with melted butter, boiled potatoes, and lingonberry sauce.

THE MAKING OF LUTEFISK

It's no surprise that America's largest lutefisk processor — indeed, one of the *only* places that still makes the stuff — is in Minnesota. Olsen Fish Company, in northeast Minneapolis, has been cranking out this Nordic specialty since 1910, and sales, like the odor of the fish, are still strong. (Sorry, couldn't resist.) The company acquired its biggest rival, Mike's Fish and Seafood of Glenwood, in 2006, and may now be the largest lutefisk plant in the world.

Lutefisk starts out as fresh cod, which is caught, filleted, and kiln-dried in Norway until stiff. The stockfish, as it's now called, is shipped to Olsen's. Some is bought in that form by East Africans who have moved to the Twin Cities, but the bulk of it is turned into lutefisk. The fish is soaked in water for several days, then skinned. Next it's soaked for several days in lye (*lut* means "lye" in Norwegian) until it's soft. The fish is then soaked in clear water for about a week, with frequent changes of water, to remove the lye; it also spends time in a hydrogen peroxide bath to lighten the color. The lutefisk is now ready to cook. Hungry yet?

Recipe from HOWIE WALBERG

Värmland Potato Sausage

This version of Swedish potato sausage uses only salt, pepper, and onions for seasoning the mixture of potatoes, beef, and pork, skipping the nutmeg and allspice found in some other Swedish potato sausage recipes. The resulting sausage has a clean, meat-and-potatoes flavor that is surprisingly rich and savory. Potato sausage is served at Thanksgiving and Christmas, and occasionally at Easter, in many Minnesota households where Scandinavian traditions are held dearly. (For more information on potato sausage, see page 207.) **Note:** You should be familiar with preparing cased sausage before attempting this recipe. The casings, which are sold packed in salt and are available at a good butcher shop, must be soaked overnight. You will need a large metal or plastic pan that holds at least 4 gallons and a sausage stuffer for this recipe.

ABOUT 22 POUNDS; 15–20 RINGS

1½ pounds beef casings, refrigerated overnight in water to cover

15 pounds Yukon Gold, russet, or white potatoes

3 medium yellow onions, each cut vertically into 8 wedges

4 pounds ground beef

2 pounds ground pork

3½ tablespoons salt, or as needed

2½ teaspoons freshly ground black pepper, or as needed

1. Drain and rinse the casings, then re-cover with fresh cold water. Peel the potatoes and cut them into chunks that will fit into the feed tube of your food processor, transferring the chunks to a kettle of cold water as you work.

2. Prop the large pan up on one end so it sits at an angle. Place a colander over a large mixing bowl. Drain the potatoes. Fit the food processor with the plastic chopping blade, attach the cover, and turn the empty machine on. Start dropping potatoes through the feed tube, including a few onion wedges with each batch, until the machine is a bit more than half full (if you don't have enough in the food processor, the mixture won't be processed finely enough). Process until the mixture is the texture of chopped coleslaw, about a minute after the last potatoes have been added, scraping down as needed. Transfer to the colander and let it drain while you chop another batch. While the next batch is processing, stir the batch in the colander to help extract the starchy liquid. When the next batch is chopped, transfer the first batch to the large pan, spooning the potatoes toward the top of the pan so the starchy liquid drains into the bottom of the pan. Continue until all potatoes and onions have been processed and added to the pan, then drain for about 5 minutes longer.

Recipe continues on page 206

3. Spoon the starchy liquid out of the large pan, adding it to the bowl that was under the colander. This liquid should not be poured down the sink without running a strong stream of water; it can be fed to livestock, if you have any.

4. Add the beef and pork to the pan with the potatoes. Mix with your hands in a kneading, rolling motion for about 5 minutes; the mixture should feel somewhat firm. Sprinkle the salt and pepper over the top and knead for several minutes longer, until the mixture is becoming sticky. Fry a small patty and taste it to check for seasoning; knead in additional salt and/or pepper if you feel it needs it, but don't overseason it; the flavor will "bloom" during the cooking process.

5. Once the mixture is well combined and seasoned to your taste, stuff the casings without delay; the potatoes will turn black if you wait too long. Before stuffing, drain the casings again, and re-cover with cold water. Use a sausage stuffer to fill the casings evenly and plumply, but don't overfill because the sausages will plump up during cooking. Use scissors to cut off the casing when the stuffed portion is about 12 inches long, leaving about 1½ inches of unfilled casing at each end. Hold the sausage in a loop shape and gently drop it into a gallon-size, freezer-weight ziplock bag. Seal and place on a baking sheet. Continue until all of the sausage mixture has been cased and bagged, stacking no more than three deep on the baking sheets to avoid putting too much pressure on the sausages. Freeze without delay. The sausages will keep in the freezer for months.

6. To cook the sausages, preheat the oven to 350°F. Place a frozen loop of sausage in a flat baking dish that holds it comfortably. Add ¼ inch of water to the dish. Cover with foil and bake for 1 hour, turning and re-covering midway through. Turn the sausage again and bake, uncovered, for 30 minutes, turning midway through. Drain and cool the baked sausage and refrigerate, covered, overnight; this allows the flavors to bloom.

7. When you are ready for the final preparation, place the cooked sausage in a skillet and add about ¼ inch of water. Cover and cook over medium heat until warmed through, 15 to 20 minutes. Cut into 1- to 2-inch lengths to serve.

MAKING POTATO SAUSAGE

Howie Walberg, a Minnesotan of Swedish and Norwegian heritage, doesn't characterize his family's potato sausage recipe as Swedish. "Most Swedish potato sausage has nutmeg and allspice in it, and it also has more meat in proportion to the potatoes," he mused when we were talking about the recipe that has been handed down in his family for at least four generations. I did some research after talking with Howie and learned that the version of potato sausage his family makes is attributed to the Värmland district of Sweden (on the border with Norway) — and Howie can trace his ancestry back to his great-grandfather, John Nilson Walberg, who was born in the Värmland district in 1849 and immigrated to America in 1910.

This anecdote illustrates how food can provide a lens into the past, providing information that enriches our understanding of our ancestors. We also learn to appreciate the modern conveniences that we use to prepare heirloom recipes. Howie reflected back to his youth, helping his father prepare the family's annual batch of potato sausage. "We had to grind everything by hand, and we stuffed the casings by pushing the mixture through a funnel. Later on, I got an antique cast-iron sausage stuffer, and that was a lot better than doing it by hand with a funnel. Now, I use a food processor and an electric sausage stuffer. I can make a batch of sausage in a few hours, rather than the whole day it used to take."

One cold day in late fall, I watched Howie and his wife, Cheri, prepare a batch of potato sausage at their Annandale farm; Howie's son Kipp, along with daughter-in-law Carey, were also there to learn how to prepare the traditional family recipe. Although it was cold outside on that November day, the atmosphere in the house was warm as everyone participated in this special ritual, laughing and telling stories as the work progressed. And I know that when the Walbergs gathered together to celebrate Thanksgiving and Christmas and enjoy the fruits of the day's labor, everyone was warmed once again to be taking part in a delicious family tradition.

Howie Walberg

Recipe from MAVIS PETERSEN

Ham Hock and Kale with Potatoes

This delicious, deeply flavored dish is a classic example of the sum being more than the parts. I got the basis for this German-style farmhouse recipe from a discussion with Mavis Petersen, who has lived most of her life on the farm she shares with her husband, Roy, near Wheaton, in western Minnesota. Although they are both retired now, Roy actively farmed for decades, and they also had a huge kitchen garden. Kale was their favorite garden produce, and this was way before it was fashionable. "Years ago I won first prize for my kale at the Traverse County Fair," Mavis mused when we were chatting. "Of course, I was the only one who entered any!" Mavis uses a ham bone that has been picked over but still has some meat on it. I like to use a hock that is fairly meaty, but it's up to you. I also like to perk it up by adding a little cayenne pepper hot sauce to my bowl.

4 SERVINGS

1 ham hock or ham bone (see headnote)

2 quarts water

1 large celery stalk, cut into several pieces

½ onion, cut into large chunks

1 bay leaf

1½ pounds red or Yukon Gold potatoes

¼ cup white rice

1 bunch curly green kale, heavy ribs removed

Salt and freshly ground black pepper

1. Combine the ham hock, water, celery, onion, and bay leaf in a soup pot. Bring to a boil, then reduce the heat so the mixture bubbles gently and cook for 1½ hours. Remove the ham hock and set it aside on a plate to cool. Strain the broth through a fine-mesh strainer into a Dutch oven, discarding the contents of the strainer. You should have about 4 cups broth; refrigerate any extra for other uses.

2. Cut the potatoes into halves or quarters, depending on their size. Add them to a large pot of salted water. Bring the water to a boil, and cook until the potatoes are tender, 15 to 20 minutes. If the potatoes are done before the kale is ready, drain them and keep warm.

3. After you start heating the water for the potatoes, pick the meat off the ham hock, adding it to the broth in the Dutch oven; discard the bone. Return the broth to a boil, then reduce the heat to medium and stir in the rice. Cook, stirring occasionally, until the rice is just tender, 10 to 15 minutes.

4. While the rice is cooking, coarsely chop the kale into 1-inch chunks; you should have 5 to 6 cups. When the rice is just tender, add the kale to the Dutch oven. Cook over medium heat, stirring occasionally, until the kale is tender, 10 to 15 minutes. Add salt and pepper to taste.

5. Serve in soup plates or bowls, ladling the kale-rice mixture over the potatoes.

Köttbullar: Swedish Meatballs

This comes from the recipe collection of Elaine Anderson, a second-generation Swede who lived in Cokato, a small town about an hour west of Minneapolis; it was graciously shared by her youngest daughter, Margaret Anderson. It uses no cream in the gravy, a point that surprised me. The day I asked Margaret about this, three of the seven Anderson siblings were present, and all had something to say. "Mom never used cream," said Sharon, a middle daughter. "I think cream is an IKEA thing," added eldest son Joel. Margaret noted, "We always had boiled potatoes for Christmas, and I remember Mom saving the water for meatball gravy." All agreed that Elaine's meatballs were the most authentic — and the best.

5 SERVINGS

1 egg

⅔ cup dry breadcrumbs

¼ cup finely minced onion

½ teaspoon salt

¼ teaspoon freshly ground black pepper

¼ teaspoon ground allspice

1 pound ground beef

1 tablespoon vegetable oil, or as needed

1 (10.5-ounce) can beef consommé

4 tablespoons salted butter

¼ cup all-purpose flour

1½ cups potato water (see Note)

Pinch of freshly grated nutmeg

Mashed potatoes, for serving (see Note)

Note: Potato water is the water in which potatoes have been boiled. Prepare the mashed potatoes while the meatballs are baking, timing it so the potatoes and meatballs are done at about the same time; use the potato water to make the gravy. In place of the potato water, you could use 1½ cups water with 1 teaspoon flour stirred in.

1. Preheat the oven to 325°F. Beat the egg in a large mixing bowl. Stir in the breadcrumbs, onion, salt, pepper, and allspice. Set aside for 10 minutes. Add the ground beef to the breadcrumb mixture and mix very well with your hands. Shape into 1-inch balls, packing firmly; you should have about 55 meatballs.

2. Warm the oil in a large skillet over medium heat. Add half of the meatballs and brown gently on all sides, shaking the skillet to turn them. (**Tip:** The meatballs won't shake loose unless they are properly browned on the bottom.) Use tongs to gently transfer the meatballs to a 9- by 13-inch baking dish. Cook the remaining meatballs, adding a little more oil if needed. Transfer to the baking dish. Set the skillet aside, retaining the drippings. Add ½ cup of the consommé to the baking dish. Cover tightly with foil and bake for 40 minutes.

3. Transfer the meatballs to a warm serving dish, retaining the pan juices; cover the meatballs and keep warm while you prepare the gravy.

4. Melt the butter in the skillet with the drippings over medium heat. Sprinkle the flour into the skillet, whisking constantly. Cook, whisking constantly, for 3 minutes. Add the potato water, the remaining consommé (a bit less than 1 cup), the liquid from the meatball baking dish, and the nutmeg, whisking constantly. Cook, whisking frequently, until the gravy has thickened, 3 to 5 minutes. Serve the gravy with the meatballs and mashed potatoes.

Smørrebrød: Danish Open-Faced Sandwiches

There are many versions of these classic Danish sandwiches, which are served throughout the day. Prepare several types of *smørrebrød* and arrange them on a platter for an elegant buffet item; offer one of each variety per guest. Tradition dictates that when multiple *smørrebrød* are offered, those featuring fish are eaten first, followed by those topped with meat, and finishing with cheese or vegetable versions. To avoid spilling the toppings, *smørrebrød* are eaten with knife and fork. **Note:** *Rugbrød* is the classic bread for most of the *smørrebrød* listed here. It's a dense, moist, chewy sourdough rye bread shot through with whole rye kernels, cracked rye, and flax or sunflower seeds. The loaf is small, typically about 3 by 5 inches, and it is cut into slices about ¼ inch thick.

PICKLED HERRING *SMØRREBRØD* (per sandwich)

- 1 slice *rugbrød* (see headnote) or other dense, whole-grain rye bread
- 1½ teaspoons unsalted butter, slightly softened
- 4–5 chunks pickled herring, drained and lightly blotted with paper towels
- ½ thin slice small-diameter red onion, rings separated
- A few small sprigs dill (fronds, not seed heads)

GRAVLAX *SMØRREBRØD* (per sandwich)

- 1 small, thin slice light rye bread, such as Jewish rye or limpa
- 1 teaspoon unsalted butter, softened
- ½ teaspoon honey-Dijon mustard
- 3 paper-thin slices Gravlax (page 200)
- 1 cherry tomato or grape tomato, very thinly sliced
- Small cluster of watercress or microgreens
- ½ very thin slice lemon

ROAST BEEF AND PICKLE *SMØRREBRØD* WITH HORSERADISH (per sandwich)

- 1 slice *rugbrød* (see headnote) or other dense, whole-grain rye bread
- 1½ teaspoons unsalted butter, slightly softened
- 1 thick-cut slice rare roast beef (from the deli)
- 1–2 cornichons or other very small pickles, thinly sliced
- 1–2 teaspoons finely diced red or white onion
- 1 teaspoon prepared horseradish

CHEESE AND VEGETABLE *SMØRREBRØD* (per sandwich)

- 1 slice *rugbrød* (see headnote) or other dense, whole-grain rye bread
- 1½ teaspoons unsalted butter, slightly softened
- 1 leaf butter lettuce, gem lettuce, or other similar greens
- 1–2 slices semisoft washed-rind cheese, such as Époisses or Pont l'Évêque
- 1 small radish, thinly sliced
- 2 thin slices seedless cucumber
- 1 teaspoon snipped fresh chives

BEET ROOT AND EGG *SMØRREBRØD* (per sandwich)

- 1 slice *rugbrød* (see headnote) or other dense, whole-grain rye bread
- 2–3 teaspoons cream cheese, softened
- 4–5 whole fresh chive scapes (the hollow, tubular stems)
- 1 small pickled beet, thinly sliced and patted dry
- 1 tablespoon coarsely chopped hard-boiled egg

Spread the bread with the butter or the cream cheese, using enough to coat the bread fairly thickly. Arrange the toppings attractively on the buttered bread, in the order listed.

Recipe from JEAN FLATEN BORGERDING

Norwegian Lefse

Although popular throughout the Scandinavian countries, lefse (*LEFF-seh*) is most closely associated with Norway. This thin, tender flatbread is traditionally smeared liberally with soft butter and sprinkled with sugar, then rolled up and eaten out of hand. This recipe comes from Jean Flaten Borgerding, a second-generation Norwegian-American who hails from Roseau, a town in northwestern Minnesota. (See page 215 for more information on making lefse.) **Note:** This recipe requires advance potato preparation the day before.

To make this recipe, you will need a potato ricer, a lefse griddle (or other large flat griddle), a round pastry board with a fitted pastry cloth (or a large pastry cloth), a grooved rolling pin covered with a cloth sock, a lefse turner, and a stack of thin cotton or linen tea towels.

15 TO 20 LEFSE

5 pounds russet potatoes, peeled and cut into 2-inch chunks

¾ cup (1½ sticks) salted butter, melted

½ cup sugar

½ cup heavy cream

1 teaspoon salt

3 cups bread flour or all-purpose flour (see Note), or as needed

1. Bring a large pot of salted water to a boil. Add the potatoes and boil until just tender. Drain well. Press while still warm through a potato ricer into a large mixing bowl. Stir the butter, sugar, cream, and salt into the warm riced potatoes, mixing well. Let cool, then refrigerate overnight.

2. When you're ready to prepare the lefse, heat the griddle until a few drops of water sprinkled on the surface dance vigorously. Add 2 cups of the flour to the potato mixture and mix thoroughly with a sturdy wooden spoon. The dough should be smooth and somewhat silky; stir in a little additional flour if needed. Roll the dough into balls about 2 inches in diameter, transferring them to a plate in the refrigerator as you work.

3. Generously flour the pastry cloth and the rolling-pin sock, rubbing the flour gently into the pastry cloth. Shape one dough ball into a flattened patty about 3 inches across. Pat between your hands until the edges and both sides are smooth. Place on the floured cloth. Roll the dough from the center outward, rotating the rolling pin a quarter-turn after each stroke; at the end of each stroke, sweep the rolling pin upward slightly so it is raised above the cloth. Continue rolling until the circle is about 14 inches across; it will be very thin.

Recipe continues on page 214

4. Slide the pointed end of the lefse turner carefully underneath the circle at the center, with the flat side of the turner facing down and the handle angled upward very slightly so the tip is pressed gently against the cloth. When the turner is all the way underneath and the tip has come out on the far side, lay the turner flat against the cloth and use a gentle sawing motion to slide it underneath half of the circle until it slips out the side. Reinsert the turner at the center and slide it underneath the opposite side. Reinsert the turner at the center, then lift the circle off the cloth.

5. Hold the circle above the heated griddle so the edge of the circle aligns with the edge of the griddle. Lower the edge of the circle onto the griddle, then rotate the turner quickly and smoothly away from that edge to "unroll" the circle onto the griddle. Cook until the surface is covered with small bubbles and the bottom is lightly spotted, 30 to 45 seconds. Slide the turner underneath the center of the circle, then lift the circle and unroll it back onto the griddle with the uncooked side down. Cook until the second side is lightly spotted; the second side cooks more quickly.

6. Lift the cooked lefse with the turner and unroll it onto a clean tea towel; cover with another towel. Use a clean, wadded-up cloth to quickly wipe any crumbs off the griddle. Reflour the pastry cloth and rolling-pin sock.

7. Roll out and cook another lefse, then unroll it over the first, staggering it slightly; re-cover with the second towel. Prepare a third lefse and unroll it over the other cooked lefse; re-cover with the second towel. When the fourth lefse is cooked, lay it on top of the second towel and cover with a third towel. Repeat until all dough has been rolled and cooked, stacking three lefse between towels in each layer.

8. For storage, fold the cooled lefse individually into quarters. Stack in ziplock bags. The lefse can be refrigerated for several days or frozen for several months, but it is far superior if eaten fresh, the day it is made.

Note: Jean uses a special flour from Canada that is milled from hard wheat. This type of flour has more protein than all-purpose flour and produces more gluten, which helps provide structure to the lefse. Readily available bread flour is a good choice, although many lefse makers use all-purpose flour.

MAKING LEFSE

Many cultures can claim a signature flatbread: the Mexican tortilla, the chapati served in India, the Ethiopian injera, and the French crèpe, to name a few. In the Scandinavian countries — Norway, Sweden, Denmark, and Finland — it's lefse, which is made in several styles with slight variations.

The lefse that's most common in Minnesota is a paper-thin version made with potatoes and flour. It's prepared throughout the state by Minnesotans of Scandinavian descent, particularly around the winter holidays. Some churches and other organizations sell lefse in November and December, and it's sold at markets in towns with large Scandinavian populations.

Although it has few ingredients, lefse can be tricky to make. Jean Borgerding, whose recipe is on page 213, gave me some tips. "You can't use too much flour," she noted, as she rubbed a liberal amount into her pastry cloth and cloth rolling-pin cover. She refloured both each time she rolled out another lefse; once, distracted by my questions, she forgot to reflour the cloth, and the lefse stuck. Lesson learned.

Jean also demonstrated how she lifts the rolling pin up at the end of each stroke, sweeping it away from the dough. "This helps prevent the edge of the dough from folding over on itself," she explained.

Lefse turners are flat sticks with tapered edges that are made for handling the thin dough. It took me a few tries to emulate Jean's deft wrist movements when using the turner to unroll the dough onto the griddle; the first lefse I attempted slid off the stick at the wrong time and crumpled into an undignified mess.

Jean also noted that the griddle needs to be very hot, so that the lefse will cook quickly before it dries out. "Don't let it get too brown, though," she cautioned, lifting the edge of a cooking lefse with her turner to check the underside.

After our morning lefse-making session, we enjoyed a traditional Norwegian luncheon of smoked salmon, fudgelike gjetost cheese, sliced tomatoes and cucumbers, rye bread, cream cheese, and, of course, warm lefse with butter and sugar. Raising her glass of aquavit, Jean gave me the best tip of the day: "Lefse are best when fresh and warm, right off the griddle." I'll drink to that.

Recipe from MAVIS PETERSEN

Grittwurst: Pork and Barley Sausage

Depending on the dialect spoken by the cook, this loose sausage may be called *gritt, stupfgoetta, gritzwurst,* or *kupfwurst.* I encountered this dish across Minnesota, in farming communities that had been settled by Germans. This dish offered a way for farm families to utilize as much of a slaughtered animal as possible. It was traditionally made by simmering a hog's head and picking off the meat, which was then chopped or ground; cooks these days usually use pork shoulder, although some use stewing beef. Barley or steel-cut oatmeal is cooked in the broth, and everything is mixed together. Some versions include a bit of allspice in the blend, which adds a nice flavor.

ABOUT 5 POUNDS (15–20 SERVINGS)

3 pounds lean boneless pork shoulder, cut into 3-inch chunks

1 large onion, cut into 1-inch chunks (Mavis does not use this, but I like it as an option)

2 chicken bouillon cubes, or 2 teaspoons chicken bouillon granules

3 bay leaves

½ teaspoon freshly ground black pepper

1½ teaspoons salt

1 (1-pound) box pearled barley

Vegetable oil, for frying

1. Combine the pork, onion, bouillon, bay leaves, pepper, and ½ teaspoon of the salt in a Dutch oven. Add water to cover the meat completely. Bring to a boil, then adjust the heat so the liquid boils gently and cook until the meat is very tender, about 3 hours. Transfer the meat to a large bowl and set aside. Discard the bay leaves. Let the broth settle, and skim off most of the fat.

2. Measure the defatted broth, and add water if necessary to equal 7 cups. Bring the broth to a boil in the Dutch oven. Add the barley. Cover and adjust the heat so the mixture is simmering. Cook until the barley is very tender, about 50 minutes; stir frequently near the end to prevent scorching.

3. While the barley is cooking, pick through the pork, discarding gristle or excess fat. Grind with a meat grinder fitted with a medium plate (I use a 6 mm plate), or chop in a food processor.

4. When the barley is tender, add the ground pork and remaining 1 teaspoon salt. Stir with a wooden spoon, then mix with your hands once it has cooled a bit; it will be sticky. Pack 1-pound portions into quart-size, freezer-weight ziplock bags, pressing the mixture flat so the packages are easy to store. Over-wrap with freezer paper and freeze until needed (you may also cook a batch immediately, without freezing).

5. To serve, thaw the sausage mixture. Fry in a skillet over medium heat with a little oil. Mavis mixes in a little water and stirs it so it's loose, then serves it spread on bread. Others form patties, fry until crisp, and serve them on buttered toast or pancakes; it is often topped with maple syrup when served this way.

Knife-and-Fork Italian Sausage Sandwiches

Variations on this sandwich have been served in St. Paul since before Prohibition days; it also has been on the menu at some Italian restaurants on the Iron Range (see page 221) for nearly as long. Often going under the potentially offensive moniker "Hot Dago," it is always based on Italian sausage — typically a patty, but occasionally a link — that is generally topped with warm marinara sauce and blanketed with melted cheese. Additional toppings may include fried peppers and onions, giardiniera, or pickled peperoncini peppers. The quality of the ingredients is paramount in this simple construction.

2 SANDWICHES

½ pound hot or mild Italian sausage, casing removed if cased

1 tablespoon extra-virgin olive oil, or as needed

2 (5-inch) lengths of baguette, split horizontally

1¼ cups marinara sauce, preferably homemade

2–4 thin slices provolone cheese, depending on size and your preference

⅓ cup purchased giardiniera-style relish, drained and chopped coarsely, or Pickled Italian Giardiniera (page 224)

1. Divide the sausage into two portions. Shape each portion into an oblong patty about 3 by 5 inches. Warm 1 teaspoon of the oil in a medium skillet over medium heat. Add the sausage patties and cook, turning once or twice, until the centers reach 165°F, about 10 minutes.

2. Meanwhile, brush the insides of the baguette pieces with the remaining 2 teaspoons oil. Warm a griddle or large cast-iron skillet over medium heat. Place the bread, cut side down, on the griddle, pressing down slightly with a spatula. Cook until lightly browned, 3 to 5 minutes. Transfer the bottoms to serving plates, with the cut side up; set the tops aside.

3. When the sausage patties are cooked through, add the marinara sauce to the skillet. Cover the skillet and cook over medium heat until the sauce is warm, about 3 minutes. Top each patty with one or two slices cheese. Re-cover and cook until the cheese melts completely, about 2 minutes longer.

4. Spoon a few tablespoons of the sauce onto each baguette bottom. Top with a cooked sausage patty, then divide the remaining sauce between the sandwiches. Spoon the giardiniera evenly over the sandwiches. Place the baguette tops on the patties at a slight angle so about half of the sausage is exposed. Serve immediately, with knives and forks.

Iron Range Porketta Roast

Like many dishes that are tied to a particular region or ethnic group, porketta has many variations. This version uses fresh fennel as well as fennel seeds, and the pork is cooked with root vegetables to be served with the roast. Leftovers make terrific sandwiches; indeed, some families don't eat porketta as a roast on the day they cook it, instead going straight to sandwiches. If you're not serving it as a roast, you may want to skip the vegetables and use a smaller roasting pan or a Dutch oven. **Note:** This recipe requires the seasoned roast to be refrigerated overnight before cooking.

5 OR 6 SERVINGS

3 tablespoons whole fennel seeds

2 teaspoons whole black peppercorns

1½ teaspoons coarse kosher salt or sea salt

1 fresh fennel bulb, with stems and fronds

4 sprigs parsley, stems removed

6 large garlic cloves, peeled

2 teaspoons dried Italian herb blend, optional

2 tablespoons olive oil

1 (3½- to 4-pound) boneless pork shoulder

1 cup chicken broth or water

1 large white or yellow onion, sliced ¼ inch thick

2 pounds small red potatoes (2 inches across), halved

5–6 carrots, peeled and cut into 1-inch chunks

1. Combine the fennel seeds, peppercorns, and salt in a blender. Process until the fennel seeds are chopped; the mixture should have some texture rather than being completely powdered.

2. Snip the fronds from the fennel bulb. Cut the bulb into quarters. Remove and discard the core from one of the quarters, then cut the cored quarter into chunks. Refrigerate the remaining bulb quarters for later use, discarding the stems. Measure ¼ to ⅓ cup of fronds, tightly packed; discard any remaining fronds. Place the fennel fronds, cut-up bulb quarter, parsley, garlic, and herb blend, if desired, in a food processor. Add the fennel seed mixture. Pulse until finely chopped. Add the oil and pulse a few times to mix.

3. Butterfly the pork roast as follows (or have the butcher do it when you buy it): Place the roast on a cutting board, with one short end facing you. Hold a chef's knife parallel to the cutting board, ¾ to 1 inch above the board. Cut into the roast from the right-hand edge (if you're right-handed); you'll be cutting a slab along the bottom of the roast. When you have cut through to within 1 inch of the left side of the roast, roll the uncut portion of the roast to the left to expose the slab (which is still attached to the rest of the roast). Continue cutting and rolling until the entire roast is opened up and has become a slab ¾ to 1 inch thick. Now cut a few ½-inch-deep slashes into the top surface of the meat.

4. Rub about two-thirds of the fennel mixture over the opened roast. Roll the roast back up, then tie in several places with kitchen string. Rub the outside with the remaining fennel mixture. Wrap in plastic wrap and refrigerate overnight.

5. When you're ready to cook, preheat the oven to 325°F. Unwrap the roast and place it in a roasting pan. Pour the broth around the edges. Cover and bake for 3 hours. After 3 hours, remove the cores from the reserved fennel quarters, then slice the quarters about ½ inch thick. Transfer the roast to a heatproof platter. Scatter the fennel and onion in the bottom of the roasting pan, stirring to coat with the drippings. Return the meat to the pan, turning it upside down so the side of the roast that had been facing down is now facing up. Arrange the potatoes and carrots around the sides of the roast. Re-cover and bake for 1½ hours longer, or until the roast is very tender. Transfer the roast to a deep heatproof platter and tent loosely with foil. Increase the oven temperature to 400°F. Stir the vegetables to coat with drippings, then bake, uncovered, for 15 minutes longer.

6. Use a slotted spoon to transfer the vegetables to a serving bowl. Pull the roast apart with forks and moisten the meat with some of the drippings. Serve the meat with the vegetables.

Iron Range Pasties

There are many opinions on what constitutes the perfect pasty. Everyone agrees that it is a folded-over pastry filled with meat, potatoes, and onions, but then the bickering starts. Should the crust be made with cut-in butter so it's flaky like a piecrust, or is it better to use lard, kneading the dough so the finished pasty holds up to rough handling? Is ground beef acceptable, or must it be hand-chopped? Should there be pork in addition to the beef? Is it better to make the filling with cooked or raw meat? Rutabagas or carrots — or both? Happily, all are delicious. The crust here is a compromise, using both butter and lard, with just a little kneading. The filling uses ground beef, but feel free to hand-chop a chunk of round steak; add some chopped-up pork, too, if you like. Note that the rutabagas and carrots here are diced more finely than the potato so that they will all cook evenly.

6 SERVINGS

CRUST

- 3 cups all-purpose flour, plus more for handling dough
- ½ teaspoon salt
- ½ cup (1 stick) unsalted butter, cut into ½-inch chunks
- ¼ pound chilled lard, cut into ½-inch chunks
- ¾ cup ice water

FILLING

- 1½ cups peeled and diced potatoes
- ¾ cup finely chopped onion
- ½ cup peeled and finely diced rutabaga
- ½ cup peeled and finely diced carrots
- 3 tablespoons chopped fresh parsley, optional
- ¾ pound ground beef
- ½ teaspoon salt
- ¼ teaspoon freshly ground black pepper
- Ketchup, for serving (see Note)

Note: Some prefer gravy as an accompaniment when the pasties are served warm. My husband like his with horseradish, but don't tell anyone hailing from the Iron Range (see box at right).

1. **Make the crust:** Combine the flour and salt in a food processor. Pulse a few times to mix. Add the butter and lard. Pulse a few times, until the mixture resembles very coarse sand. With the motor running, pour the ice water through the feed tube in a thin stream, processing until the mixture begins clumping together. Transfer to a lightly floured work surface and knead a few times. Divide into six equal portions, shaping each firmly into a flat disk about 3 inches across. Wrap and refrigerate for at least 1 hour or up to 1 day.

2. **Make the pasties:** Preheat the oven to 375°F and lightly grease a large baking sheet. Stir together the potatoes, onion, rutabaga, carrots, and parsley, if desired, in a large mixing bowl. Add the ground beef, salt, and pepper. Mix very well with your hands; this is more difficult than it may seem, and requires a fair amount of mixing.

3. On a lightly floured work surface, roll a pastry disk into an 8-inch circle. Mound one-sixth of the filling (about ¾ cup) in the center. Brush the edge with water, then fold the pastry in half over the filling, stretching the top portion as necessary to align the two halves. Seal the edges with a fork. Lightly brush the sealed edge with water, then turn the edge inward to form a rolled-over border. Press together well. Transfer the pasty to the baking sheet, and cut a few small slits in the top of the crust. Repeat with the remaining ingredients.

4. Bake for 50 minutes to 1 hour, or until lightly browned. Serve warm or cold, accompanied by ketchup.

THE IRON RANGE

In the late 1800s, rumors of gold near Lake Vermilion brought an influx of people to northeastern Minnesota, joining the legion of loggers who had arrived a decade earlier to harvest timber. The gold rush was a bust, but in the 1890s, a very large deposit of hematite was discovered in what became known as the Mesabi Range, and the iron boom was on.

For the next 75 years, the Mesabi Range was responsible for over half of the nation's total iron ore output, assisting considerably with the nation's need for steel during World War II. Two more deposits in northeastern Minnesota, the Cuyuna and the Vermilion Ranges, were developed after the turn of the century. Collectively, these three deposits gave the area its name, the Iron Range.

Workers came from Scandinavian countries, Cornwall and other parts of the British Isles, Italy, and Eastern Europe, bringing with them their own foods and cultures. The Iron Range today retains the diverse flavors brought by these immigrants.

Porketta is one of the most iconic Iron Range foods. It's loosely based on the classic Italian dish *porchetta,* which is a boned, spit-roasted suckling pig fragrant with garlic and herbs. The Range version is much simpler, typically prepared with a butterflied pork shoulder roast that is seasoned with fennel, garlic, and black pepper before being rolled and tied; it's slow-roasted and pulled apart or, less commonly, sliced. It's generally served as a sandwich, although some families prepare it with root vegetables and serve it like a pot roast.

Pasties are meat-and-potato-filled hand pies that hail from Cornwall, a peninsula on the southwestern tip of England that was originally a big mining area. When most mines were idled in the late 1800s, Cornish miners immigrated to Michigan, Canada, and Minnesota (as well as Brazil and other places), bringing their food along with them. The pasty originally had a tough crust so it could be carried in a miner's pocket without breaking; modern pasties are less utilitarian and feature more tender crusts.

Other foods that reflect the area's cultural diversity include Czechoslovakian *potica,* a paper-thin pastry rolled up with ground walnuts and spices; *sarma,* a stuffed cabbage roll from Eastern Europe; Italian loose-meat sausage sandwiches; and knishes, a contribution from ethnic Jews. Famous Iron Rangers include Bob Dylan, wine baron Robert Mondavi, actress Jessica Lange, and peace activist Father Philip Berrigan.

THE TWIN CITIES: A MOSAIC OF FOODS

The first Chinese restaurant in Minnesota was the Canton, opened in Minneapolis by the Sing brothers in 1883. In those days, it seemed exotic. Since then, restaurateurs from all corners of the globe have brought flavors of their homelands to enrich the local dining scene. Numerous specialty markets also make it possible for Twin Cities cooks to buy ingredients ranging from asafetida to za'atar. Although the Twin Cities don't boast anything on the scale of New York's Chinatown, there are areas where foods from a particular region hold sway.

EAT STREET is a 17-block stretch on Nicollet Avenue South in Minneapolis dominated by Asian restaurants and shops. Eat Street isn't entirely Asian, though; tucked between the pho restaurants, Chinese markets, and banh mi take-out joints are restaurants offering German, Greek, East African, and Mexican foods, as well as a number of blended or New American eateries.

EAST LAKE STREET holds Minneapolis's main concentration of Hispanic restaurants and markets. In addition to numerous stand-alone shops, many are found in the Midtown Global Market. This enclosed marketplace, in a 1920s-era former Sears building, is home to more than 40 internationally themed businesses. Education and entertainment programs are offered weekly in the central courtyard, which is ringed with restaurants and shops. Camel burgers, pho, tortas and tamales, open-faced Scandinavian sandwiches . . . they're all here. Over a million people visit the market every year. It's also the home of Kitchen in the Market, an innovative shared kitchen space used by caterers, food-truck operators, and startup food entrepreneurs who need access to a licensed commercial kitchen.

THE MIDTOWN FARMERS' MARKET, just east of Midtown Global Market, is a neighborhood source for fresh, locally grown foods. It reflects the cultural diversity of the area, and includes Hmong, Latino, and Native American vendors (including Dream of Wild Health, page 104). Nearby, the Minneapolis American Indian Center and Little Earth of United Tribes mark the heart of the Twin Cities' American Indian community, the largest urban population of Native Americans in the country. Little Earth is a public housing complex geared toward assisting Natives and is home to members of 32 different tribes. The Little Earth Urban Farm garden, established in 2010, provides residents with fresh food as well as the opportunity to work the land in ways similar to methods used by their forebears.

THE CEDAR-RIVERSIDE AREA OF MINNEAPOLIS (also known as the West Bank) is one of the Twin Cities' most culturally diverse neighborhoods. Roughly half of the residents in this vibrant area are recent immigrants. Nearly one-third of Somalis residing in the United States live in Minnesota, and Cedar-Riverside holds the state's largest concentration of Somalis and other East Africans. The area hosts numerous food outlets, including halal meat stores, African restaurants, and storefronts selling take-out foods.

ST. PAUL is the center of the Italian-American community in the Twin Cities. A wave of Italian immigrants arrived in Minnesota in the early 1900s; many settled along the Mississippi River west of downtown St. Paul, eventually expanding northward into the area along 7th Street. Many Italian eateries and shops opened nearby, including Cossetta's, a neighborhood anchor since 1911, which recently enjoyed a complete remodel and expansion. North of downtown, the Swede Hollow and Railroad Island neighborhoods also saw heavy Italian influx in the 1900s and were home to many Italian shops and restaurants; Yarusso Brothers Restaurant, on Payne Avenue, has been open for more than 80 years.

THE NEIGHBORHOODS NORTH OF DOWN-TOWN ST. PAUL are home to the Twin Cities' largest concentration of Hmong, a group of clans from the mountainous regions of Southeast Asia. After the Vietnam War, many Hmong were forced off their lands into refugee camps, eventually immigrating to America; the Twin Cities is home to the country's fastest-growing Hmong population. Two

major Hmong cultural shopping hubs are Hmong-Town Marketplace on Como Avenue and Hmong Village on Johnson Street. Both are warehouses divided into stalls. Traditional Hmong foods are available, as are crafts and other goods. Although Hmong food is similar to Thai food, it typically features more herbs, as well as animal parts often shunned by Americans. I remember sitting down to a meal with a group of Hmong elders after I'd given a presentation — aided by translators — about foraging. I took a portion of larb, a dish that appears on many Thai menus, usually made with chicken or beef. This version, however, was made with tripe, and the elders watched as I took my first bite. I guess I passed the test, because my smile of appreciation was met with a lot of hand-shaking and nods of approval on their part. The language of food is universal and can transcend cultural barriers.

Pickled Italian Giardiniera

Giardiniera means "garden" or "woman who works in the garden" in Italian. This recipe is an adaptation of my Italian grandmother's hot-pepper giardiniera. Grandma Norek made hers almost entirely with hot peppers and a goodly amount of coarsely chopped garlic, with just a little celery to add bulk. It was hotter than blazes. My version is a mixed-vegetable relish with just a hint of heat. Grandma covered the pickled peppers with olive oil, but a vinaigrette-type mixture is used here (don't use olive oil for this, because it turns solid in the refrigerator). It's great on the Knife-and-Fork Italian Sausage Sandwiches (page 219), hot dogs, grilled sausage, or any other sandwich that needs a bit of crunchy kick. You will need two clean pint canning jars with lids and bands.

ABOUT 2 PINTS

1 quart cider vinegar

1 cup coarse kosher salt or canning/pickling salt (do not use iodized salt)

1 large celery stalk

1 cup very small cauliflower florets, no larger than ½ inch across

1 cup diced red bell pepper

1 cup diced carrots

3–4 serrano chile peppers, halved vertically and sliced crosswise ⅛ inch thick

3 tablespoons coarsely chopped garlic

½ cup sliced pimiento-stuffed green olives (use small olives, not large ones)

¾ cup white wine vinegar

6 tablespoons cold water

6 tablespoons sunflower oil or grapeseed oil

1. Combine the cider vinegar and salt in a large ceramic or glass bowl. Stir until the salt is completely dissolved and the mixture is clear.

2. Cut the celery in thirds lengthwise, then cut the lengths crosswise ¼ inch thick. Add to the vinegar brine, along with the cauliflower, bell pepper, carrots, serrano chile peppers, and garlic. Stir well and cover with plastic wrap. Let stand at room temperature for 24 hours, stirring several times.

3. Drain the vegetable mixture in a fine-mesh strainer (save the brine in a bottle to use as a seasoning in other recipes, or discard it). Return the vegetable mixture to the ceramic bowl. Add the olives and stir well. Pack the vegetable mixture into two clean 1-pint canning jars. Whisk together the white wine vinegar, cold water, and oil in a bowl. Add enough of the vinegar mixture to each jar to completely cover the vegetables, pressing with a spoon to submerge the vegetables in the brine. Seal with a lid and screw-top band. Shake each jar gently in a side-to-side motion to remove air bubbles, then top off with more of the vinegar mixture if necessary.

4. Store in the refrigerator. Let mellow for a few days, then shake before using. It keeps for months.

Chilaquiles with Red Sauce and Chicken

Chilaquiles is a home-style Mexican dish that's not often found in restaurants. It was created to use up leftover fried tortillas that may have gone stale and often includes other leftovers such as sauce and shredded meat. This version uses a mildly spicy red sauce, although *salsa verde*, a green sauce based on tomatillos, works just as well. The quality of the tortilla chips is important in this dish; make sure to get a premium brand that has no seasoning added other than salt.

2 SERVINGS

1 tablespoon vegetable oil

½ cup thinly sliced onion (1-inch lengths)

¼ teaspoon ground cumin

1½ cups Roasted Ranchero Sauce (page 228) or good-quality purchased salsa

2½ ounces top-quality tortilla chips, such as Whole Grain Milling tortilla chips

¾ cup shredded cooked chicken

½ cup shredded Monterey Jack cheese

2 teaspoons unsalted butter

2 eggs

Leaves from a few sprigs cilantro

¼ cup crumbled Cotija cheese or feta cheese

1. Heat the oil in a large skillet over medium heat. Reserve about half of the sliced onions. Add the remaining sliced onions and the cumin to the skillet and cook, stirring occasionally, until the onions are tender-crisp and beginning to brown, about 5 minutes. Add the ranchero sauce to the skillet and cook over medium-high heat, stirring frequently, until any thin liquid cooks away, 2 to 5 minutes. Stir in the tortilla chips and chicken, mixing very well; some of the tortilla chips will break as you stir, and that's okay. Cook for 1 to 2 minutes, stirring several times.

2. Remove the skillet from the heat and sprinkle the Monterey Jack over the top. Cover and set aside while you prepare the eggs.

3. In another skillet, melt the butter over medium heat and cook the eggs over easy. To serve, divide the tortilla mixture between the serving plates. Top each portion with a fried egg. Sprinkle with cilantro leaves and the remaining sliced onion. Sprinkle with the Cotija. Serve immediately.

Elote: Grilled Sweet Corn with Mexican Cheese

The chopped cilantro is not always included in this dish, but it adds a wonderful, fresh flavor note. Try it and see what you think. Additional variations are listed below.

4 ears sweet corn, husked

½ cup mayonnaise

1 tablespoon lime juice

1 teaspoon ground ancho chile powder or chili powder blend

½ teaspoon smoked paprika, optional

½ cup finely crumbled Cotija cheese (about 1¾ ounces)

¼ cup finely chopped fresh cilantro, optional

1. Preheat the grill for direct high-heat grilling. While the grill is heating, bring a large pot of water to a boil. Add the corn and simmer until tender, about 10 minutes. Transfer the corn to a plate.

2. While the corn is cooking, stir the mayonnaise, lime juice, ancho chile powder, and paprika, if desired, together in a small bowl. Combine the cheese and cilantro, if desired, on a large plate, mixing with your hands.

3. Grill the ears of corn, turning occasionally, until roasted-looking and darkened in spots, about 5 minutes. Remove the corn from the grill. Brush the corn liberally with the mayonnaise mixture, then roll in the cheese mixture. Serve immediately.

Variations

- Use a mixture of half mayonnaise and half sour cream (or crema, a Mexican sour cream).

- Omit the lime juice from the mayonnaise mixture. Serve each ear of corn with a lime wedge so people can add their own to taste.

- Substitute grated Parmesan cheese or finely crumbled feta cheese for the Cotija.

- Omit the ancho chile powder from the mayonnaise mixture. Serve the corn with hot sauce.

- Substitute cayenne pepper for the ancho chile powder.

- Cut the corn off the cobs and stir the kernels together in a bowl with the mayonnaise mixture and cheese.

- It's not uncommon to brush melted (or softened) butter over the grilled corn before brushing it with the mayonnaise mixture.

Roasted Ranchero Sauce

This type of salsa is made throughout Mexico, although every region — and every cook — has variations. The ancho chile, which adds a special flavor, can be found in most large grocery stores or in specialty Mexican markets. This chile is often dusty, so wash it briefly before using it. Serve this as you would any salsa, or use it in recipes; it works very well for the Chilaquiles with Red Sauce and Chicken (page 225) and is fabulous on the Duck Carnitas Tacos (page 76).

ABOUT 3 CUPS

1 dried ancho chile

1 teaspoon vegetable oil, or as needed

1½ pounds Roma tomatoes, halved vertically and cored

½ white onion, cut into several wedges

4 garlic cloves, peeled

1 serrano chile pepper, halved vertically, stem, ribs, and seeds removed

8 sprigs cilantro, thick stems removed

1½ teaspoons salt, or as needed

A few lime wedges, if needed

A bit of sugar, if needed

1. Position an oven rack at the top of the oven and preheat the broiler. Break the ancho chile open, then pull out and discard the stem. Pull the pepper apart into big chunks, picking out and discarding the seeds. Simmer the chile in a small saucepan with water to cover until the chile is soft, 5 to 7 minutes. Drain and transfer the chile to a blender.

2. Line a large rimmed baking sheet with foil. Rub the oil over the foil. Place the tomatoes, cut side down, on the baking sheet. Add the onion wedges, garlic cloves, and serrano chile pepper halves (cut side down). Broil until each vegetable piece is roasted as described below, removing individual pieces as they are done and transferring them to the blender except for the serrano halves, which you should transfer to a cutting board. **For the garlic,** broil for 7 to 13 minutes, until the surface is browned; turn over when the first side is done. **For the serrano chile pepper,** broil for 10 to 12 minutes, until the skin is blackish bronze and blistered. **For the tomatoes,** broil for 10 to 15 minutes, until large areas of the skins are blackened and the flesh is tender but not mushy. **For the onion,** broil for 12 to 18 minutes, until softened and lightly charred in spots; break apart into smaller portions as they begin to soften.

3. Scrape the blistered skin off the serrano pepper. Transfer the pepper to the blender; for a less-spicy sauce, use only half.

4. Add the cilantro and salt to the blender. Pulse a few times, then blend until fairly smooth. Taste and add additional salt, a few squeezes of lime juice, or a bit of sugar, according to preference. Refrigerate in a clean jar until ready to use. The sauce will keep for about a week.

Cantaloupe *Horchata*: Mexican Rice Drink

Horchata is a very refreshing drink that's made by blending a mixture of uncooked rice soaked in water with cinnamon and, sometimes, almonds. Although it's not difficult to make in the traditional fashion, it's a lot easier to use purchased, nondairy rice milk. Updated versions include fruits or vegetables in addition to the cinnamon. Serve it over ice for a very refreshing beverage; it's good any time of day, but it is particularly welcome on a hot, sunny afternoon.

SERVES 3

2 cups chilled rice milk

1 cup cubed cantaloupe

2 tablespoons honey

¼ teaspoon (scant) vanilla extract

¼ teaspoon ground cinnamon

Combine the rice milk, cantaloupe, honey, vanilla, and cinnamon in a blender. Process until smooth. The beverage may be served straight from the blender; for the smoothest *horchata*, strain through a fine-mesh strainer before serving. Serve over ice.

Variations

- Use 1 cup rice milk and 1 cup almond milk.

- Substitute 1 cup diced, seeded cucumber for the cantaloupe. Reduce the honey to 1 tablespoon.

- Omit the cantaloupe. Add four or five fresh mint leaves to the mixture, and increase the honey to 3 tablespoons. This version yields slightly less of the beverage, and will serve two.

- Substitute 1 cup fresh strawberries, raspberries, or blueberries for the cantaloupe.

- For an adult version, add a jigger of dark rum to the mixture.

IMMIGRANTS OF DISTINCTION

During the writing of this book, I was delighted to see that two local chefs/food entrepreneurs were honored with a special award. Chefs get awards all the time, but this one was different. It was the 2015 Immigrant of Distinction Award, given by the Minnesota/Dakotas chapter of the American Immigration Lawyers Association to Enrique Garcia Salazar and Sameh Wadi.

Enrique emigrated from Mexico in 1993 and founded La Loma with his Mexican-born wife, Noelia Urzua. From its beginnings as a coffee shop, La Loma has grown into a six-restaurant business famed for handmade tamales. La Loma also offers catering, and its wholesale division supplies frozen tamales to numerous grocery stores.

Sameh Wadi was born in Kuwait and came to Minnesota in 1997 to join his family, who had gradually moved to Minnesota over the previous decade. Sameh and his brother, Saed, founded the white-tablecloth restaurant Saffron, then the food truck World Street Kitchen, which became a bricks-and-mortar restaurant that was named one of America's top 50 new restaurants by *Bon Appétit* magazine in 2013. In 2015, Sameh authored *The New Mediterranean Table,* a book that will surely go on to great critical acclaim.

Hmong Chicken Larb

This dish has a lot of similarities to Thai larb. Many say that larb is the national dish of the Hmong; I shared larb with Hmong elders on several occasions in St. Paul, and it was considered a must-have dish whenever they gathered together for a meal. This dish is best when the chicken is hand-minced, which produces a far better texture than chopping in a food processor. **Note:** This dish is often pretty spicy; adjust the amount of hot peppers to suit your taste. If your table guests include people who can't handle the heat, serve it "Minnesota nice," with the chopped peppers (or, less traditionally, Sriracha sauce) on the side rather than in the dish.

4 OR 5 SERVINGS

1 (1¼- to 1½-pound) boneless, skinless chicken breast, cut into cubes

½ teaspoon salt, or as needed

¼ cup chicken broth

1½ tablespoons toasted rice powder (see Note)

1½ tablespoons fish sauce (see headnote on page 232)

1 tablespoon lime juice, or as needed

¼ teaspoon ground white pepper

1–3 Thai bird chile peppers, finely minced (see headnote)

1 garlic clove, minced

⅓ cup chopped fresh cilantro

¼ cup chopped fresh mint

1 tablespoon chopped fresh lemongrass, white part only

4 scallions, thinly sliced

1 head butter lettuce, Boston lettuce, or red leaf lettuce

1 lime, cut vertically into 8 wedges

2–3 carrots, peeled and sliced a generous ⅛ inch thick on a sharp diagonal

1 cucumber, sliced ⅛ inch thick

Hot cooked sticky rice or white rice, for serving

1. Mince the chicken finely with a very sharp knife. Note that it helps to roll and turn the mixture as you mince; if you're having trouble handling the full amount at once, divide it into smaller batches. The texture should be like very coarsely ground pork sausage, with some pieces up to ¼ inch across. Sprinkle the minced chicken with ¼ teaspoon of the salt.

2. Heat the broth in a large skillet over medium heat. Stir in the chopped chicken and cook, stirring constantly, until the meat turns white and most of the liquid has cooked away, 7 to 10 minutes; the largest pieces must be completely cooked through. Transfer the chicken to a large bowl (discard excess cooking liquid) and set aside until cooled to warm room temperature.

3. Add the rice powder, fish sauce, lime juice, remaining ¼ teaspoon salt, the white pepper, minced chiles, and garlic to the bowl with the chicken. Mix well with a wooden spoon. Add the cilantro, mint, lemongrass, and scallions, and stir gently to combine. Taste for seasoning, and add additional lime juice and/or salt to taste.

4. Separate the lettuce leaves and arrange on a platter, along with the lime wedges, carrots, and cucumbers. Place the larb in a pretty serving bowl. Serve with hot rice.

Note: Toasted rice powder is available at Asian markets. To make your own, toast uncooked sticky rice (also called sweet rice) in a dry cast-iron skillet over medium heat, stirring constantly, until it is golden brown, about 5 minutes. Let cool, and pound to a powder with a mortar and pestle, or grind in a clean coffee grinder.

Somali Lamb or Goat Stew

You may substitute about 2 pounds bone-in meat for the boneless meat in this tasty stew. **Note:** Injera is a thin, spongy sourdough flatbread about a foot across that is served in many parts of East Africa. *Anjero* is the Somali version; it has a similar spongy texture, but it is the size of a dinner plate or smaller. You may be able to find injera or *anjero* at a market that caters to East Africans. Naan is an Indian flatbread that also works well, and it is increasingly available in supermarkets.

6 SERVINGS

1¼ pounds boneless lamb or goat, cut into 1-inch chunks

½ teaspoon salt, or as needed

¼ cup vegetable oil

1 onion (any color), diced

1 tablespoon minced garlic

1¼ teaspoons ground turmeric

½ teaspoon ground cinnamon

½ teaspoon ground cumin

½ teaspoon ground coriander

½ teaspoon ground cardamom

½ teaspoon ground fenugreek

Pinch of ground cloves

1 (8-ounce) can plain tomato sauce

½ cup water

2 tablespoons tomato paste

1 pound russet potatoes, peeled and cut into ¾-inch cubes

2 carrots, sliced a bit thicker than ⅛ inch

½–1 serrano chile pepper, thinly sliced, then coarsely chopped

½ teaspoon freshly ground black pepper, or as needed

⅓ cup chopped fresh cilantro

One of the following, for serving: injera, *anjero*, or naan (see headnote); Italian or French bread; or hot cooked polenta or grits

1. Sprinkle the lamb with the salt. Heat the oil in a Dutch oven over medium heat. Add the onion and cook, stirring frequently, until nicely browned, about 10 minutes. Add the garlic, turmeric, cinnamon, cumin, coriander, cardamom, fenugreek, and cloves, and cook, stirring constantly, until fragrant, about 30 seconds. Add the lamb, stirring to coat with the spices. Cook, stirring several times, until lightly browned on all sides, about 5 minutes.

2. Stir in the tomato sauce, water, and tomato paste. Scrape the bottom of the Dutch oven to incorporate the crust of spices on the bottom. Adjust the heat so the mixture is simmering. Cover and cook, stirring occasionally, until the lamb is just tender, 45 to 60 minutes. (If you're using bone-in meat, it may take longer; add a little water if it seems to need it.)

3. Add the potatoes, carrots, serrano chile pepper, and black pepper. Re-cover and cook until the potato and carrot pieces are tender but not mushy, 30 to 45 minutes. Stir in the cilantro. Taste, and add salt and pepper as needed. Serve with one of the breads, or with polenta or grits.

Busy-Day Pho: Vietnamese Beef Noodle Soup

Authentic beef pho (pronounced *fuh*) features a rich broth made from marrow bones and beef chuck, simmered for hours with spices. The version here starts with beef broth, which saves quite a lot of time. Powdered gelatin helps provide some of the richness of long-simmered stock. When buying fish sauce, look for one in a glass bottle that is fairly light in color; dark fish sauce has been on the shelf too long. Three Crabs is my favorite brand, but Thai Kitchen is easier to find. Serve the pho in big soup bowls, accompanying each with a soupspoon and pair of chopsticks. Vietnamese diners I've seen usually hold chopsticks in the right hand to grab the noodles and beef, with the spoon in the left hand for the broth; slurping is considered polite.

4 GENEROUS SERVINGS

1 (3-inch) piece fresh gingerroot, halved vertically

2 large shallots, halved vertically

1 teaspoon vegetable oil, or as needed

6 cups top-quality beef broth, purchased or homemade

3 tablespoons fish sauce, or as needed (see headnote)

2 tablespoons sugar, or as needed

2 teaspoons whole fennel seeds

2 teaspoons whole coriander seeds

2 whole star anise

2 whole cloves

½–¾ pound beef sirloin steak, trimmed of exterior fat before weighing

8 ounces dried flat rice noodles

1 packet (¼ ounce) unflavored gelatin

¼ cup cold water

6 ounces fresh bean sprouts

20 sprigs cilantro, thick lower stems removed

4 leafy sprigs Thai basil or regular basil

1 lime, cut into 8 wedges

Squeeze bottle of Sriracha sauce

Squeeze bottle of hoisin sauce, or a small dish with about ½ cup hoisin sauce

1. Position an oven rack in the top position and preheat the broiler. Line a small baking sheet with foil. Place the gingerroot and shallot on the baking sheet and brush with the oil. Broil for 10 to 12 minutes, until well charred on both sides. Transfer to a 1-gallon soup pot. Add the broth, fish sauce, sugar, fennel seeds, coriander seeds, star anise, and whole cloves. Bring to a simmer over medium-high heat, then adjust the heat so the mixture simmers steadily and cook for 30 to 45 minutes.

2. While the broth is simmering, place the steak in the freezer until partially frozen, about 20 minutes. Slice very thinly against the grain, then refrigerate until needed. Near the end of the simmering time, prepare the rice noodles according to the package directions; if they are done before you are ready to serve, drain and rinse the noodles, then place in a bowl of cold water until needed. Sprinkle the gelatin over a bowl containing the ¼ cup cold water. Place the bean sprouts, cilantro, basil, and lime wedges on a serving plate.

3. Strain the simmered broth through a fine-mesh strainer into a large saucepan. Adjust the seasoning to taste, adding more fish sauce and/or sugar until the broth is savory and slightly salty. Stir in the softened gelatin.

4. Divide the noodles (drain if necessary) among four large soup bowls. Bring the broth to a boil. Add the steak slices, separating them with chopsticks. Remove from the heat and immediately divide the broth and steak between the serving bowls. Serve with the garnishes and Sriracha and hoisin sauces so diners can add what they like to their portion.

CHAPTER 7

Fairs, Festivals, and Special Events

THE OUTDOOR FESTIVAL SEASON starts early in Minnesota, when parks and other venues hold maple syrup–making demonstrations from mid-March through early April. After that, from the end of May through October, there is some sort of food-related festival or event going on somewhere in Minnesota nearly every weekend.

Many festivals are designed to highlight a specific food that's associated with the region. In early June, Bullhead Days in Waterville celebrate the homely but locally abundant fish with deep-fried bullheads and other local fare. Kolacky Days, held at the end of July, offer a chance to enjoy Czech culture and food in Montgomery, which bills itself as the Kolacky Capital of the World. Cokato's Corn Carnival, held in mid-August, recognizes the connection between the town and nearby vegetable canneries, which donate fresh corn on the cob for the event. A list of festivals is provided on page 249.

Most Minnesota counties hold a county fair in late summer, giving communities a chance to judge livestock competitions to determine which prizewinners will represent the county at the State Fair. Fairs also offer an opportunity for folks in rural areas to visit with far-flung neighbors while enjoying music, games, and, of course, fair food.

The granddaddy of all is the Minnesota State Fair. This massive, sprawling event in St. Paul is a food lover's mecca that also attracts farmers, families, teens, politicians, music fans, and others from all corners of Minnesota as well as from surrounding states and beyond.

Some farms host weekend events featuring food, music, and crafts. In the cities, food trucks are like a high-end mobile food court, offering a wide array of items at locations including downtown metro areas, farmers' markets, taprooms, fairs, and festivals. Major-league ballparks are also upping their food game, featuring stands from red-hot local restaurants as well as innovative, delicious foods from vendors unique to the ballpark. This final chapter includes 16 make-at-home recipes that let you bring some of these fun foods to your own backyard.

Food Cart Soft Pretzels

These big, soft pretzels are good served warm, with mustard. The sesame seeds are not traditional, but they are a nice addition. **Note:** I find it's easiest to roll out the ropes on a very lightly damp wooden cutting board, which holds on to the dough better than a floured work surface. If your work surface isn't wooden, flour is your best option.

6 PRETZELS

¾ cup water, warmed to about 100°F

1 teaspoon honey

¾ teaspoon active dry yeast (not quick-rise or instant yeast)

2 cups all-purpose flour

1 tablespoon firmly packed light brown sugar

½ teaspoon salt

1 tablespoon unsalted butter, melted and cooled slightly

Vegetable oil, as needed

⅓ cup baking soda

1 egg, lightly beaten with 1 tablespoon water

1½ teaspoons sea salt, pretzel salt, or other coarse salt, or as needed

1½ teaspoons sesame seeds, or as needed, optional

1. Stir together the water and honey in a small bowl. Sprinkle the yeast over the water and stir. Let sit until foamy, about 10 minutes.

2. Combine the flour, brown sugar, and salt in a food processor. Pulse a few times. Add the yeast mixture and butter. Process for 1 minute. Lightly oil a clean mixing bowl. Add the dough, turning to coat. Cover and let rise until doubled, 1½ to 2 hours.

3. Position an oven rack in the top third of the oven and preheat the oven to 425°F. Line a large baking sheet with parchment paper. Coat the parchment lightly with cooking spray.

4. Punch the dough down. Knead a few times on a lightly damp work surface (see headnote). Divide into six equal portions. Roll and stretch one portion into a 24-inch-long rope; if the rope seems too springy, let it rest for a few minutes while you start another one. Form one rope into a horseshoe on the work surface. Cross the ends over, 1 inch from the tips. Twist the crossed area once to form a short braid, then flip the ends onto the bottom of the loop to form a pretzel shape. Press the ends into the loop. Transfer to the baking sheet. Repeat with the remaining dough.

5. Bring about 5 cups water to a boil in a medium nonreactive saucepan. Gradually add the baking soda; it will foam vigorously. When the foam settles, add one pretzel and cook for 60 seconds, turning once. Use a slotted spoon to return it to the baking sheet. Repeat with two more pretzels. Add another ½ cup or so water to the saucepan and return to a boil. Boil the remaining pretzels. Brush the pretzels with the beaten egg, and sprinkle with sea salt to taste; also sprinkle with sesame seeds, if desired. Bake for 10 to 13 minutes, until the pretzels are nicely browned.

Pretzel Dogs

You can serve these on a stick if you want that State Fair vibe. They also freeze well.

Food Cart Soft Pretzels (opposite page), prepared through step 2

6 skin-on, fully cooked beef wieners

⅓ cup baking soda

3 cups very hot water

1 egg, lightly beaten with 1 tablespoon water

1½ teaspoons sea salt, pretzel salt, or other coarse salt, or as needed

2 tablespoons unsalted butter, melted

1. Preheat the oven to 375°F and line a large baking sheet with parchment paper. Coat the parchment lightly with cooking spray.

2. Punch the dough down and transfer to a lightly damp work surface, preferably wooden (see headnote on opposite page). Divide into six equal portions. Roll and stretch one portion into a rope about 24 inches long; if the rope seems too springy, let it rest for a few minutes while you start another one. Wrap the rope around a wiener in a spiral shape, keeping the ends of the wiener exposed. Pinch the dough very well at the ends to seal it together. Repeat with the remaining dough and wieners.

3. Stir the baking soda into the very hot water in a mixing bowl. One at a time, dip each wrapped wiener into the baking soda mixture, letting it soak for about 15 seconds. Transfer to the prepared baking sheet. Brush the dough with the beaten egg, and sprinkle with salt to taste. Bake for 15 to 17 minutes, until the dough is golden brown and the wieners are hot. Brush the pretzel dogs lightly with the melted butter.

FOOD TRUCKS

Since the days of the chuck wagons that served beans and biscuits to cowboys in the nascent West, people have gathered around rolling kitchens and portable pantries when it's time to eat. Ice cream trucks are a more recent example that resonates with anyone who grew up in the 1960s, when summertime play was interrupted by the ding-ding of the Good Humor truck as it made its way up the block, peddling frozen treats to kids clutching their quarters.

Fast-forward to modern times, when chic modern food trucks have become part of the urban scenery in the Twin Cities, and to a lesser extent, Duluth, Rochester, and other cities. Fare ranges from *lengua* tacos, goat burgers, and Indian-spiced mini dough-nuts to more modest foods including cupcakes, ribs, and burgers. Food trucks are self-contained, and include griddles, deep fryers, refrigerators, sanitation stations, and whatever else is needed to prepare and serve food.

Downtown Minneapolis, which has up to 200,000 people on the streets on a busy day, becomes a parking lot of food trucks from May to September.

(In the colder months, downtown denizens troll the Skyway, a system of enclosed, second-story walk-ways that connect buildings in the city core, allowing office workers to walk for blocks in their shirtsleeves even in freezing weather. The Skyway contains dozens of restaurants and other options for quick food — some of it quite good — and is extensively used at lunchtime.)

The rolling kitchens also provide needed ballast to patrons at the many craft-brewery taprooms that are proliferating around the Twin Cities and beyond. Most taprooms have no kitchens, so during busy times, they may host a food truck in the parking lot, allowing patrons to slip out between IPAs to buy tacos, pasties, and other fare offered by the food-truck-of-the-day. Taprooms and food trucks use social media to let patrons know what food will be available at a specific taproom on any given day. Food trucks are also a feature at many farmers' markets.

Food truck fairs are held several times in a typical year, at various locations in and around the greater Twin Cities metro area. Each event includes dozens of food trucks — sometimes 50 or more. Live music is part of the fun, as are beer and wine vendors. For a schedule, visit the Minnesota Food Truck Fair web-site (see Resources on page 270 for the address).

Totchos (Tater Tot Nachos)

Here's another way for Minnesotans to indulge their love of tater tots. In this dish, crisp tots replace tortilla chips for a popular dish that would be equally at home dished up from a food truck, from a stand at the State Fair, or in your backyard. A guilty, messy pleasure! For additional heat, also add a few pickled jalapeño rings to each serving.

4 OR 5 SERVINGS

1 pound ground beef, preferably grass-fed

1 cup diced onion

½ cup diced red or green bell pepper

2 garlic cloves, minced

1 tablespoon top-quality chili powder blend

1 teaspoon dried oregano

½ teaspoon ground cumin

1¼ cups chicken broth, beef broth, or water

2 tablespoons tomato paste

1¼ pounds (6–7 cups) frozen tater tots, preferably extra crispy

2 cups shredded crisp lettuce, such as iceberg

2 tomatoes, diced

1½ cups shredded Colby-Jack or cheddar cheese

2–3 radishes, thinly sliced, optional

2–3 scallions, thinly sliced

¼ cup fresh cilantro leaves

Sour cream, for serving

Prepared guacamole, for serving

Bottled hot sauce, such as Frank's RedHot, Cholula, or Tapatío, for serving

1. Preheat the oven to 425°F, or as directed on the tater tot package.

2. Cook the ground beef in a large skillet over medium heat, stirring frequently to break it up, until the meat is no longer pink, 5 to 8 minutes. Add the onion, bell pepper, and garlic. Cook, stirring occasionally, until the vegetables are beginning to soften, about 5 minutes. Spoon off excess grease. Add the chili powder, oregano, and cumin, and continue cooking, stirring occasionally, until the spices are fragrant, 2 to 3 minutes longer. Stir in the broth and tomato paste. Adjust the heat so the mixture bubbles gently and continue to cook, stirring occasionally, while you prepare the tater tots.

3. Bake the tater tots in the oven as directed on the package. Meanwhile, check on the consistency of the ground beef mixture. It should be moist and slightly saucy, but not soupy. If necessary, increase the heat slightly to reduce the liquid.

4. When the tater tots are golden brown and crisp, divide them among soup plates or wide, shallow bowls. Spoon the ground beef mixture evenly over the tots. Top evenly with the lettuce, tomatoes, cheese, radishes (if desired), and scallions, in that order. Scatter some cilantro leaves over each serving. Dollop a scoop of sour cream and guacamole on one side of each portion, or serve the sour cream and guacamole on the side so each diner can add as much as desired. Have bottles of hot sauce available so each diner can add to taste; it's nice to have more than one kind of hot sauce to cater to different preferences.

Reuben Wontons

I came up with the idea for these after snacking on the delicious Reuben egg rolls at Voyageur Brewing Company in Grand Marais. They serve their egg rolls with Thousand Island dressing, but I prefer a sweet-and-sour egg roll sauce. Although these tasty little bites seem tailor-made for a food truck or the Minnesota State Fair, I've never heard of them at either . . . yet!

ABOUT 20 WONTONS

3 ounces thin-sliced corned beef (sandwich-style slices from the deli)

¾ cup sauerkraut, or as needed, well rinsed and drained

½ cup shredded Swiss cheese

1 (1-pound) package wonton wrappers (you will use about half of the package)

Vegetable oil, for frying

Duck sauce or egg roll sauce, for serving

1. Preheat the oven to 275°F. Line a baking sheet with paper towels.

2. Chop the corned beef coarsely and transfer to a mixing bowl. Wring the sauerkraut well between doubled paper towels or a clean cloth towel to squeeze out as much moisture as you can, then measure. You need about ½ cup of wrung-out sauerkraut; if necessary, rinse, drain, and wring additional sauerkraut until you have ½ cup after wringing. Add the wrung-out sauerkraut and the cheese to the bowl with the corned beef. Mix very well.

3. Arrange four wonton skins on your work surface, separated by an inch or so. Place about 2 teaspoons of the filling in the center of each. Dip your fingertip in water and run it over two edges (around a corner) of a wonton skin. Fold the wonton together diagonally, then press the edges together very well with your fingertips, poking any filling away from the edges to ensure a good seal. Moisten one of the sharp corners on the folded edge. Push your fingertip into the center of the fold to crease it, and bring the two sharp corners together, with the dry corner on top of the moistened corner. Press together very well to seal. Place on a large plate or second baking sheet. Continue making wontons until you run out of filling.

4. Heat the oil to 365°F in a deep fryer according to the fryer directions. Fry the wontons in small batches (two to four at a time, depending on the size of your deep fryer) until richly browned and very crispy, 1 to 1½ minutes. Use a wire scoop or slotted spoon to transfer the wontons to the paper towel–lined baking sheet. Keep warm in the oven as you fry additional wontons. Serve with duck sauce.

Caramel Apple Sundaes

Several booths at the Minnesota State Fair serve variations on this easy dish, and it also appears at various county fairs and food trucks. The key to deliciousness is making your own rich caramel sauce. Some vendors sauté the apples in butter before using them, but I like the dish best when the apples are fresh and crisp, providing a nice contrast to the ice cream and caramel. If you happen to have leftover sauce, it will keep in the refrigerator for weeks in a sealed glass jar; rewarm it slightly before serving.

4 SERVINGS

CARAMEL SAUCE

- ¾ cup sugar
- 2 tablespoons water
- 2 tablespoons corn syrup
- ¼ teaspoon salt
- ½ cup heavy cream
- ½ teaspoon vanilla extract
- 2 tablespoons unsalted butter, cut into ½-inch cubes

- 1 large Honeycrisp or other juicy, crisp apple
- 1–2 pints vanilla or cinnamon ice cream
- ¼–⅓ cup coarsely chopped cocktail peanuts

1. **Make the caramel sauce:** Stir together the sugar, water, corn syrup, and salt in a small heavy-bottomed saucepan. Cook over medium heat, stirring occasionally, until the mixture begins to boil; lift the pan off the heat if it threatens to boil over. Reduce the heat to medium-low and cook, swirling the pan occasionally, until the mixture is light golden in color, about 15 minutes after the mixture starts boiling. Reduce the heat to low and add the cream in a slow stream, whisking constantly; it will spatter and foam up, so take care not to get burned. Whisk in the vanilla. Add the butter one cube at a time, whisking constantly, until all the butter has been added and incorporated. Set aside to cool for 5 to 10 minutes (resist the temptation to sample it right away, as it is very hot).

2. Meanwhile, dice the apple into pieces a bit smaller than ½ inch, discarding the core; you should have about 2 cups.

3. Place several scoops of ice cream into each serving dish. Add about ½ cup apples to each. Spoon about ¼ cup caramel sauce over the apples and ice cream. Sprinkle chopped peanuts over each serving. Serve immediately.

ROOTS FOR THE HOME TEAM, TARGET FIELD, MINNEAPOLIS

Susan Moores is a registered dietitian with some fresh ideas. Rather than preaching about obesity, dieting, and "bad" food, she is working to find ways to make people excited about healthy, fun foods. In 2012, Sue started a nonprofit program called Roots for the Home Team, which hits one out of the park when it comes to combining healthy food and fun times.

The concept is groundbreaking. At its simplest level, Roots for the Home Team sells fresh salads during weekend Minnesota Twins baseball games at Target Field. The Roots cart, located just inside gate 34, features six to eight fresh, new salads each year. But there's more to it than meets the eye.

Each spring, teens who intern with one of several area youth farm programs get together with culinary students and guest chefs at St. Paul College. The young people design salads featuring produce that they will plant, cultivate, and harvest

over the course of the season at various urban garden locations (see Young Farmers on page 104). During the games, the teens pass out salad samples and assemble orders. Proceeds are used to pay the teens, purchase produce from their urban farm programs, and support the farms' enrichment and education programs.

Bringing healthy, delicious salads to a major-league ballpark is a big score for Roots for the Home Team. It's also great for the youth, who gain self-confidence and social skills and get exposure to a side of the business world they might not see otherwise. The program also engages them in the idea of healthy food for its own sake. Rather than getting the message that salads are eaten only by dieters, they discover that the salads they've created are something people appreciate, value, and genuinely enjoy. "Lots of people come back and tell the youth that their salad was the best they ever ate," Sue noted with pride. "The program started as a way to get lovely, fresh food to Target Field, but it has turned into so much more. Everyone benefits — the fans, the community, and especially the young people. They're getting great skills they'll be able to put to use in their future." And that's a home run for everyone.

Mardi Garden Salad

This salad is as delicious as it is pretty, and it's hearty enough to make a filling meal on its own. It was one of the salads offered by Roots for the Home Team in 2015, at its food cart at Target Field, home of the Minnesota Twins. The recipe was developed by youth from the Urban Roots program (page 244), who also grew many of the ingredients used at Target Field at their gardens in East St. Paul. Score one for the home team!

8 SERVINGS

¾ pound new potatoes, cut into ½-inch chunks

1 teaspoon salt

1½ cups shredded green cabbage

1 cup whole-kernel corn, raw or previously frozen

1 (15-ounce) can black-eyed peas, rinsed and drained

1 cup matchstick-cut carrots

1 cup peeled and diced raw beets

¾ cup sliced sugar snap peas

½ cup chopped fresh cilantro

8 cups mixed salad greens

DRESSING AND GARNISHES

½ cup canola oil

¼ cup smoky barbecue sauce

¼ cup lemon juice

¾ teaspoon smoked paprika

½ cup chopped dry-roasted peanuts

Hot pepper sauce, for serving

1. Place the potatoes in a medium saucepan. Cover with water and add the salt. Bring to a boil, then reduce the heat and simmer for about 15 minutes, or until just tender. Rinse with cool water and drain well.

2. Meanwhile, mix the cabbage, corn, black-eyed peas, carrots, beets, sugar snap peas, and cilantro in a large bowl. Divide the salad greens among serving plates, or mound the entire amount on a large serving platter.

3. **Make the dressing:** Whisk the oil, barbecue sauce, lemon juice, and paprika in a small bowl.

4. Stir the drained potatoes into the bowl with the cabbage. Add the dressing and toss gently. Spoon the potato mixture on top of the greens, dividing evenly among the individual plates or mounding over the center of the platter of lettuce. Garnish with the chopped peanuts. Serve with hot pepper sauce on the side.

Wild *Gitigan* Salad

Gitigan (or *gitigaan*) is Ojibwe for "garden," and that's appropriate for this recipe that was developed by young members of Dream of Wild Health, a program that gives Native American youth a chance to reconnect with the land by working in a garden. This dish was in the 2015 lineup of salads offered at Target Field by Roots for the Home Team, an innovative food cart that sells healthy — and delicious — salads at Minnesota Twins baseball games. Many of the vegetables used in this salad at Roots for the Home Team are grown at the Dream of Wild Health farm in Hugo; see pages 104 and 244 for more details.

8 SERVINGS

1 cup wild rice, rinsed

3 cups vegetable broth

4 sprigs thyme

3 cups chopped kale, tough stems removed before chopping

2 teaspoons extra-virgin olive oil

⅛ teaspoon salt

1 (15-ounce) can black beans, rinsed and drained

1 cup chopped yellow bell pepper

1 cup matchstick-cut carrots

1 cup halved or whole ground cherries or quartered cherry tomatoes

8 cups mixed salad greens

DRESSING AND GARNISH

½ cup extra-virgin olive oil

¼ cup lemon juice

1 tablespoon lemon zest

1 teaspoon honey

Salt and cracked black pepper

½ cup shredded Parmesan cheese

1. Cook the wild rice in the broth according to the package directions, adding the thyme sprigs. Let the rice cool and remove the thyme stems.

2. Meanwhile, place the kale in a large bowl. Drizzle with the oil and salt. Use your hands to massage the oil and salt into the kale for 1 minute. Add the black beans, bell pepper, carrots, and ground cherries to the kale. Stir gently to combine. Divide the salad greens among serving plates, or mound the entire amount on a large serving platter.

3. **Make the dressing:** Whisk the oil, lemon juice, lemon zest, and honey in a small bowl.

4. Stir the cooled wild rice into the bowl with the kale. Add the dressing and toss gently. Spoon the wild rice mixture on top of the greens, dividing evenly among the individual plates or mounding over the center of the platter of lettuce. Season with salt and cracked pepper to taste, and garnish with the Parmesan.

Raspberry and Buttermilk Custard Pie
with Golden Grahams Crust

Since 2011, Al Franken, a U.S. Senator from Minnesota, has put on the annual Hotdish Cook-Off for Minnesota's congressional representatives. In 2014, Senator Amy Klobuchar's entry was titled "It's So Cold My Hotdish Froze": a chilled dessert featuring a graham cracker–type crust made from Golden Grahams, a cereal made by Minnesota's own General Mills. Brilliant! I've adapted her crust recipe for a pie rather than a casserole dish and made my own filling featuring fresh raspberries — the pride of Hopkins, Minnesota, and the star of their annual Raspberry Festival.

1 (10-INCH) PIE

CRUST

5½ tablespoons unsalted butter, melted

1½ cups very finely crushed Golden Grahams cereal (about 3½ cups before crushing)

FILLING

2 eggs

1 egg yolk

1 cup plus 2 tablespoons sugar

3 tablespoons all-purpose flour

⅛ teaspoon salt

¾ cup buttermilk

4 tablespoons unsalted butter, melted and cooled slightly

1 tablespoon lemon juice

1 teaspoon finely grated lemon zest

1 cup fresh raspberries

½ teaspoon nutmeg, preferably freshly grated

1. Preheat the oven to 375°F. **Prepare the crust:** Brush the inside of a 10-inch pie plate with a bit of the melted butter. Stir together the remaining butter and the crushed cereal in a mixing bowl. Press firmly into the pie plate. Bake for 10 to 12 minutes; the crust should turn darker and just begin to firm up to the touch. Set on a wire rack while you prepare the filling.

2. **Prepare the filling:** Whisk the eggs and egg yolk in a large bowl until well blended. Whisk in the sugar, flour, and salt. Add half of the buttermilk and half of the melted butter, then whisk well. Add the remaining buttermilk and melted butter, whisking well. Add the lemon juice and lemon zest, and whisk until well blended.

3. Scatter the raspberries evenly into the crust. Pour the buttermilk filling over the raspberries, ensuring that each berry gets a coating of the filling. Sprinkle with the nutmeg. Bake for 10 minutes. Reduce the oven temperature to 350°F and bake for 25 minutes. Cover loosely with a piece of foil, and continue baking for about 15 minutes longer, or until the filling is set but still slightly wiggly in the center. Remove from the oven, and carefully run a knife between the edge of the crust and the pie plate; this makes it easier to remove the slices once the pie cools. Let cool slightly on a wire rack before serving. Serve warm or at room temperature.

FOOD FESTIVALS

All community festivals have food of some sort, but these festivals emphasize the food. Check online listings for each festival, as exact dates change from year to year.

MARCH–APRIL

- Many communities and parks hold maple syrup festivals and events in March or early April. Some of these include Grand Rapids, Lino Lakes, Sandstone, Vergas, and the University of Minnesota Landscape Arboretum in Chaska.

MAY

- Trout Days, Preston; third weekend in May

JUNE

- Cheese Festival, Pine Island; early June
- Rhubarb Festival, Lanesboro; early June
- Bullhead Days, Waterville; early June
- June Bloom Wine Event, Winona; mid-June
- Tater Daze Festival, Brooklyn Park; mid- to late June
- Fireman's Hog Roast and Street Dance, Granada; late June
- Sauerkraut Days, Henderson; last weekend in June

JULY

- Wild Rice Festival, Deer River; mid-July: "world's largest wild rice festival"
- Raspberry Festival, Hopkins; mid-July: "America's raspberry capital"
- Hot Dog Night, Luverne; mid-July
- Bar-b-que and Brew Fest, Deer River; mid-July
- Corn Capital Days, Olivia; mid- to late July
- Zany Zucchini Fest, Pine River; mid- to late July
- Blueberry Festival, Lake George; late July
- Kolacky Days, Montgomery; late July
- Blueberry Arts Festival, Ely; last full weekend in July
- Turkey Days, Frazee; last weekend in July: "home of the world's largest turkey"

AUGUST

- Pie Day, Braham; first Friday in August
- Corn Carnival, Cokato; mid-August
- Rock River Beer Fest, Luverne; mid-August
- Kernel Days, Wells; mid-August
- Turkey Barbecue Days, Ulen; mid-August
- Garlic Festival, Hutchinson; third Saturday in August
- Buttered Corn Days, Sleepy Eye; late August
- Barnesville Potato Days, Barnesville; late August
- Oktoberfest, Pierz; late August

SEPTEMBER

- Taste of the Root River Trail, Peterson and Preston; mid-September
- King Turkey Day, Worthington; mid-September
- Wild Rice Days, McGregor; Labor Day weekend

OCTOBER

- Many communities and parks hold Oktoberfest festivals and events in late September or early October. Some of these include Frazee, Grand Rapids, and Pelican Rapids.
- Harvest Fest, Stillwater; mid-October

Watermelon Wedge on a Stick with Lime and Black Pepper

The Minnesota State Fair is famous for food "on a stick." Bring some of that State Fair vibe home with this fun dish. These are perfect for a garden party, and they make an especially nice ending to a meal of spicy barbecue. Prepare these when watermelons are sweet, juicy, and deep pink; the flavor depends on the quality of the fruit. If you can find seedless watermelons, it will save you some time picking out the seeds. You will need eight sturdy wooden sticks or skewers, preferably round with a sharpened end.

8 SERVINGS

2 center-cut slices from a good-size watermelon (slices should be 7 to 8 inches across and ½ to ¾ inch thick)

3 tablespoons extra-virgin olive oil

2 tablespoons lime juice

1 tablespoon chopped fresh mint, optional

½ teaspoon coarsely ground black pepper

Pinch of ground cumin

1. Cut each watermelon slice into four wedges. Pick out the large seeds; small white seeds can be left in. Lay the wedges in a large baking dish, overlapping slightly if necessary.

2. Whisk together the oil, lime juice, mint (if desired), pepper, and cumin in a small bowl. Pour over the watermelon wedges, turning to coat. Let marinate at room temperature for 30 to 45 minutes, turning once or twice.

3. To serve, blot the wedges lightly with paper towels. Spear each on a wooden stick, pushing the stick through the rind and into the center, toward the tip of each wedge. Arrange on a serving platter.

Variation

Sprinkle a little finely crumbled feta cheese over the wedges on the serving platter.

SQUASH BLOSSOM FARM, ORONOCO

L ocal food. Local art. Local music. That's both the motto and the business model for Squash Blossom Farm, a picturesque 10-acre farmstead in the rolling hills just north of Rochester, where Susan Waughtal and Roger Nelson are living their dream and sharing the joys of an eclectic country life with farm visitors throughout the growing season.

Friends since high school, Susan and Roger shared the dream of one day living on a farm where they could celebrate art, music, and community. Susan is an artist and gardener; Roger is a musician, architect, and passionate bread baker. In 2008, with no experience in farming, they had a chance to buy a 10-acre farm complete with a 100-year-old farmhouse, granary, barn, chicken coop, and the other trappings of small-farm life. They took the plunge and haven't looked back since.

They've developed the farm with features that reflect their permaculture philosophy: an aquaponic system that allows them to both farm fish and grow produce symbiotically, a rainwater collection system, and solar panels on the barn that power the old farmhouse. The granary now houses a farm store, where they sell their farm's eggs, vegetables, honey, and other farm products, along with Susan's artwork and an eclectic selection of vintage treasures and antiques.

During summer, visitors flock to the farm to enjoy food, music, and plain old country fun at the farm's Summer Sundays, which take place from June through September. The Annual Farm Fair and Cow Puja, held at the end of September, is a celebration marking the end of summer and honoring the farm's animals, particularly the cows. LaFonda, the dalmatian-spotted milk cow, and Jitterbug, a jet black Dexter heifer, are decorated for the event, and visitors — particularly kids — enjoy meeting the gentle animals along with the farm's chickens and turkeys. Artisans are on hand to demonstrate their craft, from blacksmithing to wool spinning to spoon carving. Local bands provide music throughout the day, and there's plenty of good food. The highlight is the traditional Puja blessing, a ceremony led by members of a local Hindu temple in which participants offer special treats to the cows and receive the cows' blessing in return.

Susan and Roger keep bees for honey and pollination. Farm-grown vegetables, eggs, and honey are used in their breads, pastries, and pizzas. The wood-fired oven in the new commercial kitchen allows the baking of several pizzas or 30 loaves of sourdough bread at a time. Their hearth-baked breads can be found at the Rochester Downtown Farmers' Market, co-ops, and local restaurants. Squash Blossom Farm also offers a limited number of vegetable and egg CSA shares and plans to offer a bread CSA option down the road.

Blue Ribbon Honey Pecan Pie

One of the highlights at the Minnesota State Fair is the Ag-Hort Building, which houses both the Minnesota honey and bee culture exhibit and the area where entries in juried competitions for foods featuring honey are displayed. This pie recipe won a 2012 blue ribbon in the hotly contested baking category. It was graciously shared by Shannon Gardner, a top-notch baker who notes, "My day job involves editing cookbooks, an appealing way to marry vocation and avocation."

1 (9-INCH) PIE

Pastry for single 9-inch piecrust

2 teaspoons heavy cream, or as needed

1 cup Minnesota clover honey

3 eggs, beaten

3 tablespoons butter

1 teaspoon vanilla extract

Pinch of nutmeg, preferably freshly grated

1 cup chopped pecans

⅓ cup pecan halves

1. Preheat the oven to 325°F. Fit the pastry into a 9-inch pie plate, fluting the edges decoratively. Brush the edges with the cream. Refrigerate until needed.

2. Bring the honey to a boil in a medium saucepan, watching carefully so it doesn't boil over. Remove from the heat. Quickly add the eggs and mix well. Stir in the butter, vanilla, and nutmeg, then add the chopped pecans and stir well. Pour into the pie shell. Sprinkle with the pecan halves. Bake for 30 to 45 minutes, until set in the center.

MINNESOTA STATE FAIR, ST. PAUL

Billed as the Great Minnesota Get-Together, the Minnesota State Fair is the last big gasp of summer. In a state that may be snow-covered for nearly half of the year, that's a big deal — and so is the fair, which takes place on its permanent grounds in St. Paul for 12 days, ending on Labor Day. It's the largest state fair in the country when ranked by daily attendance; on one record-setting day in 2014, over 250,000 people came through the gates.

THERE'S A LOT TO SEE AND DO. The large, vibrant midway and other rides and attractions throughout the fairgrounds attract families and offer places for teens to hang out. Exhibits in the Department of Natural Resources Building educate visitors about Minnesota's natural wonders; the giant outdoor fishpond is stocked with finny critters that give people a chance to actually see what they've been trying to catch all summer. Demonstration barns and a milking parlor provide city dwellers with a look at farm life, and youth come from across the state to show livestock, poultry, rabbits, and other critters. Musical and other performances take place throughout the day at various stages, and nightly at the grandstand, where they are followed by a fireworks display. And of course there's food . . . lots and lots of food, which is the main attraction for some fairgoers.

When it comes to food, the Minnesota State Fair is famous for one thing: food on a stick. Offerings on-a-stick include alligator sausage, deep-fried candy bars, bacon (plain or chocolate dipped), ostrich, nut rolls, grilled chops, bacon-wrapped turkey tenderloins, chocolate-covered cheesecake, pretzel dogs, mashed potatoes (yes,

indeed, and in two varieties), frozen Key lime pie, fruit chunks (fresh, or battered and fried), fried cookie dough, and lots more. One booth offers spaghetti and meatballs on a stick; it's a bit of creative advertising, because only the meatballs are on a stick, while the saucy spaghetti is served in an accompanying dish. Of course, there are the on-a-stick standbys of caramel apples, cotton candy, and corn dogs (at dozens of booths scattered across the fairgrounds, in regular or foot-long sizes; one is never far from a corn dog). Phew!

Plenty of other non-stick foods are sold — some commonplace, some not so much. Popcorn and caramel corn, ice cream, sodas, fresh-squeezed

lemonade, mini doughnuts, fresh potato chips, and French fries are found at state and county fairs all over. But how about beer gelato, Middle Eastern grilled lamb testicles, and bison hot dogs? Specialties like Iron Range pierogi, walleye mac and cheese, beef-tongue tacos, and birch beer give nod to Minnesota's rich and varied heritage. Grease-weary fairgoers will also find simple, fresh fruit, as well as sushi and frozen apple cider push-ups.

THE CREATIVE ACTIVITIES BUILDING is home to numerous juried food competitions, and the bee and honey area in the Ag-Hort Building has competitions especially for foods prepared with honey. Of course, there are also competitions for just about everything else, from crocheting to woodworking.

EMPIRE COMMONS, formerly called the Dairy Building (a name that remains etched in the public memory and is still used), is home to numerous agricultural and environmentally oriented booths, as well as delicious ice cream. But the big draw is the carved butter sculpture busts of Princess Kay of the Milky Way and her court. A new princess is elected annually by the Midwest Dairy Association, chosen from a pool of 12 young women with backgrounds in the dairy industry. Each day during the fair, one of the finalists sits in a refrigerated, rotating glass booth (wearing a jacket, of course; we're not unkind in Minnesota) while a sculptor carves her likeness from a 90-pound block of grade A butter. Each butter head takes about 6 hours to complete, and at the end of the fair, the models take their sculptures home. This unusual event was created to highlight

Minnesota's claim as "butter capital of the nation," and although other states have butter carving, the use of a live model is apparently unique to Minnesota.

There's so much more to see at the Minnesota State Fair that it's worth the trip. If you're in the area just before Labor Day, plan to spend a day . . . and wear loose pants.

Beer-Battered Deep-Fried Cheese Curds

Cheese curds are made in the beginning stage of cheese production, before the cheese is pressed and formed. Fresh cheese curds squeak when eaten, and these are the best for eating out of hand. Curds lose their freshness (and their squeakiness) within a day or two, but they can still be used for deep frying, although squeaky curds are better. Wisconsin is better known for cheese production than Minnesota, but some curds are made in Minnesota — and we can also lay claim to very famous deep-fried cheese curds served at the Minnesota State Fair. The most popular fried curds come from the Mouth Trap in the Food Building, and on a busy day multiple lines snake all the way through the building and out the doors. Choose good-size curds for deep frying, separating any that may have clumped together.

Vegetable oil, for frying
¾ cup all-purpose flour
8 ounces cheese curds, room temperature
1½ tablespoons cornmeal
¼–½ teaspoon garlic powder
¼ teaspoon baking powder
¼ teaspoon salt
¾ cup beer
A few drops of hot pepper sauce

1. Begin heating the oil in a deep fryer according to the fryer directions; it needs to be at 375°F when you start cooking. Line a plate with paper towels. Place ¼ cup of the flour in a plastic bag. Add the cheese curds and shake to coat. Transfer the floured curds to a plate. Whisk the remaining ½ cup flour, the cornmeal, garlic powder, baking powder, and salt together in a medium bowl. Whisk in the beer and hot pepper sauce.

2. When the oil reaches 375°F, dip three or four floured cheese curds into the batter. Lift them out with chopsticks or tongs and let excess batter drip back into the bowl. Drop the curds, one at a time, into the oil. Cook for 1 to 1½ minutes, until golden brown; use a slotted spoon or wire skimmer to transfer the curds to the paper towel–lined plate. (Near the end of the frying time for each batch, if you see any pinholes developing in the crust of any of the curds, remove all the curds immediately or they may start leaking cheese.)

3. Continue battering and frying the curds a few at a time; if the oil temperature drops, let it heat again to 375°F before adding more curds. Ideally, the curds should be eaten within minutes of coming out of the fryer, so you may want to serve them in small batches as you continue to fry the remaining curds. Save the last two batches for yourself!

Pickle-Brined Chicken Nuggets with Dill-Horseradish Sauce

Save the juice from a jar of dill pickles, then use it to brine chicken chunks for this fair-style treat.

1 pound boneless, skinless chicken breast, cut into 1-inch chunks

1 cup liquid from a jar of dill pickles

DILL-HORSERADISH SAUCE

1 cup mayonnaise

2 tablespoons snipped dill fronds

2 teaspoons prepared horseradish

1 teaspoon Dijon mustard

1 teaspoon seasoned rice vinegar

½ teaspoon sugar

Vegetable oil, for frying

¾ cup plus 2 tablespoons buttermilk

1¼ cups all-purpose flour

¾ teaspoon baking powder

½ teaspoon salt

½ teaspoon paprika

½ teaspoon dry mustard

½ teaspoon freshly ground black pepper

¼ teaspoon dried thyme

1. Combine the chicken chunks and pickle brine in a ceramic bowl. Cover and refrigerate for 30 minutes, stirring occasionally. After 30 minutes, drain and discard the brine. Pat the chicken dry and refrigerate in a covered bowl until you're ready to cook.

2. **Make the dill-horseradish sauce:** Stir together the mayonnaise, dill, horseradish, mustard, vinegar, and sugar in a small bowl. Cover and refrigerate until needed.

3. Preheat the oven to 275°F. Line a baking sheet with paper towels. Begin heating the oil in a deep fryer according to the fryer directions; it needs to be at 365°F when you start cooking. Add the ¾ cup buttermilk to the bowl with the chicken, stirring to coat. In another mixing bowl, whisk together the flour, baking powder, salt, paprika, dry mustard, pepper, and thyme. Add the remaining 2 tablespoons buttermilk. Whisk until the flour looks shaggy, with a mix of small and large clumps; don't overmix it.

4. When the oil reaches 365°F, remove five chunks of chicken from the buttermilk, letting the excess drip off (it's a good idea to count the nuggets as you add them to the flour mixture, which is so shaggy that you could easily lose track of a nugget). Toss them in the flour mixture, moving them around with a spoon to help the shaggy crumbs adhere. Carefully drop the chicken into the hot oil, using a pair of chopsticks (the best option, if you're comfortable with them) or a slotted spoon. Cook until richly browned, 2½ to 3½ minutes, stirring once and being careful to avoid jostling the crumbs off. Transfer to the prepared baking sheet and keep warm in the oven while you fry the remaining chicken. Serve with the dill-horseradish sauce.

Mini Corn Dogs on a Stick

Deep-fried hot dogs on a stick are found all over the grounds of the Minnesota State Fair, and each vendor has its own style. Some, such as Poncho Dogs, use a batter that contains a lot of cornmeal; others, such as Pronto Pup, use a smoother, floury batter that doesn't have the grainy texture associated with cornmeal. The recipe here is for a cornmeal-style batter. At home, it's lots easier to deep-fry mini dogs, because home fryers typically aren't tall enough to hold a standard-length hot dog. If you can find actual mini hot dogs, great; otherwise, cut full-size hot dogs into smaller pieces as described, or use mini smoked links such as Hillshire Farm Lit'l Smokies. You will need 32 (or more) thin bamboo skewers, 8 to 10 inches long.

32 MINI CORN DOGS

Vegetable oil, for frying

BATTER

1 cup yellow cornmeal (standard, not coarse grind)

¾ cup all-purpose flour

3 tablespoons sugar

1½ teaspoons baking powder

¾ teaspoon salt

¼ teaspoon baking soda

¼ teaspoon onion powder, optional

⅛ teaspoon finely ground black pepper

1 egg

1½ cups whole milk, or as needed

8 hot dogs, each cut into 4 chunks, or mini hot dogs (see headnote)

Yellow mustard, for serving

Ketchup, for serving

1. Begin heating the oil in a deep fryer according to the fryer directions; it should be 355 to 360°F when you start frying. Preheat the oven to 250°F. Line a plate with paper towels.

2. **Make the batter:** Whisk together the cornmeal, flour, sugar, baking powder, salt, baking soda, onion powder (if desired), and pepper in a mixing bowl. In a small bowl, beat the egg and 1 cup of the milk. Whisk the milk mixture into the cornmeal mixture. Add additional milk as needed; the batter should be thick enough to cling to a spoon.

3. Spear one hot dog piece lengthwise on the sharp end of each skewer. Dip one skewered hot dog into the batter, rolling it around to coat completely, then hold it above the batter and twirl the skewer so the batter coats the hot dog evenly, with no drips. Fry the hot dogs two or three at a time, turning them to brown evenly; they will float, and you may find it easier to hold on to the ends of the skewers and push the tips down to submerge the hot dogs completely in the oil. Cook until richly browned, 3 to 4 minutes. Drain on the paper towel–lined plate while you fry the next batch; as you finish a batch, transfer the previous batch to a baking sheet and keep warm in the oven while you continue frying. The batter may thicken as you continue; thin it with a little more milk as necessary. When all the hot dogs are fried, transfer to a serving plate. Serve with mustard and ketchup.

Note: You will probably have some batter left after you fry all the hot dogs. You can cut dill pickles into ¾-inch chunks, which you can dip in batter and fry to serve alongside the hot dogs.

Honey and Sunflower Ice Cream

The bee and honey area of the Ag-Hort Building sells some of the best ice cream at the Minnesota State Fair. Sweetened with honey and shot through with sunflower seeds, it's available in plain and chocolate — and you can get one scoop of each, if you like. Here's my make-at-home version, which will give you a taste of summer year-round. The custard needs to chill for at least 6 hours (or as long as 24 hours) before churning, so plan accordingly.

3 egg yolks

1 egg

¾ cup honey

1½ cups heavy cream

1 cup whole milk

¾ teaspoon vanilla extract

⅓ cup roasted unsalted sunflower seeds

ABOUT 1¼ QUARTS

1. Prepare your ice cream machine for use; many have a canister that must be frozen for at least 24 hours before using.

2. Whisk the egg yolks in a medium mixing bowl until lighter in color and somewhat thickened, about 2 minutes. Add the whole egg and honey, and whisk until smooth. Place a fine-mesh strainer over a large heatproof mixing bowl.

3. Stir the cream and milk together in a heavy-bottomed medium saucepan. Heat over medium heat until bubbles appear around the edges. Whisk about 1 cup of the warm cream into the honey mixture, then add the honey mixture to the saucepan, whisking constantly until smooth. Cook over medium-low heat, stirring constantly with a wooden spoon, until the mixture reaches 175°F, 3 to 5 minutes; be sure to stir around the edges of the saucepan, where the custard may overcook and form curds. Immediately pour the mixture through the strainer into the clean mixing bowl. Stir in the vanilla. Let cool for 20 minutes, then cover with plastic wrap, laying it directly on the surface of the mixture. Chill for at least 6 hours, or up to 24 hours.

4. Churn the mixture in the prepared ice cream machine according to the manufacturer's directions, adding the sunflower seeds during the last minute or two. Transfer the ice cream to a freezer container and freeze until firm, 3 to 4 hours. If the ice cream is too stiff to scoop when you're ready to serve it, let the container stand at room temperature for 10 minutes before scooping.

Thai Peanut-Caramel Popcorn

The thick caramel on this popcorn, enriched with peanut butter and Thai spices, makes this a delicious change from the regular caramel corn found at fairs and festivals. This stuff is pretty addictive, once you get into it.

6 cups popped popcorn (from about 3 tablespoons popcorn kernels)

1 cup very coarsely crushed peanuts (crushed in a plastic bag with a rolling pin)

1 teaspoon soy sauce

¼ teaspoon baking soda

1 cup firmly packed light brown sugar

½ cup (1 stick) unsalted butter, melted

⅓ cup peanut butter

⅓ cup light corn syrup

1 tablespoon hoisin sauce

1 tablespoon toasted sesame oil

1 teaspoon Sriracha or other hot pepper sauce

½ teaspoon finely minced fresh gingerroot

¼ teaspoon finely minced garlic

1. Preheat the oven to 250°F. Line a large rimmed baking sheet with parchment paper. Coat a very large mixing bowl with cooking spray. Add the popcorn and peanuts to the bowl. Stir together the soy sauce and baking soda in a small bowl.

2. Stir together the brown sugar, melted butter, peanut butter, corn syrup, hoisin sauce, oil, Sriracha, gingerroot, and garlic in a heavy-bottomed medium saucepan. Bring to a boil, then reduce the heat to medium and cook, stirring constantly, for about 5 minutes. The mixture will be foamy and should pull together into a soft, taffylike mass, coming slightly away from the edges of the pan; take care not to burn the thin coating that will form on the bottom of the pan. Remove from the heat. Stir the soy sauce mixture again, and stir it into the peanut butter mixture.

3. Immediately pour the peanut butter mixture over the popcorn and peanuts, tossing with two large wooden spoons as though mixing a salad to distribute the hot mixture as best you can; the popcorn and peanuts will not be evenly coated, and that's fine. Spread as evenly as possible on the prepared baking sheet.

4. Bake for 45 minutes, stirring every 15 minutes to distribute the caramel more evenly. Remove from the oven and let the popcorn cool on the baking sheet. Break up into clusters. The popcorn will keep for a week or longer in a tightly sealed container at room temperature.

INTERNATIONAL EELPOUT FESTIVAL, WALKER

Eelpout is a fish with an image problem. Although they're delicious when cooked, with firm, sweet white meat, eelpout are supremely ugly, with a nasty habit of winding their slimy, eel-like bodies around the arms of anglers who catch them. They also have an identity problem, because they're really not eelpout; they're burbot. The fish became locally known as eelpout when Scandinavian immigrants thought that the fish they were catching in Minnesota were the same as the true eelpout they knew from the Old Country.

The eelpout is a deep-water dweller most of the year and is seldom caught by anglers in the open-

water season. In winter, however, eelpout come into shallower water to spawn, and they are often caught by ice anglers hoping to catch walleyes or something — anything — else.

Walker, a town of about 1,100 in north-central Minnesota, decided to make lemonade from lemons (and also increase winter tourism) by initiating the International Eelpout Festival, which has been held annually since 1979. For three days in February, over 10,000 festivalgoers descend on Leech Lake, Minnesota's third-largest lake.

Mid-February is typically the coldest time in Minnesota, so part of the fun is checking out the visitors' winter wear, which includes snowmobile suits, fur caps (the more outlandish, the better), and mukluks. It also includes bathing suits and costumes, which brave festivalgoers don for the Polar Pout Plunge, a leap into the frigid waters through a huge hole cut into the ice. There is also a bikini-clad ice-fishing team. You can't say that Minnesotans don't know how to have a good time.

Other highlights include sled dog races, beer pong, chainsaw carving, an on-the-ice auto race, multiple bands, a bar made out of carved ice, an overabundance of adult beverages — and, of course, lots of fishing and fishing contests, including a prize for the largest eelpout. Food tents and trucks serve up fried eelpout nuggets and other specialties. With all the booths, ice-fishing shacks, trailers, and stages on the ice, Leech Lake looks like a refrigerated version of Florida's spring break.

Poor Man's Lobster (Eelpout)

This is the most common way to prepare eelpout (burbot), which, although ugly to look at and disgusting to catch, is a fish that deserves more respect in the kitchen. The meat is white, sweet, and flaky without being dry. Commercial fisherman Harley Toftey (page 26), who occasionally catches eelpout while fishing for lake herring in Lake Superior, says, "Someone should figure out a way to farm eelpout, because it's really delicious. You just have to get over the way they look!"

3 OR 4 SERVINGS

1 cup (2 sticks) salted or unsalted butter

½–1 teaspoon chopped garlic, optional

1 quart chicken broth

1 cup water

¼ cup firmly packed light brown sugar

1 tablespoon salt

1 pound skinless eelpout loin, cut into 1½-inch chunks

1. Melt the butter in a small saucepan over medium-low heat. Add the garlic, if desired, and simmer for a few minutes. Remove from the heat and keep warm.

2. Combine the broth, water, brown sugar, and salt in a large saucepan. Bring to a boil. Add the fish chunks. Return to a boil, and cook until the fish chunks rise to the surface, 5 to 8 minutes. Use a slotted spoon to transfer the fish to a serving dish, removing smaller pieces as they finish cooking. Serve with the melted garlic butter; generally, this is served family-style, with each diner dipping fish into the butter, a chunk at a time, but if you prefer, you can pour the melted butter over the fish in the serving dish.

Variations

- Substitute 5 cups lemon-lime soda, such as 7UP, for the chicken broth and water. Omit the brown sugar.

- Add 2 tablespoons Old Bay seasoning to the chicken broth mixture. Let it simmer for about 10 minutes before adding the fish.

- Use water in place of the chicken broth; increase the salt to 1½ tablespoons.

- Add 1 to 2 tablespoons lemon juice, or a cut-up lemon, to the chicken broth mixture.

Resources

Featured Organizations

Ames Farm
Watertown, Minnesota
952-955-3348
www.amesfarm.com
@amesfarmhoney

Bois Forte Band of Chippewa
Nett Lake, Minnesota
800-221-8129
www.nettlakewildrice.com
Nett Lake Wild Rice

Community Supported Agriculture
Local Harvest
www.localharvest.org/csa
@LocalHarvestorg

Dockside Fish Market
Grand Marais, Minnesota
218-387-2906
http://docksidefishmarket.com

Dream of Wild Health
Hugo, Minnesota
651-439-3840
http://dreamofwildhealth.org

The Growler
http://growlermag.com
@growlermag

Land Stewardship Project
Multiple locations; see website for details.
http://landstewardshipproject.org

Locally Laid Egg Company
Wrenshall, Minnesota
612-245-0450
www.locallylaid.com
@LocallyLaidEggs

Minneapolis Farmers Market
Minneapolis, Minnesota
612-333-1718
www.mplsfarmersmarket.com

Minnesota Food Truck Fair
Multiple locations; see website for details.
www.mnfoodtruckfair.com
@MNFoodTruckFair

Minnesota Grown
Minnesota Department of Agriculture
St. Paul, Minnesota
800-657-3878
http://minnesotagrown.com

Minnesota Hop Growers Association
www.mhga.org

Minnesota Mycological Society
Eagan, Minnesota
http://minnesotamycological society.org

Principle Six (P6)
Cooperative Trade Movement
612-719-9724
http://p6.coop

Red Lake Nation Fishery
Redby, Minnesota
877-834-2954
www.redlakewalleye.com

Serious Eats
212-488-6304
www.seriouseats.com
@seriouseats

Seward Community Co-op
Minneapolis, Minnesota
612-230-5555
http://seward.coop

Shepherd's Way Farms
Nerstrand, Minnesota
507-663-9040
www.shepherdswayfarms.com
@Shepswayfarms

Smude's Sunflower Oil
Pierz, Minnesota
320-468-6925
http://smudeoil.com
@SmudeOil

Squash Blossom Farm
Oronoco, Minnesota
507-252-9639
www.squashblossomfarm.org

Urban Roots
St. Paul, Minnesota
651-228-7073
http://urbanrootsmn.org
@urbanrootsmn

White Earth Land Recovery Project
Callaway, Minnesota
800-973-9870
http://nativeharvest.com
White Earth Wild Rice

Whole Grain Milling
Welcome, Minnesota
507-728-8489
www.wholegrainmilling.net

Wild Acres Processing
Pequot Lakes, Minnesota
218-820-5748
www.wildacresprocessing.com

Women's Environmental Institute and Amador Hill Farm
www.w-e-i.org

Recipes by Category

Index

Page numbers in *italic* indicate photos.

Scotch Eggs with Horseradish-Mustard Sauce, 168, *169*
hot dogs
    Mini Corn Dogs on a Stick, 261
    Pretzel Dogs, 237
Hummus with Olive Garnish, Navy Bean, 189

I

Icebox Pickles, 92–93, *93*
ice cream
    Caramel Apple Sundaes, 243
    Honey and Sunflower Ice Cream, 263
ice fishing, 32, *32–33*
immigrants
    awards granted to, 229
    culinary traditions and, 191
International Eelpout Festival, 266, *266, 267*
Iron Range, 221
    Iron Range Pasties, 220
Iron Range Porketta Roast, 218–19
Iron Skillet Pizza Dough, 106
Iron Skillet Pizza with Roasted Tomato, Pesto, and Mozzarella, 107
Iron Skillet Pizza with Sweet Peppers, Red Onions, and Salami, 107
Italian Giardiniera, Pickled, 224
Italian Sausage Sandwiches, Knife-and-Fork, 217

J

Jelly, Small-Batch Wild Cherry, 59
juniper berries
    Bison Jerky with Juniper Berries and Mustard Seeds, 195
    Cranberry Juniper Twist Cocktail, 85
    Grilled Venison Loin with Honey, Juniper, and Black Pepper Glaze, 80, *81*
    Juniper Bitters, 84

K

kale
    Ham Hock and Kale with Potatoes, 208
    Kale, Bacon, and Ricotta Dumplings, 117
    Warm Winter Market Salad, 125
    Wild *Gitigan* Salad, 246, *247*
Kimbler, Tammy, 167, *167*
Knife-and-Fork Italian Sausage Sandwiches, 217
Köttbullar: Swedish Meatballs, 209

L

lakes, *4*, 5
    Lake Superior, 8, *9*
lamb
    Bolognese-Style Pasta with Lamb, 176
    Lamb and Pork Breakfast Sausage, 159
    Somali Lamb or Goat Stew, 231
Larb, Hmong Chicken, 230
Latte, Oatmeal Stout, 135
lefse
    making, 215, *215*
    Norwegian Lefse, *212*, 213–14
lettuce
    Hmong Chicken Larb, 230
    Totchos (Tater Tot Nachos), 240
limes/lime juice
    Busy-Day Pho: Vietnamese Beef Noodle Soup, 232
    Watermelon Wedge on a Stick with Lime and Black Pepper, 250, *251*
Liver Pâté, Venison, 82
Locally Laid Egg Company, 170, *170*
Lutefisk, 203

M

manoomin. *See* wild rice
map, Minnesota, 3
maple syrup, 37, 39, *39*
    Home-Cured Maple Bacon, 160–61
    Maple-and-Cream Butter, 181
    Maple Candy with Walnuts, 196–97
    Maple-Cinnamon Apples, 38
Mardi Garden Salad, *244*, 245
marinara sauce
    Knife-and-Fork Italian Sausage Sandwiches, 217
Marinated Cucumbers with Dill, 94
Mediterranean Shepherd's Salad, 103
Mexican Rice Drink (Cantaloupe *Horchata*), 229
microgreens
    Roasted Pumpkin Soup with Curry Oil and Microgreens, 122, *123*
Mini Corn Dogs on a Stick, 261
Minnesota State Fair, 256–57, *256, 257*
Minnesota Wild Rice Soup, 67
Molten Cheeseburger with Grass-Fed Beef, 152–54, *153*
Moores, Susan, 244
morels
    cleaning, 44
    Crab-Stuffed Morel Mushrooms, 50, *51*
    Golden Toasts with Crispy Morels, Green Pea Spread, and Ham, 48, *49*
    Morel Cream Sauce with Roasted Shallots and Garlic, 44
    Morel Rings in Clarified Broth, 45
Mousse with *Sauce Verte*, Salmon or Trout, 18
mozzarella cheese
    Iron Skillet Pizza with Roasted Tomato, Pesto, and Mozzarella, 107
    Iron Skillet Pizza with Sweet Peppers, Red Onions, and Salami, 107

More Great Books from Storey?
You Betcha!

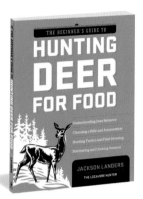

By Jackson Landers

Deer hunting is the most inexpensive, environmentally friendly way to get organic, grass-fed meat. From choosing the right rifle to butchering and then using the meat, this book is the perfect guide — even if you've never held a gun before.

By Teresa Marrone

From apples to watermelon, asparagus to zucchini, and basil to beef, you'll find detailed instructions for drying with a dehydrator, an oven, or the sun. And more than 140 recipes help you use your dried foods in a range of delicious dishes.

By John Manikowski

This tasty collection of 150 flavorful and richly varied recipes for freshwater and saltwater fish includes step-by-step directions for building your own smoker — in your backyard or in the wild!

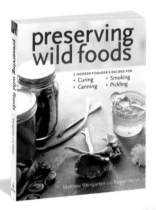

By Matthew Weingarten & R

Forage wild ingredients from tr. rivers, and preserve the old-world methods. Doz. you how to cure, can, sm. bounty.